Better Homes and Gardens®

Knitting Year-Round

Better Homes and Gardens® Books
Des Moines, Iowa

Better Homes and Gardens® Books
An imprint of Meredith® Books

Knitting Year-Round

Editor: Carol Field Dahlstrom
Writer: Ann E. Smith
Pattern Editor: Gayle Bunn
Technical Editor: Susan M. Banker
Designer: Catherine Brett
Copy Chief: Terri Fredrickson
Copy and Production Editor: Victoria Forlini
Editorial Operations Manager: Karen Schirm
Managers, Book Production: Pam Kvitne, Marjorie J. Schenkelberg, Rick von Holdt
Contributing Copy Editor: Margaret Smith
Contributing Proofreaders: Judy Friedman, Colleen Johnson, Jeanne Ledoux
Photographers: Ed Gohlich, Peter Krumhardt, Scott Little, Andy Lyons Cameraworks
Technical Illustrator: Chris Neubauer Graphics, Inc.
Electronic Production Coordinator: Paula Forest
Editorial and Design Assistants: Kaye Chabot, Mary Lee Gavin, Karen McFadden

Meredith® Books
Editor in Chief: Linda Raglan Cunningham
Design Director: Matt Strelecki
Executive Editor, Food and Crafts: Jennifer Dorland Darling

Publisher: James D. Blume
Executive Director, Marketing: Jeffrey Myers
Executive Director, New Business Development: Todd M. Davis
Executive Director, Sales: Ken Zagor
Director, Operations: George A. Susral
Director, Production: Douglas M. Johnston
Business Director: Jim Leonard

Vice President and General Manager: Douglas J. Guendel

Better Homes and Gardens® Magazine
Editor in Chief: Karol DeWulf Nickell

Meredith Publishing Group
President, Publishing Group: Stephen M. Lacy
Vice President-Publishing Director: Bob Mate

Meredith Corporation
Chairman and Chief Executive Officer: William T. Kerr

In Memoriam: E. T. Meredith III (1933–2003)

All of us at Better Homes and Gardens® Books are dedicated to providing you with information and ideas to create beautiful and useful projects. We welcome your comments and suggestions. Write to us at: Better Homes and Gardens Books, Crafts Editorial Department, 1716 Locust Street—LN112, Des Moines, IA 50309-3023.

If you would like to purchase any of our crafts, cooking, gardening, home improvement, or home decorating and design books, check wherever quality books are sold. Or visit us at: bhgbooks.com

Cover Photographs: Andy Lyons

You'll love the projects!

Creating a knitting book takes so many wonderful steps—working with talented knitting designers, choosing glorious yarns, and watching the yarn transform into exquisite knitted pieces of all kinds. But one of the best parts of creating *Knitting Year-Round* was photographing the people who modeled each project. We loved hearing their comments. On one cold day while we shivered and photographed the hat and scarf set, one model said she was toasty warm and loved how she looked. The sweet 5-month-old baby girl dressed in pink giggled the whole time she was photographed. The mother of our baby boy model commented on the soft and lovely feel of the tiny sweater set and how easily she could dress him. When a little girl came to model her brightly colored holiday sweater, she couldn't stop smiling because she loved the colors so much. The teenager modeling the ducky sweater said she certainly would find a place in her closet for this fun-to-wear piece. Even the little dog loved his made-to-order outfit and pranced around showing off his new look.

We know you'll love making the projects in this book as much as our models loved wearing them.

3

contents

As the leaves transform to a new palette and the air turns crisp, wrap yourself and those you love in knit creations. From cozy cardigans for kids to V-necks and jackets for you, you'll find wonderful wearables for autumn.

Autumn

Winter

Knitting for the merry winter months is great fun when you have more than two dozen patterns awaiting! Take your pick from snugly mittens, hats, scarves, sweaters, vests, and jackets—plus throws and purses!

When the freshness of spring hits, be ready with colorful stitches to show off your knitting talents. Create attractive short sleeve sweaters, sweet baby projects, sharp sleeveless men's cardigans, and more, ranging from easy to advanced.

pages 110–151

Spring

Summer

Warm up your knitting needles for a variety of projects that are perfect for summer. Pick a favorite from sun-splashed crop tops, cardigans, sweaters, and tank tops for girls of all ages.

pages 152–184

Get ready for cooler weather with trendy sweaters, striking outerwear, and snugly throws to keep you toasty warm. From easy-to-knit vests and lovely shawl-collar cardigans to jackets embellished with scallops, lace patterns, and bobbles, you're sure to find something wonderful to knit for one of nature's most colorful seasons...

Autumn

NORTHWOODS CARDIGAN
Accented with side-slash
pockets and a shawl collar, this
moose motif sweater makes a
graphic autumn statement. The
color pattern that forms the
boxes is easy to create, as
described in the instructions
beginning on page 24.

great outdoors

LIVELY IVY An easy-to-knit textured pattern with horizontal panels of intarsia leaves, like that of inlayed mosaic, make this a favorite sweater for the season. Set-in sleeves and a wide turtleneck accent the two-tone green sweater. Instructions begin on page 27.

CROPPED PULLOVER
Bursting with color, this geometric sweater has square armholes and stockinette-stitched hems. The color pattern is a 12-stitch repeat that uses two colors in each row for easy knitting. Instructions begin on page 29.

autumn pattern

LITTLE GLOWWORM CARDIGAN AND HAT

Worked in easy stockinette stitch, this sweater is accented with bold checked borders. To make the cardigan for a boy, simply change the side of the button band. The hat, worked on a circular needle, includes eyelets, a drawstring, and a lower edge that rolls naturally. Instructions begin on page 30.

cuddly

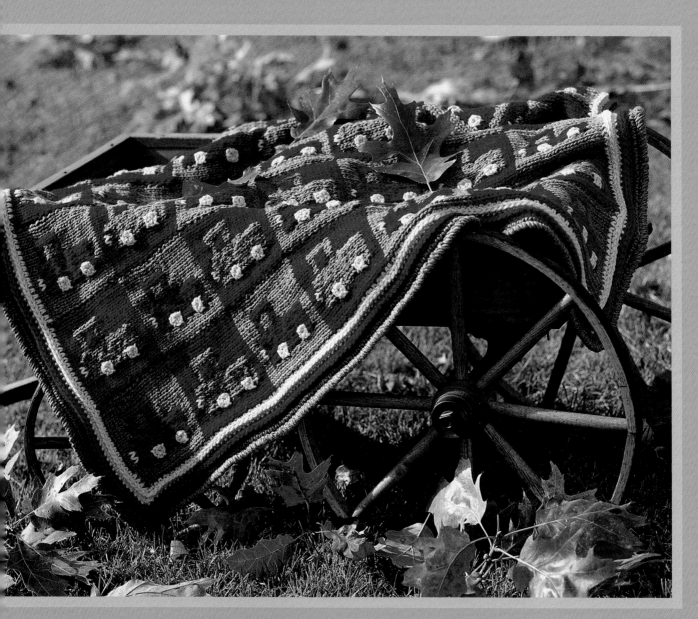

TRUCKS THROW The perfect size for nap time, this acrylic throw is assembled in stockinette panels from side to side, making the truck motifs easy to work. The headlights are duplicate stitched and the wheels are embroidered using spider stitch. For a quick finish, crochet the borders in simple stitches. Chart and instructions begin on page 32.

JR. ACCOUNTANT VEST
Designed for boys, this smart vest is worked in black and gray, but the design would be cute for girls as well. The easy-to-knit pattern forms little boxes that are bordered by lines. The vest hangs straight and has a crossed V-neck front. Instructions begin on page 33.

boyish charm

"FALL BACK" RAGLAN

Size 10½ needles make this a quick knitting project. The sweater is knit in rounds from the neck to the underarm. Then the contrasting areas are worked back and forth in stockinette stitches. A dot pattern on the lower body keeps it interesting. Instructions begin on page 35.

TARTAN JACKET

Stockinette stripes of paprika, gold, and two shades of green accent this pretty wool jacket. The look of tartan is created with duplicate stitch embroidery, working vertical lines one at time. Instructions begin on page 36.

fall for color

CHANCE ENCOUNTER

Here's a striking straight-style sweater that's easy to knit with size 10 needles and stockinette stitches. You choose whether to knit in the motifs or work them with duplicate-stitch embroidery. A stylish garter-stitch collar is worked along the V-neck. The back and dropped-shoulder sleeves are worked in the main color. Instructions begin on page 38.

open air

SCALLOPED HEM JACKET
A library of interesting pattern stitches, including a wide triangle, garter-stitch ridges, scallops, bobbles, and a lace pattern make up this relaxed long-line jacket. Scalloped hem borders accent the garment. Instructions begin on page 40.

SCALLOPS AND SQUARES THROW Make this lovely throw in one piece by knitting stockinette stitch and reverse stockinette stitch squares, alternating with a simple scalloped pattern. Eyelets at even intervals along each border make adding the fringe easy. The finished size is approximately 43×55 inches. Instructions begin on page 43.

solid warmth

FAIR ISLE SWEATER

Fair Isle patterns make the knitting exciting on this casual crew-neck sweater. The set-in sleeves are short, as is the length, making it a perfect wearable for in-between weather. Instructions begin on page 44.

BRIGHT CARDIGAN AND HAT

Colorful garter-stitch ridges border the simple-to-knit Fair Isle patterns. For boys or girls, work the cardigan in one piece to the underarm. The unusual tassel on the cap is actually a braid. Instructions begin on page 45.

design elements

Northwoods Cardigan

photos on pages 8–9

SKILL LEVEL: Intermediate

SIZES: S (MEDIUM, L, XL)
Note: *The pattern is written for the smallest size with changes for larger sizes in parentheses. When only one number is given, it applies to all sizes. For ease in working, before you begin, circle all numbers pertaining to the size you are knitting.*

FINISHED MEASUREMENTS:
Bust (buttoned): 42½ (44½, 47¾, 51½)"
Length: 25½ (26, 26½, 26½)"

MATERIALS:
- Brown Sheep Lamb's Pride Worsted, 85% wool/15% mohair, worsted weight yarn (190 yards per skein): 5 (5, 6, 6) skeins of Brown Heather (M02) for MC; 1 (1, 2, 2) skein(s) of Crème (M10) for Color A; and 2 (2, 3, 3) skeins of Raspberry (M83) for Color B.
- Size 8 (5mm) knitting needles or size needed to obtain gauge
- Size 7 (4.5mm) knitting needles
- Size 6 (4.25mm) knitting needles; 29-inch-length circular needle
- 5 buttons
- Yarn needle

GAUGE:
In St st and color patterns using largest needles, 18 sts and 24 rows = 4"/10cm.
TAKE TIME TO CHECK YOUR GAUGE.

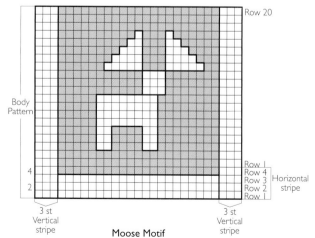

Body Pattern

Row 20

4
2

Row 1
Row 4
Row 3 Horizontal
Row 2 stripe
Row 1

3 st
Vertical
stripe

3 st
Vertical
stripe

Moose Motif

SPECIAL ABBREVIATIONS:
Sl 1: Slip next stitch purlwise and with the yarn on WS.
Ssk (slip, slip, knit): Slip next 2 sts knitwise, one at a time to right-hand needle, insert tip of left-hand needle into fronts of these 2 sts and k them tog.
Yb: Yarn back
Yf: Yarn forward

STITCHES USED:
Horizontal Stripes (a multiple of 2 sts + 1 st; a rep of 4 rows)
Row 1 (RS): With Color A, (k1, sl 1) across, ending k1.
Row 2: With Color A, p.
Row 3: With MC, (k1, sl 1) across, ending k1.
Row 4: With MC, p.

Vertical Stripes (over 3 sts; a rep of 4 rows).
Row 1 (RS): With color A, k1, sl 1, k1.
Row 2: With color A, p3.
Rows 3–4: With MC, rep Rows 1–2.
Rep Rows 1–4 for Vertical Stripes.
Note: *When working Vertical Stripes, use long strands of Color A for each individual stripe. When changing color, bring new color from under present color for a twist to prevent holes. Use a separate strand of color A for working each Moose Motif; or work later with duplicate-stitch embroidery.*

INSTRUCTIONS:
BACK
Beg at lower edge with smallest needles and color B, cast on 85 (89, 97, 105) sts.
Ribbing
Row 1 (WS): P1; (k1, p1) across.
Row 2: K1; (p1, k1) across.
Rep Ribbing Rows 1–2 to approx 3" from beg, ending with a RS row and inc 10 sts evenly spaced across last row—95 (99, 107, 115) sts. With largest needles and MC, p 1 row. Work Horizontal Stripe, Rows 1–4.

Body Pattern
Row 1 (RS): With MC, k10 (12, 16, 20); (Row 1 of Vertical Stripe over 3 sts, with MC, k21) 3 times, Row 1 of Vertical Stripe over 3 sts, with MC, k10 (12, 16, 20).
Row 2: Working Row 2 of Vertical Stripe, p across MC sts.
Row 3: Working Row 3 of Vertical Stripe, k across MC sts.
Row 4: With MC, p across.
Rows 5–20: Rep Rows 1–4.
Rows 21–24: Rep Horizontal Stripe. Noting placement for each moose (see diagrams on *page 26*), rep these 24 rows for Body Pattern to approx 17 (17, 17, 16½)" from beg, ending with a WS row.
Armhole Shaping
Bind off 6 sts at beg of next 2 rows—83 (87, 95, 103) sts. Work even to approx 24½ (25, 25½, 25½)" from beg, ending with a WS row.
Neck Shaping
Work in pattern across first 28 (29, 32, 35) sts; join new strands and bind off center 27 (29, 31, 33) sts; work to end of row. Working sides separately and at the same time, dec 1 st each neck edge. Work even to approx 25½ (26, 26½, 26½)" from beg, ending with a WS row. Bind off rem 27 (28, 31, 34) sts for each shoulder with MC.

RIGHT FRONT
Beg at lower edge with smallest needles and Color B, cast on 41 (43, 47, 51) sts. Rep Ribbing as for Back, inc 4 sts evenly spaced across last RS row—45 (47, 51, 55) sts. With larger needles and MC, p 1 row. Work Horizontal Stripe, Rows 1–4.
Body Pattern
Row 1 (RS): K8 with MC, Row 1 of Vertical Stripe over 3 sts, k21 MC, Row 1 of Vertical Stripe over 3 sts, k10 (12, 16, 20) with MC. Pattern is now set.
Pocket Opening
Bind off 6 sts at side seam at beg of next row—39 (41, 45, 49) sts. Cont in est pat until pocket opening measures approx 6", ending with a RS row. **Next Row:** Cast on 6 sts—45 (47, 51, 55) sts. Cont in est pat to approx 17 (17, 17, 16½)" from beg, ending with RS row.

Armhole Shaping

Bind off 6 sts at beg of next row—39 (41, 45, 49) sts. Work even to approx 19½ (20, 20½ 20½)" from beg, ending with a WS row.

Neck Shaping

K1, ssk, work in pat to end. P 1 row. Dec every 2nd row 7 (9, 11, 14) times more, then every 4th row 4 (3, 2, 0) times—27 (28, 31, 34) sts. Work to same length as Back, ending with a WS row. Bind off straight across with MC.

LEFT FRONT

Work as for Right Front to Body Pattern.

Row 1, Pocket Opening (RS): With MC, bind off first 6 sts, with 1 st on right needle, k3 (5, 9, 13) with MC, Row 1 of Vertical Stripe over 3 sts, k21 MC, Row 1 of Vertical Stripe over 3 sts, k8 MC—39 (41, 45, 49) sts. Cont est pat until pocket opening measures approx 6", ending with a WS row.

Next Row: Cast on 6 sts. Cont in est pat to approx 17 (17, 17, 16½)" from beg, ending with a WS row.

Armhole Shaping

Bind off 6 sts at beg of next row—39 (41, 45, 49) sts. Work even to approx 19½ (20, 20½, 20½)" from beg, ending with a WS row.

Neck Shaping

Work across to last 3 sts, k2tog, k1. P 1 row. Dec every 2nd row 7 (9, 11, 14) times more, then every 4th row 4 (3, 2, 0) times. Complete as for Right Front.

SLEEVES (make two)

Beg at lower edge with smallest needles and Color B, cast on 39 (39, 43, 43) sts. Rep Ribbing as for Back to approx 3" from beg, ending with a RS row. With largest needles and MC, p 1 row. Work Horizontal Stripe, Rows 1–4.

Body Pattern

Row 1 (RS): K18 (18, 20, 20) MC, Row 1 of Vertical Stripe over 3 sts, with MC k to end. Pattern is now set. Beg with next RS row, including new sts into pattern as they accumulate, inc each edge every 4th row 9 (13, 15, 23) times, then every 6th row 9 (7, 6, 0) times—75 (79, 85, 89) sts. Work even to approx 20" from beg,

Northwoods Cardigan
continued from page 25

ending with a WS row. Change to Color B and k 2 rows. Bind off loosely and knitwise.

Pocket Linings (make two)
With larger needles and MC, cast on 27 sts. Beg with a p row, work St st for 31 rows. Bind off loosely.

FINISHING
Join shoulder seams. Set in sleeves, sewing bound off sts to sleeve sides for square armholes.

Pocket Ribbing (make two)
With the RS facing, using smallest needles and Color B, pick up and k25 sts evenly spaced along pocket opening. Work Ribbing as for Back for 9 rows. Bind off in ribbing. Sew ribbed edges to sides of pocket opening. Using matching colors, join underarm and side seams, leaving pocket ribs free. Sew pocket lining to Back pocket opening so that the RS of lining will be against the WS of front. Sew lining to front around 3 sides. Rep for opposite side.

Left Front Band
With the RS facing, using smallest needles and Color B, pick up and k85 (87, 89, 91) sts evenly spaced from first V-neck, shaping row to lower edge. Work Ribbing as for Back for 9 rows. Bind off in ribbing.

Right Front Band
With the RS facing, using smallest needles and Color B, pick up and k85 (87, 89, 91) sts evenly spaced from lower edge to first V-neck shaping row. Work Ribbing as for Back for 3 rows.

Buttonhole Row: Rib 7 sts; * bind off 3 sts, with 1 st on right needle, rib 11 more sts—12 sts bet buttonholes; rep from * for 5 buttonholes, ending rib to end. **Next Row:** Rib across and cast on 3 sts over each buttonhole. Rib 4 more rows. Bind off in ribbing.

Collar
With the WS facing, using smaller needles and Color B, begin just above the Right Band to pick up and k31 sts evenly spaced to shoulder. Pick up and k33 (35, 37, 39) sts evenly spaced along back neck, and 31 sts evenly spaced to left band—95 (97, 99, 101) sts.

Row 1 (RS of collar): P1; (k1, p1) across.
Row 2: (K1, p1) 30 (31, 32, 33) times. Yb, sl 1, yf, sl st back onto left-hand needle; turn.
Row 3: K1; (p1, k1) 12 (13, 14, 15) times. Yb, sl 1, yf, sl st back onto left-hand needle; turn.
Row 4: P1; (k1, p1) 9 (10, 11, 12) times. Yb, sl 1, yf, sl st back onto left-hand needle; turn.
Row 5: K1; (p1, k1) 6 (7, 8, 9) times. Yb, sl 1, yf, sl st back onto left-hand needle; turn.
Row 6: Rib across.
Rows 7–9: Rib 95 (97, 99, 101) sts.
Rows 10–14: With needle one size larger than you have been using, rib across.
Rows 15–19: With largest needle, rib across.
Row 20: K1, k2tog, rib to last 3 sts, ssk, k1.

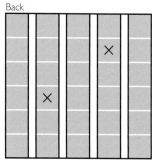

Moose Motif Placement
Back

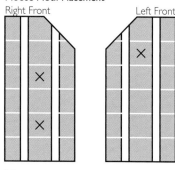

Moose Motif Placement
Right Front   Left Front

✕ Moose placement

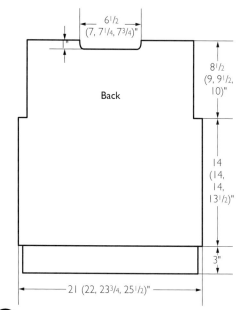

Back

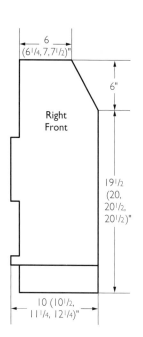

Right Front

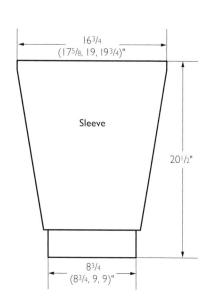

Sleeve

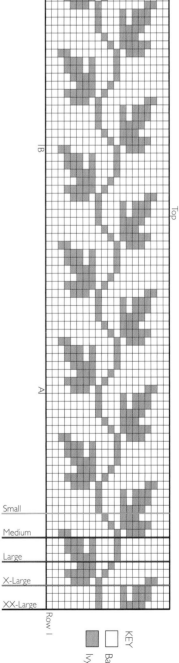

Row 21: P1, k2tog, rib to last 3 sts, ssk, p1.

Rows 22–31: Rep Rows 20–21—71 (73, 75, 77) sts. In rib, bind off 3 sts at beg of next 4 rows. Bind off rem 59 (61, 63, 65) sts. Sew front bands to corresponding collar ribbing. With the RS of collar facing and largest needles, pick up and k103 (105, 107, 109) sts evenly spaced around collar. Inc 1 st each edge every row, k 4 rows. Bind off loosely and knitwise on WS. Sew increased edges to side edges of ribbing. Sew buttons opposite buttonholes. Weave in loose ends on WS of fabric.

Lively Ivy
photo on page 10

SKILL LEVEL: Intermediate

SIZES: S (MEDIUM, L, XL, XXL)
Note: The pattern is written for the smallest size with changes for larger sizes in parentheses. When only one number is given, it applies to all sizes. For ease in working, before you begin, circle all numbers pertaining to the size you are knitting.

FINISHED MEASUREMENTS:
Bust: 40 (43, 46½, 50, 53)"
Length: 22 (22½, 23, 23½, 24)"

MATERIALS:
- Muench Yarns, G118 Via Mala, 100% merino wool, bulky weight yarn

(74 yards per skein): 9 (10, 11, 12, 13) skeins of Khaki (07) for MC and 4 (4, 5, 5, 5) skeins of Green (22) for CC
- Size 10 (6mm) knitting needles or size needed to obtain gauge
- Circular knitting needle, 16-inch length: Sizes 8 (5mm), 9 (5.5mm), and 10 (6mm)
- Yarn needle

GAUGE:
In Body Pattern, using largest needles,15 sts and 20 rows = 4"/10cm. TAKE TIME TO CHECK YOUR GAUGE.

SPECIAL ABBREVIATIONS:
Sl 1: Slip next st purlwise and with yarn on WS.
Ssk: Slip next 2 sts knitwise, one at a time to right-hand needle, insert tip of left-hand needle into fronts of these 2 sts and k them together.
P2tog-b: Turn work slightly, insert needle from left to right into back loops of 2nd and 1st sts, and p these 2 sts tog.

STITCHES USED:
Textured Pattern (a multiple of 3 sts; over 19 rows)
Row 1 (WS): With MC, p1, k1; (p2, k1) across, ending p1.
Row 2: K1, p1; (sl 1, k1, yo, pass slipped st over k1 and yo, p1) across, ending k1.
Rows 3–6: Rep Rows 1–2.

Row 20

XX-Large
X-Large
Large
Medium
Small

B

Top

A

Small
Medium
Large
X-Large
XX-Large

Row 1

KEY

Ivy and Vines (MC)

Background (CC)

Lively Ivy

continued from page 27

Row 7: Rep Row 1.
Row 8: K1, p1; (k2, p1) across, ending k1.
Rows 9–12: Rep Rows 7–8.
Rows 13–18: Rep Rows 1–2.
Row 19: Purl.
Note: Ivy inserts are worked in St st from a chart, reading from right to left for RS rows and from left to right for WS rows. Carry color not in use loosely along WS of fabric. When changing color, bring next color from under present color for a twist to prevent holes. Ivy and vines are worked with MC on a background of CC. Before you begin, study the chart. Notice that each size has a partial leaf on at least one side. For best results, do not work the partial leaves.

INSTRUCTIONS:
BACK
Beg at lower edge with MC, cast on 75 (81, 87, 93, 99) sts. * Work Textured Pattern Rows 1–19. Beg and ending at your size, work Chart Rows 1–20. With MC, k 1 row*. **For Body Pattern;** rep from * to * again, then rep Textured Pattern Rows 1–18 to required length. AT THE SAME TIME, when piece measures approx 14½" from beg, end with a WS row.
Armhole Shaping
Bind off 5 (6, 7, 8, 9) sts at beg of next 2 rows. **Dec Row (RS):** K1, ssk, pattern to last 3 sts, k2tog, k1. **Next Row (WS):** P1, p2tog, pattern to last 3 sts, p2tog-b, p1. Rep Dec Row.

Work 1 row even. Rep last 2 rows 1 (2, 3, 4, 5) time(s) more—57 (59, 61, 63, 65) sts. Work even to approx 20½ (21, 21½, 22, 22½)" from beg, ending with a WS row.
Neck and Shoulder Shaping
Work pattern on first 17 (18, 19, 19, 20) sts; join another strand of yarn and bind off center 23 (23, 23, 25, 25) sts, work to end of row. Working sides separately and at same time, dec 1 st each neck edge. Work even on rem 16 (17, 18, 18, 19) sts for each shoulder to approx 22 (22½, 23, 23½, 24)" from beg, ending with a WS row. Bind off knitwise and loosely.

FRONT
Work as for Back to approx 18 (18½, 19, 19½, 20)" from beg, ending with a WS row.
Neck Shaping
Work est pattern on first 23 (24, 25, 25, 26) sts; join a new strand and bind off center 11 (11, 11, 13, 13) sts; work to end of row. Working sides separately and at the same time decreasing as for armholes, dec 1 st each neck edge every row 4 times and every other row 3 times—16 (17, 18, 18, 19) sts rem. When piece measures same as Back, end with a WS row. Bind off knitwise and loosely.

SLEEVES (make two)
Beg at lower edge with MC, cast on 33 (36, 39, 39, 42) sts. Work Textured Pattern as for Back to approx 4" from beg, ending with a WS row. *For Chart on page 27,* with CC, k1 (2, 4, 4, 5) st(s); work from A–B on chart, then with CC, k to end. AT THE SAME TIME, keeping 1 st each edge in St st and including new sts into pattern as they accumulate, inc 1 st each edge every 4th row 0 (0, 0, 2, 2) times, every 6th row 3 (3, 7, 10, 10) times, and every 8th row 6 (6, 3, 0, 0) times. After completing chart, work Body Pattern as for Back, using first chart worked to line up the leaves when knitting chart for second time. Work even on 51 (54, 59, 63, 66) sts to approx 18" from beg, ending with a WS row.
Cap Shaping
Bind off 5 (6, 7, 8, 9) sts at beg of next 2 rows.

Dec Row (RS): K1, ssk, pattern to last 3 sts, k2tog, k1. **Next Row:** P1, p2tog, pattern to last 3 sts, p2tog-b, p1. *Rep Dec Row. Work 1 row even.* Rep last 2 rows 7 times more. Bind off 3 (3, 4, 4, 4) sts at beg of next 2 rows then bind off 3 (4, 4, 5, 5) sts at beg of next 2 rows. Bind off rem 9 (8, 9, 9, 10) sts.

FINISHING
Join shoulder seams. Set in sleeves. Join underarm and side seams.
Collar
With the RS facing, using smallest circular needle and MC, beg at right shoulder seam on back, pick up and k72 (72, 72, 75, 75) sts evenly spaced around neck. DO NOT JOIN. Working back and forth, work Rows 1–6 of Textured Pattern. Change to circular needle one size larger. Work Rows 7–12. Change to largest circular needle. Work Rows 1–12 twice then rep Row 1. Bind off loosely in ribbing. Join collar seam.

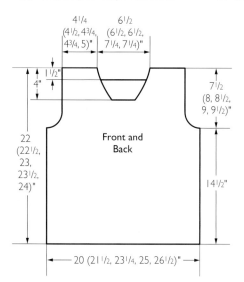

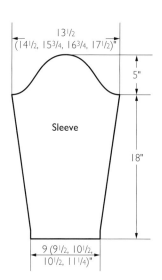

Cropped Pullover

photo on page 11

SKILL LEVEL: Intermediate

SIZES: S (M, LARGE, XL)
Note: *The pattern is written for the smallest size with changes for larger sizes in parentheses. When only one number is given, it applies to all sizes. For ease in working, before you begin, circle all numbers pertaining to the size you are knitting.*

FINISHED MEASUREMENTS:
Bust: 34½ (40½, 46½, 52½)"
Length: 18 (19, 20, 20½)"

MATERIALS:
- Classic Elite's Sand, 100% cotton, worsted weight yarn (77 yards per hank): 6 (6, 7, 8) hanks of Orange (6485) for Color A; 6 (6, 6, 7) hanks each of Gold (6402) for Color B and Ultramarine (6493) for Color C; and 5 (5, 5, 6) hanks of Fuchsia (6434) for Color D

- Size 8 (5mm) knitting needles or size needed to obtain gauge
- Size 6 (4.25mm) knitting needles
- Size 10 (6mm) knitting needles
- Yarn needle

GAUGE:
In Geometric Pattern with size 8 needles, 16 sts and 26 rows = 4"/10cm. TAKE TIME TO CHECK YOUR GAUGE.

STITCHES USED:
Geometric Pattern (a multiple of 12 sts + 9 sts; a rep of 16 rows) See chart.

Note: *Use intarsia technique throughout, meaning use a separate strand for each color area; DO NOT CARRY UNUSED COLOR ALONG BACK OF WORK. When changing color,*

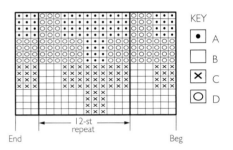

bring next color from under present color for a twist to prevent holes.

INSTRUCTIONS:
BACK
Beg at lower edge with size 6 needles and Color A, cast on 62 (73, 84, 95) sts.
Facing for Hem
Work St st to approx 1½" from beg ending after WS row, inc 7 (8, 9, 10) sts evenly across last row—69 (81, 93, 105) sts.
Body Pattern
For Turning Row: change to size 10 needles, and work Row 1 of Geometric Pattern. Change to size 8 needles, cont in Geometric Pattern, and work even to approx 8½ (9, 9½, 9½)" from Turning Row, ending after a WS row.
Armhole Shaping
Bind off 6 (6, 12, 12) sts at beg of next 2 rows—57 (69, 69, 81) sts. Work even to approx 17 (18, 19, 19½)" from Turning Row, ending after WS row.
Shoulder Shaping
Bind off 5 (7, 7, 9) sts at beg of next six rows. Bind off rem 27 sts.

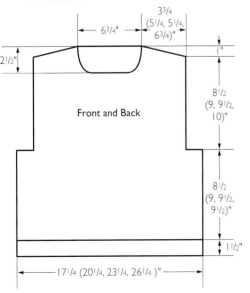

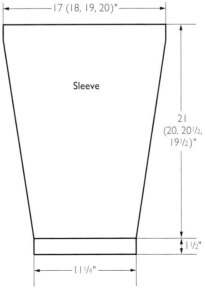

Cropped Autumn Pullover

continued from page 29

FRONT

Work as for Back until piece measures approx 15½ (16½, 17½, 18)" from Turning Row, ending after Row 8 or 16 of pattern.

Neck Shaping

Work in pattern across first 21 (27, 27, 33) sts; slip center 15 sts onto holder; join new strands of yarn, and work to end of row. Work sides at once with separate balls of yarn, and bind off 2 sts each neck edge twice, then dec 1 st each neck edge every other row twice—15 (21, 21, 27) sts rem for each shoulder. Complete shoulders as for Back.

SLEEVES (make two)

Beg at lower edge with size 6 needles and Color A, cast on 40 sts.

Facing for Hem

Work St st to approx 1½" from beg ending after WS row, inc 5 sts evenly across last row—45 sts.

Body Pattern

For Turning Row: change to size 10 needles, and work Row 1 of Geometric Pattern. Change to size 8 needles, and work even in Geometric Pattern until piece measures approx 1½" from Turning Row. Beg with next RS row, including new sts into pattern as they accumulate, inc at each edge every 4th row 0 (0, 0, 4) times, every 6th row 0 (4, 11, 14) times, every 8th row 5 (10, 5, 0) times, then every 10th row 7 (0, 0, 0) times—69 (73, 77, 81) sts. Work even to approx 21 (20, 20½, 19½)" from Turning Row, ending after WS row. Bind off.

FINISHING

Join left shoulder seam.

Neckband

With RS facing using size 8 needles, begin at back neck to pick up and k27 sts with correct colors. With correct colors, pick up and k16 sts along side of neck, k15 sts from holder, and pick up and k16 sts along next side of neck—74 sts. Working back and forth, continue Geometric Pat until band measures approx 2¼" from beg. **Next Row:** Change to size 10 needles, and

work one more row in pattern. **Next Row:** Change to size 6 needle, cont in St st with Color A only, and dec 8 sts evenly around—66 sts. Cont until band measures approx 5" from beg. Bind off very loosely. Sew left shoulder seam, including side of neckband. Loosely whipstitch facings at lower edges and neckline to WS of sweater. Set in sleeves, sewing bound off sts to sleeve sides for square armholes. Sew sleeve and side seams.

Little Glowworm Cardigan and Hat

photos on pages 12–13

SKILL LEVEL: Easy

SIZES: Girls' size 4 (6, 8, 10)
Note: The pattern is written for the smallest size with changes for larger sizes in parentheses. When only one number is given, it applies to all sizes. For ease in working, before you begin, circle all numbers pertaining to the size you are knitting.

FINISHED MEASUREMENTS:
Chest (buttoned): 30½ (32, 34½, 36)"
Length: 16 (18, 20, 22)"

MATERIALS:
- Muench Yarns, Bali, 50% cotton/50% acrylic, sport weight yarn (100 meters per ball): 4 (5, 6, 7) balls of Royal Blue (40) for MC and for all sizes; 1 ball of Lime (44) for CC
- Size 5 (3.75mm) 29-inch circular knitting needle or size needed to obtain gauge
- Size 4 (3.5mm) knitting needles
- Tapestry needle
- 5 JHB International buttons (Catty Pillar #22801, size 1⅛")

GAUGE:
In St st with larger needles, 20 sts and 28 rows = 4"/10cm.
TAKE TIME TO CHECK YOUR GAUGE.

STITCHES USED:
Border (a multiple of 4 sts + 3 sts; a rep of 2 rows)
Row 1 (WS): With MC, (k3, p1) across, ending k3.

Row 2: With MC, k.
Rep Rows 1–2 for Border.

Checks (a multiple of 4 sts + 3 sts)
Row 1 (WS): With MC, p.
Row 2: * K3–CC, k1–MC; rep from * across, ending k3–CC.
Row 3: * P3–CC, p1–MC; rep from * across, ending p3-CC.
Row 4: Rep Row 2.
Row 5: Rep Row 1.
Row 6: With MC, k.
Row 7: Rep Row 3.
Row 8: Rep Row 2.
Row 9: Rep Row 3.

Notes: The lower body is worked back and forth in one piece to the armhole, using a circular needle to accommodate the large number of stitches. When working the Checks pattern, loosely carry color not in use along WS of fabric. To change color, bring next strand from under present strand for a twist to prevent holes.

INSTRUCTIONS:
LOWER BODY

With larger needle and MC, cast on 147 (155, 167, 175) sts. Rep Border Rows 1–2 for 3 total times. Rep Checks Rows 1–9 once. With MC, beg with a k row, work in St st until piece measures approx 9 (10½, 12, 13½)" from beg, ending with a WS row.

Armhole Shaping

K35 (35, 39, 43); bind off 1 (3, 3, 1) st(s); with 1 st on right needle k across next 74 (78, 82, 86) sts; bind off 1 (3, 3, 1) sts; k to end.

LEFT FRONT

Cont in St st on last 35 (35, 39, 43) sts until piece measures approx 14 (16, 18, 20)" from beg, ending with a RS row.

Neck Shaping

At beg of neck edge, bind off 5 (5, 8, 11) sts once, 3 sts once, 2 sts once, and 1 st twice. Cont as est on rem 23 (23, 24, 25) sts to approx 16 (18, 20, 22)" from beg, ending with a WS row. Bind off.

BACK

With the WS facing, join MC and p across 75 (79, 83, 87) sts. Work even to approx 16 (18, 20, 22)" from beg, ending with a WS row. Bind off.

RIGHT FRONT

With the WS facing, join MC and p across 35 (35, 39, 43) sts. Reversing neck shaping, work as for Left Front.

SLEEVES (make two)

Beg at the cuff with larger needle and MC, cast on 31 (35, 35, 39) sts. Rep Border Rows 1–2 for 3 total times. Rep Checks Rows 1–9 once. With MC, beg St st, inc 1 st each edge every row 2 (2, 0, 0) times, every 4th row 16 (17, 21, 22) total times—67 (73, 77, 83) sts. Work even to approx 13 (14, 15, 16)" from beg, ending with a WS row. Bind off loosely and knitwise.

FINISHING

Join shoulder and sleeve seams. Set in sleeves.

Neckband

With the RS facing, using smaller needles and CC, pick up and k69 (73, 73, 77) sts evenly spaced around neck.

Row 1 (WS): P1; (k3, p1) across.

Row 2: Knit.

Rep Rows 1–2 for 3 times more then rep Row 1 again. Bind off knitwise.

Left Front Band

With the RS facing, using smaller needles and CC, pick up and k84 (95, 100, 117) sts evenly spaced along edge. K9 rows. Bind off knitwise.

Right Front Band

With the RS facing, using smaller needles and CC, pick up and k, as for Left Band. K3 rows. **Row 4:** K10 (9, 10, 11); * bind off 2 sts, k14 (17, 18, 22) more sts—15 (18, 19, 23) sts between buttonholes; rep from * for 5 buttonholes, ending k to end.

Row 5: K across and cast on 2 sts over each buttonhole. K 4 more rows. Bind off knitwise. Sew buttons opposite buttonholes. Weave loose ends along WS of fabric.

FOR HAT

photos on pages 12–13

SKILL LEVEL: Easy

SIZE: 24-inch circumference

MATERIALS:
- 2 balls of Lime Bali
- Size 7 (4.5mm) 16-inch circular needle
- 1 set of size 7 (4.5mm) double-pointed needles (dpn)
- 1 ring-type stitch marker

GAUGE:
Using a double strand of yarn, 16 sts and 24 rnds = 4"/10cm.

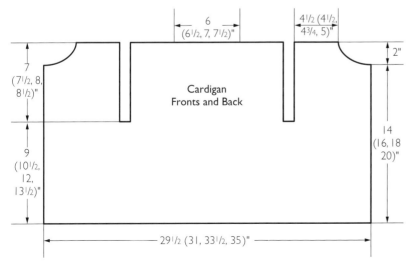

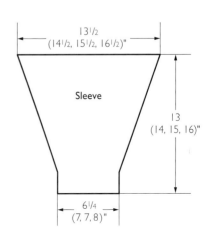

Little Glowworm Hat
continued from page 31

TIE
Using a double strand of yarn, cast on 135 sts. Bind off.

HAT
With a double strand of yarn and circular needle, cast on 96 sts. Being careful not to twist the sts, join. Place a marker to indicate beg of rnd. K 20 rnds.

Eyelets
(K4, yo, k2tog) around. K 20 rnds.

Crown Shaping
Rnd 1: [(Sl 1 st purlwise, k1, pass slipped stitch over k st—SKP made), k12, k2tog] 6 times.
Rnd 2: K84.
Rnd 3: (SKP, k10, k2tog) 6 times.
Rnd 4: K72.
Rnd 5: (SKP, k8, k2tog) 6 times.
Rnd 6: K60.
Rnd 7: (SKP, k6, k2tog) 6 times.
Rnd 8: K48. Change to dpns. Arrange sts onto dpns with 16 sts on each of 3.
Rnd 9: (SKP, k4, k2tog) 6 times.
Rnd 10: K36.
Rnd 11: (SKP, k2, k2tog) 6 times.
Rnd 12: K24.
Rnd 13: (SKP, k2tog) 6 times.
Rnd 14: K12.
Rnd 15: (K2tog) 6 times—6 sts rem.
Cut yarn leaving an 8" tail. Thread tail into yarn needle and back through rem 6 sts. Secure tail on WS of fabric. Thread tie through the eyelets; try on child; tie to fit. Let lower edge roll.

Trucks Throw
photo on page 14

SKILL LEVEL: Intermediate

SIZE: Throw measures approx 31×40"

MATERIALS:
- Bernat Berella "4," 100% acrylic, worsted weight yarn (195 yards per ball): 4 balls of Dark Oxford Heather (8893) for Color A; 3 balls of Claret (1532) for Color B; and 1 ball of Light Tapestry Gold (8886) for Color C
- Size 7 (4.5mm) knitting needles or size needed to obtain gauge
- Yarn needle
- Size G/6 (4.5mm) crochet hook

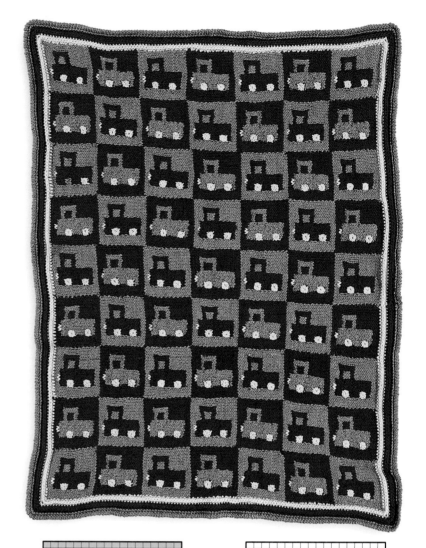

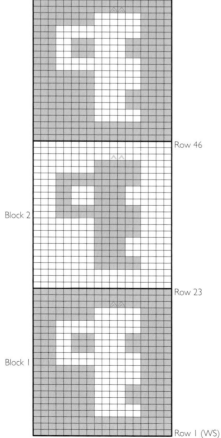
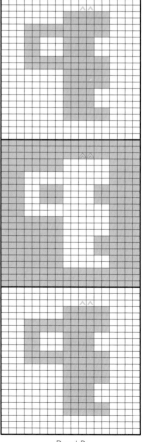

Block 2
Block 1
Row 46
Row 23
Row 1 (WS)
Panel A
Panel B

GAUGE:

In St st and color pattern, 18 sts and 24 rows = 4"/10cm.
TAKE TIME TO CHECK YOUR GAUGE.

Note: The throw is worked from side to side and in 9 panels. This St st project is worked from a chart, reading from right to left for RS rows and from left to right for WS rows. Loosely carry color not in use along WS of fabric. When changing color, bring next strand from under present strand for a twist to prevent holes. Lights and wheels on each truck are worked later with embroidery stitches.

INSTRUCTIONS:

PANEL A (make 5)

Block 1: Beg at lower edge with Color A, cast on 18 sts. Using A as the background color and B as motif color, beg with a p row and work through completion of Row 23.
Block 2: Using B as the background color and A as motif color, work through completion of Row 46. Rep Rows 1–46 twice more, then rep Rows 1–23. Bind off loosely and knitwise.

PANEL B (make 4)

Block 1: Beg at lower edge with Color B, cast on 18 sts. Using B as the background color and A as motif color, beg with a p row and work through completion of Row 23.
Block 2: Using A as the background color and B as motif color, work through completion of Row 46. Rep Rows 1–46 twice more, then rep Rows 1–23. Bind off loosely and knitwise.

FINISHING

Alternating panels, sew together.
Border
With the RS facing, using crochet hook, join Color C with a slip st in any corner. Ch 1, 3 sc in same st as joining. Work 16 sc evenly across first block; * work 17 sc evenly across each block to last block before corner, 16 sc across with 3 sc in corner, then 16 sc across next block; rep from * around. Join with a slip st in back loop of first sc.
Rnd 2: Ch 1, sc in back lp of each sc around, working 3 sc in each corner. At end, join with a slip st in first rem front lp.

Rnd 3: Slip st in each rem front lp around. Fasten off.
Rnd 4: With the RS facing, join color B with a slip st in any sc along side of Rnd 2. Ch 1, sc in each sc around working 3 sc in each corner. At end, join with a slip st in back lp of first sc.
Rnds 5–6: With Color B, rep Rnds 2–3.
Rnd 7: With the RS facing, join Color A with a slip st in any sc along side of Rnd 5. Ch 1, sc in each sc around working 3 sc in each corner. At end, join with a slip st in both lps of first sc.
Rnd 8: Working from left to right rather than from right to left, ch 1, sc in each sc around for reverse sc. At end, join and fasten off.

Embroidery

Thread Color C into yarn needle. Work 2 stitches with duplicate st on front of each truck as shown on charts.
Wheels (make two for each truck with spider stitch embroidery):
Step 1: Bring needle threaded with color C up from back to front in the center of the wheel space. (See illustration, *below.*)
Step 2: Leaving a tail at back, take needle through at #1.
Step 3: Take needle and yarn through center from back to front and then through at #2. Continue taking needle through center from back to front and then through the next number.
Step 4: Bring needle and yarn from back to front at 8.
Step 5: Take yarn under first thread to left then over next thread; rep around. Then take yarn over first thread and under next thread around.
Step 6: At end, take yarn to back and secure ends in place.

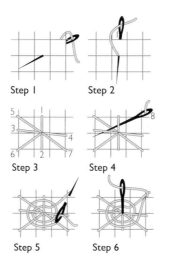

Step 1   Step 2

Step 3   Step 4

Step 5   Step 6

Jr. Accountant Vest

photo on page 15

SKILL LEVEL: Easy

Note: The pattern is written for the smallest size with changes for larger sizes in parentheses. When only one number is given, it applies to all sizes. For ease in working, before you begin, circle all numbers pertaining to the size you are knitting.

SIZES: Boys' size 6 (8, 10, 12, 14)

FINISHED MEASUREMENTS:

Chest: 31½ (33½, 35, 37, 39)"
Length: 17 (18½, 20, 21½, 23)"

MATERIALS:

- Chester Farm's Cestari 3-ply, 100% wool, DK weight yarn (290 yards per skein): 1 (1, 2, 2, 2) skein(s) of Midnight Black for Color A and 1 (1, 2, 2, 2) skein(s) of Natural Medium Gray for Color B
- Size 7 (4.5mm) knitting needles or size needed to obtain gauge
- Size 5 (3.75mm) 16-inch circular needle
- Yarn needle

Jr. Accountant Vest

continued from page 33

GAUGE:
In Body Pattern with larger needles, 17 sts and 22 rows = 4"/10cm.
TAKE TIME TO CHECK YOUR GAUGE.

SPECIAL ABBREVIATIONS:
Sl 1: Slip one stitch purlwise with yarn on WS of fabric.

Ssk (slip, slip, knit): Slip next 2 sts knitwise, one at a time to right-hand needle, insert tip of left-hand needle into fronts of these 2 sts and k tog.

STITCHES USED:
Border [a multiple of 4 sts + 3 (7, 3, 7, 3) sts; a rep of 14 rows]
Row 1 (RS): With B, k 1 (3, 1, 3, 1); (sl 1, k3) across, ending sl 1, k 1 (3, 1, 3, 1).
Row 2: With B, p1 (3, 1, 3, 1); (sl 1, p3) across, ending sl 1, p1 (3, 1, 3, 1).
Row 3: With A, k.
Row 4: With A, p.
Rows 5–8: Rep Rows 1–4.
Rows 9–10: With B, rep Rows 1–2.
Row 11: With A, k.
Row 12: With A, k.
Row 13: With A, p.
Row 14: With A, p.
Rep Rows 1–14 twice for Border.

Body Pattern [a multiple of 8 sts + 3 (7, 3, 7, 3) sts; a rep of 12 rows]
Row 1 (RS): With B, k 1 (3, 1, 3, 1); (p1, k3) across, ending p1, k 1 (3, 1, 3, 1).

Row 2: With B, p 1 (3, 1, 3, 1); (k5, p3) across, ending k1, p 1 (3, 1, 3, 1).
Rows 3–4: With A, rep Rows 1–2.
Rows 5–6: With B, rep Rows 1–2.
Row 7: With A, k 1 (3, 1, 3, 1); (p1, k3) across, ending p1, k1 (3, 1, 3, 1).
Row 8: With A, p 1 (3, 1, 3, 1), k1; (p3, k5) across, ending p 1 (3, 1, 3, 1).
Rows 9–10: With B, rep Rows 7–8.
Rows 11–12: With A, rep Rows 7–8.
Rep Rows 1–12 for Body Pattern.

INSTRUCTIONS:
BACK
Beg at lower edge, with larger needles and A, cast on 67 (71, 75, 79, 83) sts. K 1 row, p 1 row, k 1 row. Rep Border Rows 1–14 twice. Begin Body Pattern, working to approx 11½ (12½, 13½, 14½, 15½)" from beg, ending with a WS row.

Armhole Shaping
At each armhole edge, bind off 5 sts once, 3 sts once, 2 sts once, and 1 st 1 (2, 2, 3, 3) time(s)—45 (47, 51, 53, 57) sts. Cont pattern to approx 17 (18½, 20, 21½, 23)" from beg, ending with a WS row. With last color used, bind off knitwise and loosely.

FRONT
Work as for Back to approx 10½ (11½, 12½, 13½, 14½)" from beg, ending with a WS row.

Neck Shaping
In pattern work first 33 (35, 37, 39, 41) sts; place center st onto a holder; join a new strand and work to end of

row. Work sides separately and at the same time as follows:
Row 1: Cont est pattern across.
Row 2: Work pattern to last 3 sts, k2tog, k1; on next side k1, ssk, pattern to end.
Rep these 2 rows for 7 (6, 6, 5, 6) times more, then dec as est every 4th row 3 (4, 5, 6, 6) times. AT THE SAME TIME, when piece measures 11½ (12½, 13½, 14½, 15½)" from beg, shape armholes as for Back. With 11 (12, 13, 14, 15) sts rem for each shoulder, work to same length as Back, ending with a WS row. With last color used, bind off knitwise and loosely.

FINISHING
Join shoulder seams.
Neckband
With the RS facing, using smaller circular needle and Color B, begin at V-neck and k1 from holder. Pick up and k34 (37, 40, 42, 45) sts evenly spaced to shoulder, 24 (24, 26, 26, 28) sts along back neck, and 34 (37, 40, 42, 45) sts evenly spaced along opposite side of V-neck—93 (99, 107, 111, 119) sts.

Ribbing, Row 1 (WS): P1; (k1, p1) across. **Row 2:** K1; (p1, k1) across. Rep Rows 1–2 once, then rep Row 1 again. Bind off in ribbing. Cross left side of ribbed band over right side and sew in place.

Arm Bands (make two)
With the RS facing, using smaller circular needle and color B, pick up and k71 (77, 83, 89, 95) sts evenly spaced along armhole opening. Work Ribbing Rows 1–2 as for neckband; then rep Row 1 again. Bind off in ribbing. Join side seams.

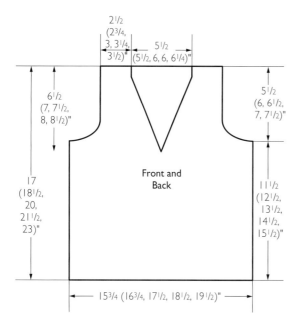

2½
(2¾,
3, 3¼,
3½)"   5½
        (5½, 6, 6, 6¼)"

6½
(7, 7½,
8, 8½)"

5½
(6, 6½,
7, 7½)"

Front and
Back

17
(18½,
20,
21½,
23)"

11½
(12½,
13½,
14½,
15½)"

←— 15¾ (16¾, 17½, 18½, 19½)" —→

Fall Back Raglan

photo on page 16

SKILL LEVEL: Easy

SIZES: SMALL (M, L, XL)
Note: *The pattern is written for the smallest size with changes for larger sizes in parentheses. When only one number is given, it applies to all sizes. For ease in working, before you begin the pattern, circle all numbers pertaining to your size.*

FINISHED MEASUREMENTS:
Chest: 40½ (43, 45½, 48)"
Length: 25 (26, 27¼, 28)"

MATERIALS:
- Lion Brand Wool-Ease Chunky, 86% acrylic/10% wool/4% viscose, bulky weight yarn (153 yards per ball): 2 (2, 3, 3) balls of Wheat (402) for Color A; 3 (4, 4, 4) balls of Foliage (187) for Color B; and 1 (1, 2, 2) ball(s) of Appleton (141) for Color C

- Size 10½ (6.5mm) circular knitting needle 29-inch length, or size needed to obtain gauge
- Set of 4 size 9 (5.5mm) double pointed knitting needles (dpn); size 9 straight needles
- 10 ring-type stitch markers
- Yarn needle

GAUGE:
In St st and color pattern with larger needle, 13 sts and 19 rows = 4"/10 cm.
TAKE TIME TO CHECK YOUR GAUGE.

SPECIAL ABBREVIATION:
M1: Lift running thread before next stitch onto left-hand needle and knit in its back loop to make one stitch.

Note: *This pullover is worked from the neck down, knitting every round for St st. After dividing for the garment sections, the pieces are worked back and forth in St st (knit on RS rows, purl on WS rows).*

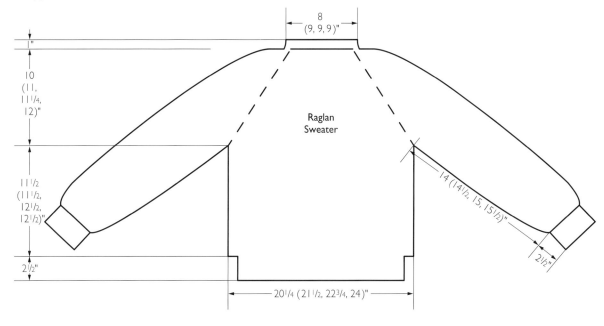

Fall Back Raglan
continued from page 35

INSTRUCTIONS:
With dpns, and Color A, cast on 56 (64, 64, 64) sts. Arrange onto 3 needles with 19 (21, 21, 21) sts on 1st and 2nd needles and 18 (22, 22, 22) sts on 3rd needle. Place a double marker to mark beg of rnd; join and work 5 rnds of k1, p1 ribbing.
Note: The double marker is in center of right sleeve and is not referred to in the following directions; slip it on every rnd.

BACK
Set-Up for Yoke
With larger needle, k3 (5, 4, 4), place marker (pm), k1, pm, k 20 (20, 22, 22), pm, k1, pm, k 6 (10, 8, 8), pm, k1, pm, k20 (20, 22, 22), pm, k1, pm, k3 (5, 4, 4).
Yoke Pattern
Rnd 1: * K to marker, M1, sl marker, k1, sl marker, M1; rep from * 4 total times—64 (72, 72, 72) sts.
Rnd 2: K around slipping markers. Rep Rnds 1–2 until there are 240 (264, 272, 288) total sts. Leaving a tail to weave in later, cut yarn.
Dividing Round
Removing markers, slip first 27 (31, 31, 33) sts onto a strand of yarn for first half of right sleeve. Join Color C and with larger needle, k across next 66 (70, 74, 78) sts for back. Slip 54 (62, 62, 66) sts onto a strand of yarn for sleeve. Slip 66 (70, 74, 78) sts onto a strand of yarn for front. Slip last 27 (31, 31, 33) sts onto a strand of yarn for 2nd half of right sleeve. Working back and forth on back sts only, p 1 row. Work 3 more St st rows with Color C. Change to Color B and work 3 St st rows.
Lower Body Pattern
Row 1 (RS): * With B, k3, k1-A; rep from * across, ending k2-B.
Row 2: With B, p.
Row 3: With B, k.
Row 4: Rep Row 2.
Row 5: With B, k1; * k1-C, k3–b; rep from * across, ending k1-C, k4–B.
Rows 6–8: Rep Rows 2–4.
Rep Rows 1–8 until piece from top of color C stripe measures approx 11½ (11½, 12½, 12½)", ending with

Row 2 or Row 6. With color B k across next row, dec 1 st—65 (69, 73, 77) sts. P 1 row. Change to smaller needles.
Ribbing (worked with Color B)
Row 1 (RS): K1; (p1, k1) across.
Row 2: P1; (k1, p1) across.
Rep Ribbing Rows 1–2 for 4 times more. Bind off in ribbing.

LEFT SLEEVE
With the RS facing, return 54 (62, 62, 66) sts to larger needle. Join Color C and k across. Work 4 more St st rows. Change to Color B and work 3 St st rows. Work Lower Body Pattern, Rows 1–2 as for Back. Cont in est pattern, dec 1 st each edge on next row, then every 6th row 8 (1, 1, 2) time(s), every 4th row 0 (10, 10, 10) times. Work even on 36 (38, 38, 40) sts to approx 14 (14½, 15, 15½)" from beg, ending with Row 4 or Row 8 and dec 1 st in last row—35 (37, 37, 39) sts. Change to smaller needles and work Ribbing as for Back.

FRONT
With the RS facing, return 66 (70, 74, 78) sts to larger needle. Join Color C and work 5 St st rows, beg with a k row. Change to Color B and work 3 St st rows. Complete as for Back, beg with Lower Body Pattern.

RIGHT SLEEVE
Work as for Left Sleeve.

FINISHING
Using matching colors, join underarm and side seams. Weave in loose ends on WS of fabric.

Tartan Jacket
photo on page 17

SKILL LEVEL: Intermediate

SIZES: S (MEDIUM, L, XL)
Note: The pattern is written for the smallest size with changes for larger sizes in parentheses. When only one number is given, it applies to all sizes. For ease in working, before you begin, circle all numbers pertaining to the size you are knitting.

FINISHED MEASUREMENTS:
Bust: 44 (48, 52, 56)"
Length: 23½ (24, 24½, 25)"

MATERIALS:
- Patons Classic Wool, 100% Pure New Wool, worsted weight yarn (223 yards per ball): 6 (6, 7, 8) balls of Natural Mix (229) for MC; 1 ball each of Paprika (238) for Color A, Forest Green (241) for Color B, Old Gold (204) for Color C, and Leaf Green (240) for Color D
- Size 7 (4.5mm) knitting needles or size needed to obtain gauge
- Size 5 (3.75mm) knitting needles
- Yarn needle
- 7 JHB International buttons (#92777 Scottish Thistle, size ⅞")

GAUGE:
In St st with larger needles, 20 sts and 26 rows = 4"/10cm.
TAKE TIME TO CHECK YOUR GAUGE.

Note: Horizontal stripes are knitted while vertical stripes are worked with duplicate stitch embroidery later. For best results when stitching the vertical stripes, work from bottom to top one row and one color at a time.

INSTRUCTIONS:
BACK
Beg at the lower edge, with smaller needles and MC, cast on 109 (119, 129, 139) sts.
Ribbing
Row 1 (WS): P1; (k1, p1) across.
Row 2: K1; (p1, k1) across.
Rep Ribbing Rows 1–2 to approx 1" from beg, ending with a WS row. Change to larger needles. K across next row, inc 1 st—110 (120, 130, 140) sts. Beg with a p row, work 9 rows St st (p WS rows, k RS rows).
For Body Pattern: * With A, k. With MC, work 3 rows; 1 row Color B; 3 rows MC; 1 row Color C; 3 rows MC; 1 row Color D; 3 rows MC; 1 row Color A; 19 rows MC. Rep from * for the 36–row Body Pattern. When piece measures approx 14½" from beg, end with a WS row.
Armhole Shaping
Bind off 10 (13, 16, 19) sts at beg of the next 2 rows—90 (94, 98, 102) sts. Cont in pattern until piece

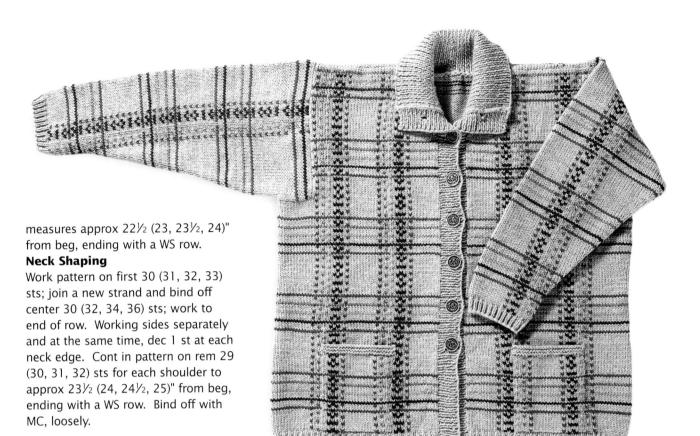

measures approx 22½ (23, 23½, 24)" from beg, ending with a WS row.

Neck Shaping
Work pattern on first 30 (31, 32, 33) sts; join a new strand and bind off center 30 (32, 34, 36) sts; work to end of row. Working sides separately and at the same time, dec 1 st at each neck edge. Cont in pattern on rem 29 (30, 31, 32) sts for each shoulder to approx 23½ (24, 24½, 25)" from beg, ending with a WS row. Bind off with MC, loosely.

Pocket Linings (make two)
With larger needles and MC, cast on 25 sts. Beg with a p row, work St st to approx 6" from beg, ending with a WS row. Place sts onto a holder.

RIGHT FRONT
Beg at the lower edge, with smaller needles and MC, cast on 51 (57, 63, 67) sts. Rep Ribbing Rows 1–2 as for Back to approx 1" from beg, ending with a WS row. Change to larger needles and k across next row, inc 1 (0, 0, 0) st—52 (57, 63, 67) sts. Work 9 more St st rows. Work in Body Pattern as for Back to approx 7" from beg, ending with a WS row.

Pocket Joining
With MC, k13 (15, 18, 19) sts, place next 25 sts onto a holder, with RS of pocket lining facing, k25 from holder, k rem 14 (17, 20, 23) sts. Cont pattern to approx 14½" from beg, ending with a RS row.

Armhole Shaping
Bind off 10 (13, 16, 19) sts at beg of next row—42 (44, 47, 48) sts. Cont pattern to approx 18½ (19, 19½, 20)" from beg, ending with a WS row.

Neck Shaping
Dec 1 st at neck edge every row 4 times, then every other row 9 (10,

12, 12) times. Work even on rem 29 (30, 31, 32) sts to same length as Back, ending with a WS row. With MC, bind off loosely.

LEFT FRONT
Reversing pocket opening, armhole and neck shapings, work as for Right Front.

SLEEVES (make two)
Beginning at the lower edge with smaller needles and MC, cast on 49 (51, 53, 55) sts. Work Ribbing as for Back to approx 1" from beg, ending with a WS row. Change to larger needles and k across, inc 1 st—50

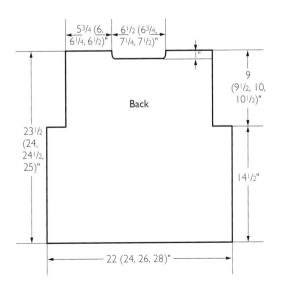

Back

5¾ (6, 6¼, 6½)"

6½ (6¾, 7¼, 7½)"

9 (9½, 10, 10½)"

23½ (24, 24½, 25)"

14½"

22 (24, 26, 28)"

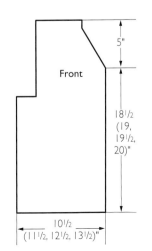

Front

5"

18½ (19, 19½, 20)"

10½ (11½, 12½, 13½)"

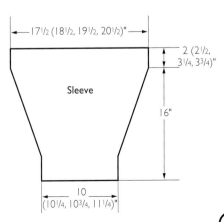

Sleeve

17½ (18½, 19½, 20½)"

2 (2½, 3¼, 3¾)"

16"

10 (10¼, 10¾, 11¼)"

Tartan Jacket
continued from page 37

(52, 54, 56) sts. Work 9 more St st rows. Beg Body Pattern. When piece measures approx 3" from beg, inc 1 st each edge every other row 0 (0, 4, 6) times then every 4th row 19 (20, 18, 17) times. Work even on the 88 (92, 98, 102) sts to approx 18 (18½, 19¼, 19¾)" from beg, ending with a WS row. Bind off loosely with MC.

FINISHING
Block pieces to measurements.
Embroidery
Right Front: Working from right to left, skip first 9 (11, 14, 15) sts; work from A–B on Right Front chart; skip 10 sts; work from A–B; leave last 11 (14, 17, 20) sts unworked. Left Front chart is a mirror image of Right Front.
Back: Working from right to left, skip 11 (14, 17, 20) sts; work from B–A on Left Front chart; skip 10 sts; work from B–A on Left Front chart. Skip 24 (28, 32, 36) sts. Work from A–B on Right Front chart, skip 10 sts, work from A–B on Right Front chart, leave last 11 (14, 17, 20) sts unworked.
Sleeves: Working from right to left, skip 2 (3, 4, 5) sts; rep B–A of Left Front chart, skip 24 sts, rep A–B of Right Front chart, leave rem 2 (3, 4, 5) sts unworked. Join shoulder seams. Sew in sleeves, sewing bound off sts to sleeve sides for square armholes. Join underarm and side seams.

Pockets
With the RS facing, slip sts from pocket holder onto smaller needle. Join MC and k 5 rows for garter st band. Bind off loosely and knitwise on WS of fabric. Sew sides of garter st band to fronts. Sew pocket linings in place.

Collar
With the RS facing, using smaller needles and MC, pick up and k 25 sts evenly spaced along right V-neck, 43 (43, 45, 45) sts along back neck, and 25 sts along left V-neck. Work Ribbing as for Back to 4½" from beg, ending with a WS row. Bind off in ribbing.

Left Front Band
With the RS facing using smaller needles and MC, pick up and k 149 (151, 153, 155) sts evenly spaced along edge. Work Ribbing as for Back for 9 rows. Bind off in ribbing.

Right Front Band
Work as for Left Band to completion of 3rd ribbing row. **Row 4 (RS):** Rib 34 (36, 38, 40); * bind off 3 sts, rib 13 more sts—14 sts between buttonholes; rep from * across for 7 buttonholes, ending rib to end. **Row 5:** Rib across and cast on 3 sts over each buttonhole. **Rows 6–9:** Rib. Bind off in ribbing. Sew buttons opposite buttonholes. Weave in loose ends on WS of fabric.

Chance Encounter
photos on pages 18–19

SKILL LEVEL: Intermediate but easy

SIZES: S (MEDIUM, L, XL)
Note: The pattern is written for the smallest size with changes for larger sizes in parentheses. When only one number is given, it applies to all sizes. For ease in working, before you begin, circle all numbers pertaining to the size you are knitting.

FINISHED MEASUREMENTS:
Bust: 40 (44, 48½, 53)"
Length: 24 (25, 26, 27)"

MATERIALS:
- Patons Shetland Chunky, 75% acrylic/25% wool, bulky weight yarn (148 yards per ball): 6 (6, 7, 8) balls of Bottle Green (3206) for MC; 3 (4, 4, 5) balls of Aqua Haze Heather (3205) for Color A; 1 ball each of Nugget Gold (3608) for Color B and Black (3040) for Color C
- Size 10 (6mm) straight knitting needles or size needed to obtain gauge
- Size 9 (5.5mm) straight knitting needles
- 16-inch circular needle; sizes 8 (5mm), 9 (5.5mm), and 10 (6mm)
- Yarn needle

GAUGE:
In St st and color patterns using largest needle, 15 sts and 20 rows = 4"/10cm. TAKE TIME TO CHECK YOUR GAUGE.

Note: The bodice portion of the front is worked in St st from a chart, reading from right to left for RS rows and from left to right for WS rows. Loosely carry color not in use along WS of fabric. To change color, bring next color from under present color for a twist to prevent holes. When working the horse and rider, use separate strands for each motif. Small areas

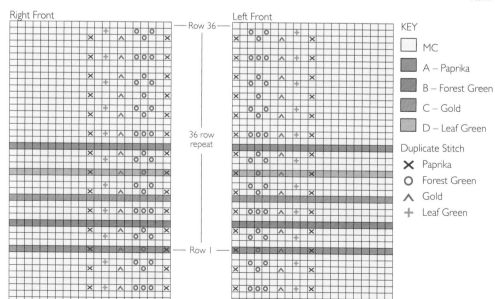

Right Front — Row 36 — 36 row repeat — Row 1

Left Front

KEY
- ☐ MC
- ▨ A – Paprika
- ▨ B – Forest Green
- ▨ C – Gold
- ▨ D – Leaf Green

Duplicate Stitch
- ✕ Paprika
- ○ Forest Green
- ∧ Gold
- ✛ Leaf Green

such as the diamonds along the side edges are best worked in duplicate stitch embroidery after the knitting is completed. Or if desired, work the entire chart in duplicate stitch.

INSTRUCTIONS:
BACK
Beginning at the lower edge with smaller needles and MC, cast on 75 (80, 90, 95) sts.
Ribbing
Row 1 (WS): P1; (k3, p2) across, ending k3, p1.
Row 2: Knit.
Rep Ribbing Rows 1–2 to approx 2" from beg, ending with a WS row. Change to larger needles and k across next row, inc 0 (3, 1, 4) sts evenly spaced—75 (83, 91, 99) sts. Work St st (p WS rows, k RS rows) until piece measures approx 23 (24, 25, 26)" from beg, ending with a WS row.
Neck Shaping
K first 28 (31, 34, 37) sts; join a new strand and bind off center 19 (21, 23, 25) sts; k to end of row. Working sides separately and at the same time, dec 1 st each neck edge. Work even on 27 (30, 33, 36) sts for each shoulder to approx 24 (25, 26, 27)" from beg, ending with a WS row. Bind off loosely.

FRONT
Work as for Back to approx 11½ (12½, 13½, 14½)" from beg, ending with a WS row. Begin Chart with Row 1 and work through completion of Row 29. Cont in St st with Color A until piece measures approx 20 (21, 22, 23)" from beg, ending with a WS row.
Neck Shaping
K first 37 (41, 45, 49) sts; join a new strand of A, bind off center st and k to end of row. Working sides separately and at the same time, dec 1 st each neck edge every row 4 (6, 8, 10) times and every other row 6 (5, 4, 3) times. Work even on rem 27 (30, 33, 36) sts for each shoulder to same length as Back, ending with a WS row. Bind off loosely.

SLEEVES (make two)
Beg at the lower edge, with smaller needles and MC, cast on 35 sts. Work Ribbing as for Back to approx 2" from beg, ending with a WS row. Change to larger needles and k across next row, inc 1 st—36 sts. Cont in St st,

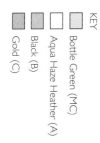

KEY
Gold (C)
Black (B)
Aqua Haze Heather (A)
Bottle Green (MC)

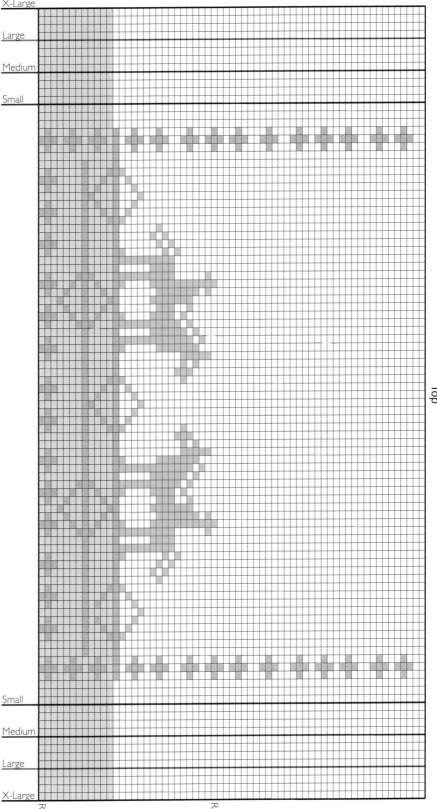

X-Large
Large
Medium
Small

Top

Small
Medium
Large
X-Large

Row 1 (RS)
Row 29

19 (21, 23, 25) sts across bound off sts at back neck; pick up 1 more st; turn. **Row 2:** K across and pick up 1 st; turn. Rep Row 2 for 7 times more, so you are at shoulders on each side —28 (30, 32, 34) sts. Working along V-neck, k across and pick up 2 sts; turn. Rep this row 5 times more—40 (42, 44, 46) sts. K across and pick up 3 sts; turn. Rep this row 7 times more—64 (66, 68, 70) sts. K across and pick up 4 sts; turn. Rep last row once more—72 (74, 76, 78) sts. Change to circular needle one size larger. K 5 rows. Change to largest circular needle. K 20 rows. Bind off loosely and knitwise. Fold collar in half toward the front.

inc 1 st each edge every 4th row 0 (0, 6, 13) times, every 6th row 6 (13, 9, 4) times, and every 8th row 5 (0, 0, 0) times. Work even on 58 (62, 66, 70) sts to approx 19½" from beg, ending with a WS row. Bind off loosely.

FINISHING

Join shoulder seams. Place markers 8¼ (8¾, 9¼, 10)" each side of shoulder seams. Sew in sleeves between markers. Join underarm and side seams.
Collar
Row 1: With the RS facing, using smallest circular needle, pick up and k

Scalloped Hem Jacket

photo on page 20

SKILL LEVEL: Intermediate

SIZES: S (MEDIUM, L, XL, XXL)
Note: The pattern is written for the smallest size with changes for larger sizes in parentheses. When only one number is given, it applies to all sizes. For ease in working, before you begin, circle all numbers pertaining to your size.

FINISHED MEASUREMENTS:
Bust: 40¼ (44, 47¼, 51, 54½)"
Length (hemmed): 26½ (27, 27½, 28, 28½)"

MATERIALS:
▪ Brown Sheep Lamb's Pride Worsted, 85% wool/15% mohair, worsted weight yarn (190 yards per skein): 7 (7, 8, 9, 9) skeins of Sunburst Gold (M 14)

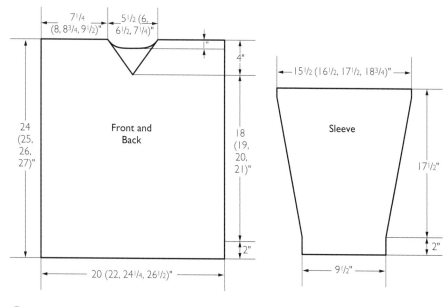

- Size 8 (5mm) knitting needles or size needed to obtain gauge
- Size 7 (4.5mm) knitting needles
- Five JHB International buttons, Autumn Festival #95180, size ⅞")
- Yarn needle

GAUGE:

In St st with larger needles, 18 sts and 24 rows = 4"/10cm.
TAKE TIME TO CHECK YOUR GAUGE.

SPECIAL ABBREVIATIONS:

Sl 1: With yarn on WS, slip next st purlwise to right-hand needle.
P2tog-b: Turn work slightly, insert needle from left to right into back loops of 2nd and 1st sts, p these two sts together.

STITCHES USED:
Scallops
Row 1 (RS): K1; * yo, k2tog; rep from * across.
Row 2: P all sts.

Garter Stitch Ridges
Row 1 (WS): Knit.
Row 2: Knit.
Row 3: Knit.

Bobble
(K1, p1, k1, p1, k1) into next st; turn. K5; turn. Bind off 4 sts.

Lace Pattern (a multiple of 20 sts + 1 st; over 10 rows)
Row 1 (RS): K1; * yo, sl 1, k1, psso, k15, k2tog, yo, k1; rep from * across.
Row 2: P2; * yo, p2tog, p13, p2tog-b, yo, p3; rep from * across, ending p2tog, p13, p2tog, yo, p2.
Row 3: K3; * yo, sl 1, k1, psso, k11, k2tog, yo, k5; rep from * across, ending yo, sl 1, k1, psso, k11, k2tog, yo, k3.
Row 4: P4; * yo, p2tog, p9, p2tog-b, yo, p7; rep from * across, ending yo, p2tog, p9, p2tog-b, yo, p4.
Row 5: K5; * yo, sl 1, k1, psso, k3, Bobble, k3, k2tog, yo, k9; rep from * across, ending yo, sl 1, k1, psso, k3, Bobble, k3, k2tog, yo, k5.
Row 6: P6; * yo, p2tog, p5, p2tog-b, yo, p11; rep from * across, ending p2tog, p5, p2tog-b, yo, p6.
Row 7: K7; * yo, sl 1, k1, psso, k3, k2tog, yo, k6, Bobble, k6; rep from *

Scalloped Hem Jacket

continued from page 41

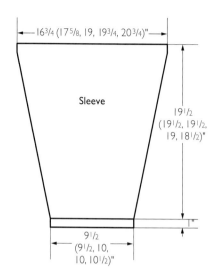

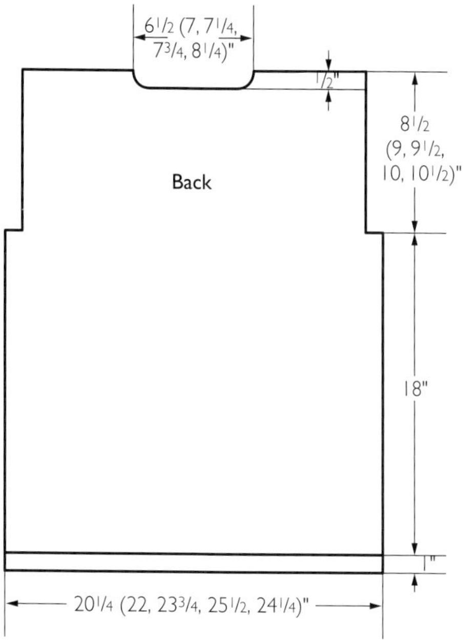

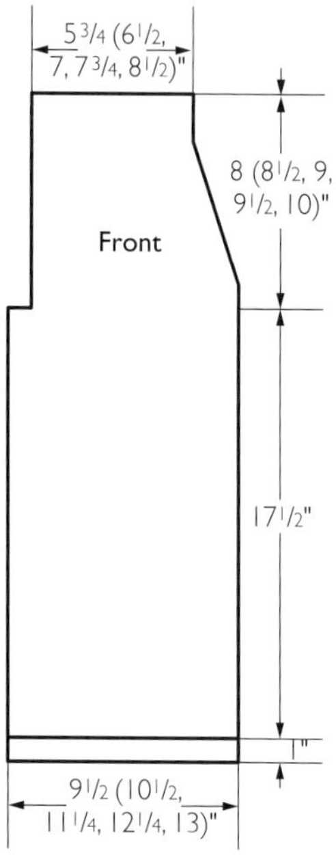

Sleeve

16¾ (17⅝, 19, 19¾, 20¾)"

19½ (19½, 19½, 19, 18½)"

9½ (9½, 10, 10, 10½)"

1"

Back

6½ (7, 7¼, 7¾, 8¼)"

½"

8½ (9, 9½, 10, 10½)"

18"

20¼ (22, 23¾, 25½, 24¼)"

1"

Front

5¾ (6½, 7, 7¾, 8½)"

8 (8½, 9, 9½, 10)"

17½"

9½ (10½, 11¼, 12¼, 13)"

1"

across, ending yo, sl 1, k1, psso, k3, k2tog, yo, k7.

Row 8: P8; * yo, p2tog, p1, p2tog-b, yo, p15; rep from * across, ending p2tog, p1, p2tog-b, yo, p8.

Row 9: K9; * yo, sl 1, k2tog, psso, yo, k17; rep from * across, ending yo, sl 1, k2tog, psso, yo, k9.

Row 10: Purl.

Note: *Read the chart from right to left for RS rows and from left to right for WS rows.*

INSTRUCTIONS:
BACK

For Border: Beg at lower edge with larger needles, cast on 91 (99, 107, 115, 123) sts. Beg with a p row, work 3 St st rows (p WS rows, k RS rows). Work Scallops Rows 1-2.

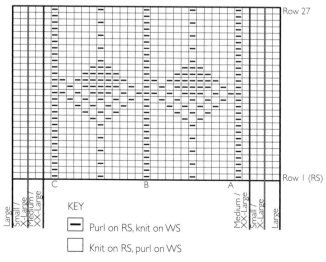

Row 27

Row 1 (RS)

C

B

A

Large
Small/X-Large
Medium/XX-Large

Medium/XX-Large
Small/X-Large
Large

KEY

▬ Purl on RS, knit on WS

☐ Knit on RS, purl on WS

Beg with a k row, work St st until piece measures approx 9" from beg, ending with a RS row. Work Garter Stitch Ridges.

For Chart: Beg at your size and work to B; rep A–B across, ending last rep at C; complete the row by working to your size. Work through completion of Row 27. Work Garter Stitch Ridges.

For Lace Pattern: Keeping 5 (9, 3, 7, 1) st(s) along each edge in St st, work the 10 pattern rows. Cont in St st for rem of Back. When piece measures approx 19" from beg, end with a WS row.

Armhole Shaping

Bind off 5 sts at the beg of the next 2 rows—81 (89, 97, 105, 113) sts. Work even to approx 27 (27½, 28, 28½, 29)" from beg, ending with a WS row.

Back Neck Shaping

K27 (30, 33, 36, 39) sts, join a new strand and bind off center 27 (29, 31, 33, 35) sts, k to end. Working sides separately and at the same time, dec 1 st at each neck edge. When piece measures approx 27½ (28, 28½, 29, 29½)" from beg, end with a WS row. Bind off 26 (29, 32, 35, 38) sts for each shoulder.

RIGHT FRONT:

Beg at lower edge with larger needles, cast on 43 (47, 51, 55, 59) sts. Beg with a p row, work 3 St st rows. Work Scallops Rows 1–2. Beg with a k row, work St st until piece measures approx 9" from beg, ending with a RS row. Work Garter Stitch Ridges.

For Chart: K3 (9, 9, 3, 9); rep A–B across, ending last rep at C; complete the row by working to your size. Work through completion of Row 27. Work Garter Stitch Ridges.

For Lace Pattern: Keeping 1 (3, 5, 7, 9) st(s) along each edge in St st, work the 10 pattern rows. Cont in St st for rem of Front. When piece measures approx 19" from beg, end with a RS row.

Armhole Shaping

Bind off 5 sts at the beg of the next row—38 (42, 46, 50, 54) sts. Work even to approx 18½" from beg, ending with a WS row.

Neck Shaping

K1, ssk, k to end. Dec every other row 3 (5, 7, 9, 11) times more, then every 4th row 8 (7, 6, 5, 4) times—26 (29, 32, 35, 38) sts rem. When piece measures same as Back, end with a WS row. Bind off.

LEFT FRONT

Work as for Right Front to Chart; begin at your size and work to B; rep A–B across, ending last rep at C; k 3 (9, 9, 3, 9). Complete as for Right Front, except on neck shaping, k across to last 3 sts, then k2tog, k1.

SLEEVES (make two)
For Border: Beg at lower edge, cast on 43 (43, 45, 45, 47) sts. Beg with a p row, work 3 St st rows. Work Scallops Rows 1-2. Beg with a k row, work St st until piece measures approx 3" from beg, ending with a WS row. Inc 1 st each edge now and then every 2nd row 0 (0, 0, 0, 2) times, every 4th row 2 (7, 13, 21, 20) times, and every 6th row 13 (10, 6, 0, 0) times—75 (79, 85, 89, 93) sts. AT THE SAME TIME, when piece measures 9" from beg, end with a RS row. Work Garter Stitch Ridges then cont in St st for rem of sleeve. Work even to approx 20½ (20½, 20½, 20, 19½)" from beg, ending with a WS row. Bind off.

FINISHING
Join shoulder seams. Sew in sleeves, joining sides to bound off sts for square armholes. Join underarm and side seams. Fold lower edge along eyelets and whip st in place; rep for sleeves.

Left Band
With the RS facing using smaller needles, beg at center of back neck to pick up and k19 (20, 21, 22, 23) sts evenly spaced to shoulder, 40 (42, 44, 46, 48) sts to V-neck, 94 sts to lower edge. K 6 rows. 153 (156, 159, 162, 165) sts. Bind off loosely and knitwise on WS of fabric.

Right Band
With the RS facing using smaller needles, beg at lower edge to pick up and k94 sts to V-neck, 40 (42, 44, 46, 48) sts to shoulder, and 19 (20, 21, 22, 23) sts along back neck. K 3 rows. 153 (156, 159, 162, 165) sts.
Buttonhole Row: K41 sts; * bind off 2 sts, with 1 st on right needle, k9 more sts—10 sts bet buttonholes; rep from * for 5 buttonholes, ending k to end. **Next Row:** K across and cast on 2 sts over each buttonhole. K 1 row. Bind off loosely and knitwise on WS of fabric. Join back neck seam. Sew buttons opposite buttonholes.

Scallops and Squares Throw
photo on page 21

SKILL LEVEL: Easy

SIZE: Throw measures approx 43×55"

MATERIALS:
- Lion Brand Wool-Ease, Article 620, 80% acrylic/20% wool, worsted weight yarn (197 yards per ball): 9 balls of Cranberry (138)
- Size 8 (5mm) 29-inch circular knitting needle or size needed to obtain gauge

GAUGE:
In Body Pattern, 20 sts and 24 rows = 4"/10cm.
TAKE TIME TO CHECK YOUR GAUGE.

STITCHES USED:
Garter Stitch—Knit every row.

Scallops (over 18 sts; a rep of 4 rows)
Row 1 (RS): Knit.
Row 2: Purl.
Row 3: (K2tog) 3 times, (yo, k1) 6 times, (k2tog) 3 times.
Row 4: Knit.
Rep Rows 1–4 for Scallops.

Squares (over 15 sts; a rep of 12 rows)
Row 1 (RS): P5, k5, p5.
Row 2: K5, p5, k5.
Rows 3–6: Rep Rows 1–2.
Row 7: K5, p5, k5.
Row 8: P5, k5, p5.
Rows 9–12: Rep Rows 7–8.
Rep Rows 1–12 for Squares.

Note: *The throw is worked back and forth on a circular needle to accommodate the large number of stitches.*

INSTRUCTIONS:
Beg at the lower edge, cast on 216 sts.
Border
Row 1 (RS): Knit.
Row 2: Knit.

Scallops and Squares Throw
continued from page 43

Row 3: K8; * k2tog, yo, k14, k2tog, yo, k15; rep from * across, ending k2tog, yo, k8.
Rows 4–6: Knit.

Body Pattern
Row 1 (RS): * K18, p5, k5, p5; rep from * across, ending k18.
Row 2: * P18, k5, p5, k5; rep from * across, ending p18.
Row 3: * Scallops Row 3 over 18 sts, p5, k5, p5; rep from * across, ending Scallops Row 3 over last 18 sts.
Row 4: K23; * p5, k28; rep from * across, ending p5, k23.
Rows 5–6: Rep Rows 1–2.
Row 7: * Scallops Row 3 over 18 sts, k5, p5, k5; rep from * across, ending Scallops Row 3 over last 18 sts.
Row 8: * K18, p5, k5, p5; rep from * across, ending k18.
Row 9: K23; * p5, k28; rep from * across, ending p5, k23.
Row 10: P23; * k5, p28; rep from * across, ending k5, p23.
Rows 11–12: Rep Rows 7–8.
Rep Rows 1–12 for Body Pattern until piece measures approx 54" from beg, ending with Row 12.

Border
Rows 1–4: Knit.
Row 5: K8; * k2tog, yo, k14, k2tog, yo, k15; rep from * across, ending k2tog, yo, k8.
Rows 6–7: Knit.
Row 8: Bind off knitwise on WS of fabric.

Fringe
Cut 8 strands measuring 7" each. Holding strands together in a bundle, fold in half to form a lp. With the WS of afghan facing, take lp through first eyelet on border; take ends through lp and pull up to form a knot. Make fringe for each border eyelet along each end.

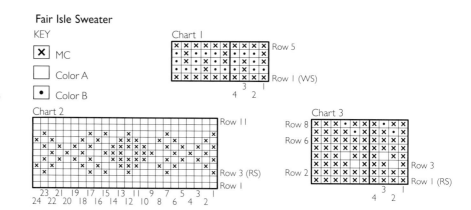

Fair Isle Sweater
KEY
☒ MC
☐ Color A
• Color B

Chart 1
Chart 2
Chart 3

Fair Isle Sweater

photo on page 22

SKILL LEVEL: Intermediate

SIZES: S (MEDIUM, L, XL, XXL)
Note: *The pattern is written for the smallest size with changes for larger sizes in parentheses. When only one number is given, it applies to all sizes. For ease in working, before you begin, circle all numbers pertaining to your size.*

FINISHED MEASUREMENTS:
Bust: 34½ (37, 39½, 42, 44½)"
Length: 18½ (19, 19½, 20, 20½)"

MATERIALS:
- Blue Sky Alpaca, 100% alpaca, sport weight yarn (134 yards per ball): 4 (5, 5, 5, 6) balls of Natural Medium Grey (0010) for MC; 1 (1, 2, 2, 2) ball(s) of Natural White (000) for Color A; for all sizes 1 ball of Red (23) for Color B
- Size 3 (3.25mm) knitting needles or size needed to obtain gauge
- Size 2 (2.75mm) knitting needles
- Tapestry needle
- Two ⅜-inch-diameter buttons
- Size C/2 crochet hook

GAUGE:
In St st and color patterns with larger needles, 26 sts and 30 rows = 4"/10cm. TAKE TIME TO CHECK YOUR GAUGE.

SPECIAL ABBREVIATIONS:
Ssk (slip, slip, knit): Slip next 2 sts knitwise, one at a time to right-hand needle, insert tip of left-hand needle into fronts of these 2 sts and k them tog.

Note: *The sweater is worked from charts, reading from right to left for RS rows and from left to right for WS rows. Loosely carry color not in use along WS of fabric. When changing color, bring new strand from under present strand for a twist to avoid holes. Twist strands at least every 5 sts.*

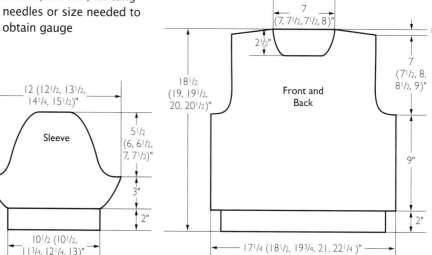

INSTRUCTIONS:
BACK
Beg at the lower edge with MC and smaller needles, cast on 111 (119, 127, 135, 143) sts.

Ribbing
Row 1 (WS): P1; (k1, p1) across.
Row 2: K1; (p1, k1) across. Rep Ribbing Rows 1–2 to approx 2" from beg, ending with a RS row. Change to larger needles and p across next row, inc 1 st–112 (120, 128, 136, 144) sts.

Begin Charts *(opposite)*
Begin Chart 1 with Row 2, rep #1–#4 across. Work through completion of Row 5. Note that the background color for this chart is MC. For Chart 2, using Color A as the background, work 2 St st rows. **Row 3 (RS):** Beg at #5 (1, 5, 1, 5) and work to #20; rep #5–#20 across, ending last rep at #20 (24, 20, 24, 20). Work through completion of Row 11. Rep Chart I as before. For Chart 3, using MC as the background, work 2 St st rows. **Row 3 (RS):** Rep #1–#4 across for all sizes. Work through completion of Row 8; then rep Rows 1–8 until piece measures approx 10½" from beg, ending with Row 2 or Row 6. Rep Chart 1, Chart 2, Chart 1 as est then rep Chart 3 for remainder of Back. AT THE SAME TIME, when piece measure approx 11" from beg, end with a WS row.

Armhole Shaping
Keeping to est pattern, bind off 9 (10, 11, 12, 13) sts at the beg of the next 2 rows. **Next Dec Row (RS):** K3, k2tog, cont chart pat to last 5 sts, ssk, k3. Work 1 row even. Rep last

2 rows 1 (2, 3, 4, 5) time(s) more—90 (94, 98, 102, 106) sts. Work even to approx 18 (18½, 19, 19½, 20)" from beg, ending with a WS row.

Shoulder and Back Neck Shaping
Bind off 11 (12, 12, 13, 13) sts at each shoulder edge once and 11 (12, 13, 14, 14) at each shoulder edge once. Bind off rem 46 (46, 48, 48, 52) sts.

FRONT
Work as for Back to approx 16 (16½, 17, 17½, 18)" from beg, ending with a WS row.

Neck Shaping
In color pattern, k34 (36, 37, 39, 39) sts; join new strand(s) and bind off center 22 (22, 24, 24, 28) sts; k to end. Working sides separately and at the same time, bind off at each neck edge 3 sts 3 times, 2 sts once, and 1 st once. Work even on rem 22 (24, 25, 27, 27) sts for each shoulder to approx 18 (18½, 19, 19½, 20)" from beg. Shape shoulders as for Back.

SLEEVES (make two)
Beg at the lower edge with smaller needles and MC, cast on 65 (65, 69, 73, 77) sts. Work Ribbing as for Back to approx 2" from beg, ending with a WS row. Change to larger needles and k next row, inc 3 (3, 7, 7, 7) sts evenly spaced—68 (68, 76, 80, 84) sts. P across. Begin Chart 3, rep #1–#4 across. On next RS row, inc 1 st each edge. Including new sts into color pattern, inc every other row 0 (4, 2, 2, 6) times then every 4th row 4 (2, 3, 3,

1) time(s)—78 (82, 88, 92, 100) sts. Work even to approx 5" from beg, ending with a WS row.

Sleeve Cap Shaping
Bind off 9 (10, 11, 12, 13) sts at the beg of the next 2 rows. **Next Dec Row (RS):** K3, k2tog, cont chart pat to last 5 sts, ssk, k3. Work 1 row even. Rep last 2 rows 3 times more— 52 (54, 58, 60, 66) sts. Rep dec row every 4th row 3 (4, 5, 5, 6) times then every other row 7 (7, 7, 8, 9) times. Bind off 3 sts at the beg of the next 4 rows. On next RS row, bind off rem 20 (20, 22, 22, 24) sts.

FINISHING
Join left shoulder seam.
Neckband
With the RS facing, using smaller needles and MC, pick up and k109 (109, 115, 115, 127) sts evenly spaced around neck. Rep Ribbing as for Back until band measures approx 1" from beg, ending with a WS row. Bind off in ribbing.

Leaving neckband open, join right shoulder seam. Set in sleeves. Join underarm and side seams. Weave in loose ends. With the RS facing, using crochet hook, join MC with a sl st at inside edge of front neck band. Ch 1, work 5 sc evenly spaced to edge; turn. Sl st in first sc; * in next sc (sl st, ch 3, sl st), sl st in next sc; rep from * again. Fasten off. Sew buttons opposite button loops.

Weave loose ends along WS of fabric.

Bright Cardigan and Hat
photo on page 23
SKILL LEVEL: Intermediate

SIZES: Children's size 4 (6, 8, 10)
Note: *The pattern is written for the smallest size with changes for larger sizes in parentheses. When only one number is given, it applies to all sizes. For ease in working, before you begin, circle all numbers pertaining to the size you are knitting.*

FINISHED MEASUREMENTS:
Chest (buttoned): 30½ (33, 35¼, 37½)"
Length: 16 (18, 20, 22)"

Bright Cardigan and Hat

continued from page 45

CARDIGAN MATERIALS:

- Muench Yarns, Bali, 50% cotton/50% acrylic, sport weight yarn (100 meters per ball): 4 (4, 5, 6) balls of Purple (69) for MC; 1 (1, 2, 2) ball(s) of Aqua (70) for Color A; and 1 ball of Orange (66) for Color B
- Size 5 (3.75mm) 29-inch circular knitting needle or size needed to obtain gauge
- Size 4 (3.5mm) knitting needles
- Tapestry needle
- 7 JHB International buttons [Peoria, (#45140, green—3), (#45141, red—2), and (#45143, yellow—2)]

GAUGE:

In St st and color patterns with larger needles, 20 sts and 28 rows = 4"/10cm. TAKE TIME TO CHECK YOUR GAUGE.

STITCHES USED:

Border (a multiple of 6 sts + 3 sts; a rep of 2 rows)
Row 1 (WS): With MC, * p1, k1, p1, k3; rep from * across, ending p1, k1, p1.
Row 2: With MC, knit.
Rep Rows 1–2 for Border.

Note: The lower body is worked in one piece to the armhole, using a circular needle to accommodate the large number of stitches. This sweater is worked from a chart, reading from right to left for RS rows and from left to right for WS rows. When changing color, bring next strand from under present strand for a twist to prevent holes.

INSTRUCTIONS:
LOWER BODY

With larger needles and MC, cast on 147 (159, 171, 183) sts. Work Border Rows 1–2 to approx 2" from beg, ending with a WS row.

Body Pattern
Rows 1–4: With Color A, k.
Row 5: With MC, k.
Row 6: With MC, p.
Row 7 (RS): Beg Row 7 Chart 1 at A and work to #4; rep #1–#4 across, ending last rep at B.
Rows 8–15: Follow the chart.
Row 16: With MC, p.
Row 17: With MC, k.
Row 18: With MC, p.
Rows 19–22: With color B, k.
Row 23: With MC, k.
Row 24: With MC, p.
Rows 25–33: Follow the chart, beg at A and work to #4; rep #1–#4 across, ending last rep at B.
Row 34: With MC, p.
Row 35: With MC, k.
Row 36: With MC, p.
Rep Rows 1–36 until piece measures approx 9 (10½, 12, 13½)" from beg, ending with a WS row.

RIGHT FRONT

Work est pat across first 36 (39, 42, 45) sts. Leave rem sts for later. Cont in color patterns until 2 total Chart 1 repeats have been completed. Rep Chart 1, Rows 1–4 again. Begin Chart

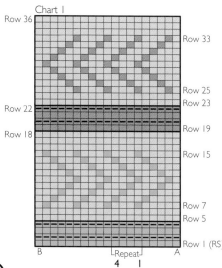

Chart 1

Chart 2

KEY

Knit on RS, purl on WS with MC

Knit on WS with Color A

Knit on WS with Color B

Aqua (A)

Orange (B)

2 at #5 (7, 5, 7) and work to #8. Rep #3–#8 across, ending last rep at #10 (9, 10, 9). AT THE SAME TIME, when piece measures approx 14 (16, 18, 20)" from beg, end with a WS row.

Neck Shaping
At beg of neck edge, bind off 6 (7, 8, 9) sts once, 3 sts once, 2 sts once, and 1 st twice. Cont as est on rem 23 (25, 27, 29) sts to approx 16 (18, 20, 22)" from beg, ending with a WS row. Bind off knitwise with MC.

BACK
Work pat across center 75 (81, 87, 93) sts. Cont in color patterns until 2 total Chart 1 repeats have been completed. Rep Chart 1, Rows 1–4 again. Begin Chart 2 at #1 (2, 1, 2) and work to #8; rep #3–#8 across, ending last rep at #9 (10, 9, 10). Work even to approx 16 (18, 20, 22)" from beg, ending with a WS row. Bind off knitwise with MC.

LEFT FRONT
Work as for Right Front to Chart 2. Begin Chart 2 at #2 (1, 2, 1) and work to #8. Rep #3–#8 across, ending last rep at #7 (9, 7, 9). Reversing neck shaping, complete as for Right Front.

SLEEVES (make 2)
With larger needle and MC, cast on 36 sts. Work Border Rows 1–2 to approx 2" from beg, ending with a WS row. With Color A, k next row, inc 3 (3, 3, 7) sts evenly spaced—39 (39, 39, 43) sts. K 3 more rows with A. With MC, k 1 row, p 1 row. Beg Chart 1 at A and work to #4; rep #1–#4 across, ending last rep at B. Pattern is now set. Inc 1 st each edge on next 3 (3, 3, 2) RS rows. Including new sts into

pattern as they accumulate, inc 1 st each edge every 4th row 11 (14, 16, 18) times—67 (73, 77, 83) total sts. Work even to approx 11 (13, 14, 15)" from beg, ending with a WS row. Bind off knitwise with MC.

FINISHING
Join shoulder and sleeve seams. Sew in sleeves.

Neckband
With the RS facing using smaller needles and MC, pick up and k75 (81, 87, 93) sts evenly spaced around neck. Rep Border Rows 1–2 for 4 times; rep Row 1 again. Bind off knitwise.

Left Front Band for Girls or Right Front Band for Boys
With the RS facing, using smaller needles and MC, pick up and k 81 (93, 105, 117) sts evenly spaced along edge. Work Border Rows 1–2 for 4 times; rep Row 1 again. Bind off knitwise.

Right Front Band
Work as for Left Band through completion of Row 3. **Row 4:** K4; * bind off 2 sts, with 1 st on right needle k 9 (11, 13, 15) more—10 (12, 14, 16) sts between buttonholes; rep from * across for 7 buttonholes, ending k to end. **Row 5:** Work est pattern across and cast on 2 sts over each buttonhole. **Rows 6–9:** Work as est. Bind off knitwise. Sew buttons opposite buttonholes.

HAT (19½-inch circumference)
■This project requires 1 ball of Purple Bali; small amounts of Aqua and Orange Bali; size 5 and 4 knitting needles; tapestry needle. Gauge is same as for Cardigan.

With smaller needles and Purple, cast on 97 sts.
Row 1 (WS): * P1, k1, p1, k3; rep from * across, ending p1.
Row 2: Knit.
Rep Rows 1–2 for 4 times more; then rep Row 1 again. Change to larger needles, beg with a p row, work 11 rows of St st, dec 1 st on last RS row—96 sts. Work Chart 2 from #1–#8 across; rep Rows 1–8 twice, then rep Rows 1–6 again.

Crown Shaping
Row 1 (RS): K1; (k2tog, k17) across.
Row 2: P91.
Row 3: K1; (k2tog, k16) across.
Row 4: P86.
Row 5: K1; (k2tog, k15) across.
Row 6: P81.
Continue is this manner, working 1 less st between decreases until 36 sts rem. P36. (K2tog) across. P18. Cut yarn, leaving a long tail. Thread tail into tapestry needle and back through rem sts. Pull up to close opening. With same tail, join sides tog.

Tassel
Cut 6 lengths of Purple, about 18" long. Hold strands tog and tie one end into an overhand knot. Pin the knot to a stable surface. Divide strands into 3 equal sections and braid them; tie into an overhand knot, leaving about 3" free for fringe. Take one knot through top of Hat. Repeat this process for the rem 2 colors. Braid the 3 braids tog; secure by tying a strand of any color beneath the first knots at the outside end of the braid.

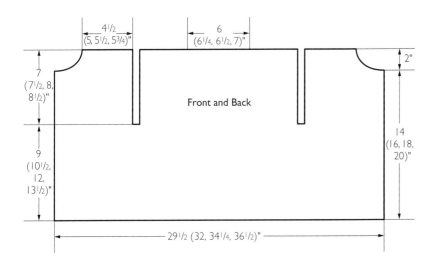

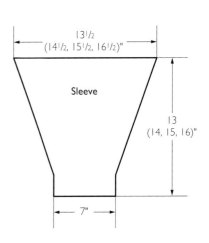

W

hether there's snow on the ground or a nip in the air, the winter months beg for knitted warmth. To take away the chill, pull on gloves, a hat, and a scarf with chunky cables and dainty Fair Isle pattern or a colorful sweater or vest. Whether knitting for yourself or for those on your gift list, this festive collection will help you make the most of...

Winter

**CABLES AND FAIR ISLE
ACCESSORY SET** This beautiful
set will keep you toasty warm
when chilly weather arrives. The
hat band is worked lengthwise
in cable pattern. Stitches are
picked up along one edge to
work the Fair Isle pattern back
and forth for the crown. Garter
stitches border each piece in the
set. The same Fair Isle pattern is
worked above the cuff on each
glove, and the cable pattern is
used for the scarf. Instructions
begin on page 78.

let it snow

CHILD'S COLORFUL PULLOVER For girls and boys, this cotton/acrylic pullover is worked in three colors with only two colors on each row. Highlights on the bandings accent the color of the narrow background stripe. Instructions begin on page 80.

CASUAL STRIPES Comfortable to wear and fun to make, this colorful pullover will brighten winter days. The zipper is easy to sew in by hand or machine. Ribs border the cuffs, collar, and lower edges of this stylish stockinette-stitch pullover. Instructions begin on page 81.

holiday bright

PERUVIAN RAGLAN AND CAP This gorgeous wool duo includes a raglan-sleeve turtleneck and a cap with ear flaps and solid color tassel. The sweater bodice and cap include contrasting intarsia patterns. Instructions begin on page 82.

inca like

HOMESPUN THROW

Here's a soft throw that's easy enough for a beginner to master. Use a double strand of yarn and size 15 knitting needles to work this quickly in one piece. Instructions begin on page 86.

BACK-TO-BASICS SWEATER

A wonderful choice for beginning knitters, this soft pullover is worked in basic stockinette stitch. The square neck and cuff details add design to this one-color beauty. Instructions begin on page 86.

simply basic

STADIUM MITTENS AND STRIPED MITTENS Here are pairs that are easy to knit yet will receive rave reviews during sledding weather. The bulky Stadium mittens, *far left*, are accented with stripes at the wrist bands. The palm side of these mittens is worked in stockinette stitch. The Striped mittens, *near left*, use four colors of yarn to create the vivid stripes. Instructions for both pairs of mittens start on page 87.

warmth

KNIT CHEX MITTENS
Darling braided tails hang
from checkerboard cuffs of
these finger-warming mittens.
A cable runs along the back
of each mitten to make this
pair anything but plain.
Instructions for the mittens
start on page 89.

ROARIN' GOOD TIME MITTS
Knit a playful pair of mittens
for each of the special kids in
your winter wonderland.
These easy-to-knit lion
mittens are finished with knit
ears, yarn manes, and
stitched features. Instructions
for the mittens start on
page 90.

playful

MATCHING VESTS If you're looking for fast projects, knit these vests that are made in wide ribs interrupted with garter stitch and stockinette stitch color work. To work the handsome V-neck, pick up an even number of stitches, then rib for 7 rows. Turn the rib to the inside and sew in place. Instructions begin on page 91.

dad & lad

RODEO DRIVE FOR LUNCH
This cardigan is worked in
stockinette stitch with panels
of lace along the bodice and
sleeves, with I-cords
accenting the wrists and
waist. A soft collar is
bordered with simple crochet
stitches. Made of cotton/wool
blend, this cardigan is
suitable for wearing any
season. Instructions begin
on page 92.

it's a wrap

RED HAT, SCARF, AND BAG
Use size 10 needles and a double strand of yarn to make these intermediate level projects. After you learn the cable patterns, each project will go lickity split. The cabled scarf is bordered by moss stitch. The constructed hat is worked from side to side and joined together at the back. Instructions begin on page 95.

cabled

CHRISTMAS STOCKINGS
Add handcrafted fun to the
holidays with a set of easy-knit
striped Christmas stockings
that hold lots of goodies.
Each stocking is worked in
stockinette stitches with
garter-stitch bands and cuffs.
Instructions begin on page 96.

deck the halls

MEN'S ARGYLE SWEATER

Two shades of gray mix with winter white for this roomy men's pullover. The argyle patterns are on the front while the back and sleeves are worked in stockinette stitch using the main color. The pullover has set-in sleeves and a crew neck of 2x2 ribs. Instructions begin on page 98.

DOG ARGYLE Pamper your pet with an argyle crewneck sized for petite, small, or medium dogs. The white areas of the pattern are worked in seed stitch while the grays are in stockinette stitch. Instructions begin on page 101.

for fido too

BUTTON-UP JACKET AND HAT
This winter white seed-stitch jacket works up quickly. The ribbed sleeves, square armholes, patch pockets, and side vents add textural details. Blanket-stitch embroidery borders the pockets and hat. Instructions begin on page 101.

SNOWFLAKE PULLOVER
This sweater's easy-knit texture surrounds a snowflake panel on the front and back. The crew neck is detailed by working the last round with a contrasting color. Instructions begin on page 104.

winter wear

CHRISTMASTIME CAPE

For a cover-up a little out of the ordinary, knit this comfy cape in stockinette stitch with a central front cable. The project works up quickly in two sections (front panel and front sides/back) to the top of the armhole openings, where the sections are joined and worked in rounds for the remainder of the garment. The cape has a turtleneck with a rolled edge. The perfect solution to shopping in warm stores during inclement weather, this cape is warm enough for protection outside yet comfortable to wear inside. Instructions begin on page 106.

so sweet

BASKETWEAVE AND BOBBLES JACKET AND CAP

Make your little angel a comfortable cardigan and stocking cap with ribbed borders and lively pattern stitches. Worsted weight yarn in gray is the main color with contrasting copper and kiwi. The jacket is made in one piece to the underarm, and the cap is worked back and forth and has a back seam. Instructions begin on page 107.

bundle up

Cables and Fair Isle Accessory Set

photos on pages 50–51

SKILL LEVEL: Advanced

SIZE:
Hat and Gloves: One size
Scarf measures approx 8×62"

MATERIALS:
- Patons Decor, 75% acrylic/25% wool, worsted weight yarn (210 yards per skein): *For Hat and Gloves:* 1 skein Burgundy (1647) for MC; and 1 skein each of Claret (1657) for A, Rich Bronze (1662) for B, Coralberry (1651) for C, and Rich Aqua (1612) for D. *For Scarf:* 3 skeins of Burgundy (1647)
- Size 3 (3.25 mm) set of four double pointed knitting needles for Gloves or size needed to obtain gauge
- Size 7 (4.5mm) knitting needles for Hat and Scarf or size needed to obtain gauge
- Cable needle
- Tapestry needle

GAUGE:
Hat and Scarf: In St st on size 7 needles, 20 sts and 26 rows = 4"/10cm.
Gloves: In St st on size 3 needles, 24 sts and 32 rows = 4"/10cm
TAKE TIME TO CHECK YOUR GAUGE.

SPECIAL ABBREVIATIONS:
Cr5B: Slip next 3 sts onto cable needle and leave at back of work. K2, then p the p st from cable needle. K2 rem sts on cable needle.
T3B: Slip next st onto cable needle and leave at back of work. K2 then p1 from cable needle.
T3F: Slip next 2 sts onto cable needle and leave at front of work. P1, then k2 from cable needle.
MB: (K1, yo, k1, yo, k1) all in next st. Turn; p5. Turn; ssk, k1, k2tog. Turn; p3. Turn; sl 1, k2tog, psso—1 st rem. Bobble complete.
Ssk (slip, slip, knit): Slip next 2 sts knitwise, one at a time to right-hand needle, insert tip of left-hand needle into fronts of these 2 sts and k them tog.

STITCHES USED:
Cable Panel (worked over 11 sts; a rep of 22 rows)
Row 1 (WS): K3, p2, k1, p2, k3.
Row 2: P3, Cr5B, p3.
Row 3: As Row 1.
Row 4: P2, T3B, p1, T3F, p2.
Row 5: K2, p2, k3, p2, k2.
Row 6: P1, T3B, p3, T3F, p1.
Row 7: K1, p2, k5, p2, k1.
Row 8: P1, k2, p5, k2, p1.
Rows 9–10: As Rows 7 and 8.
Row 11: As Row 7.
Row 12: P1, T3F, p3, T3B, p1.
Row 13: As Row 5.
Row 14: P2, T3F, p1, T3B, p2.
Row 15: As Row 1.
Row 16: As Row 2.
Row 17: As Row 1.
Row 18: As Row 4.
Row 19: As Row 5.
Row 20: P2, k2, p1, MB, p1, k2, p2.
Row 21: As Row 5.
Row 22: As Row 14.
Rows 1–22 form Cable Panel.

INSTRUCTIONS:
SCARF
With MC, cast on 38 sts.
Work 9 rows in garter St (k every row), noting first row is WS.
Row 10: K across, inc 7 sts evenly—45 sts.

Proceed in pattern as follows:
Row 1 (WS): K3, work Row 1 of Cable Panel across next 11 sts, k3, work Row 19 of Cable Panel across next 11 sts, k3, work Row 1 of Cable Panel across next 11 sts, k3.
Row 2: K3, work Row 2 of Cable Panel across next 11 sts, p3, work Row 20 of Cable Panel across next 11 sts, p3, work Row 2 of Cable Panel across next 11 sts, k3.
Cable Panels are now in position. Cont in pat until Scarf measures approx 60" ending on Row 2 of Cable Panel for Outer Panels and Row 20 of Cable Panel for Center Panel.
Next Row (WS): Knit, dec 7 sts evenly across—38 sts. Work 9 rows Garter St. Bind off knitwise (WS).

GLOVES
Right Glove: ** **Cuff: With MC and set of four needles, cast on 36 sts. Divide into 12 sts on 3 needles. Place marker to indicate beg of rnd; join.
Rnd 1: Knit.
Rnd 2: Purl.
Rnds 3–8: Rep last 2 rnds 3 times more.
Rnd 9: K 1 rnd, inc 4 sts evenly around—40 sts.
Rnds 10–11: With A, k.
Rnd 12: * With A, k1, with C, k1. Rep from * around.

Rnd 13: With C, k.
Rnd 14: With A, k.
Rnd 15: * With B, k1, with MC, k1.
Rep from * around.
Rnd 16: With MC, k.
Rnd 17: * With MC, k1, with B, k1.
Rep from * around.
Rnd 18: With A, k.
Rnd 19: With D, k.
Rnd 20: * With D, k1, with C, k1.
Rep from * around.
Rnd 21: With D, k.
Cont with A for remainder of Glove.
K 2 rnds.

Thumb Gusset: Rnd 1: P1, (inc 1 st in next st) twice, p1, k to end of rnd.
Rnds 2–5: K all k sts and p all p sts as they appear.
Rnd 6: P1, inc 1 st in next st. K to 2 sts before the next p st, inc 1 st in next st, k1, p1, k to end of rnd.
Rnds 7–8: K all k sts and p all p sts as they appear.
Rep last 3 rnds until there are 12 sts between the 2 p sts—50 sts. Work 2 rnds even. **Next Rnd:** Cast on 4 sts. Slip next 14 sts onto a thread for thumb. K to end of rnd—40 sts.
K 9 rnds **.

First Finger: K first 4 sts. Slip all but last 8 sts onto a thread. Turn. Cast on 2 sts. Turn. K last 8 sts. Divide these 14 sts onto 3 needles. Join in rnd. K 20 rnds.
* **Next Rnd:** (K2, k2tog) 3 times, k2.
Next Rnd: (K1, k2tog) 3 times, k2.
Next Rnd: (K2tog) 4 times.
Break yarn. Thread end through rem 4 sts. Draw up and fasten securely *.

Second Finger: Slip next 5 sts from thread. Turn. Cast on 2 sts. Turn. K last 5 sts. Pick up and k 2 sts at base of first finger. Divide these 14 sts onto 3 needles. K 22 rnds. Work from * to * as given for First Finger.

Third Finger: Slip next 5 sts from thread. Turn. Cast on 2 sts. Turn. K last 5 sts. Pick up and k 2 sts at base of second finger. Divide these 14 sts onto 3 needles. K 20 rnds. Work from * to * as given for First Finger.

Fourth Finger: Slip last 8 sts from thread. Pick up and k 2 sts at base of third finger. Divide these 10 sts onto 3 needles. K 16 rnds. **Next Rnd:** (K2tog) 5 times. **Next Rnd:** (K2tog) twice, k1. Break yarn. Thread end through rem 3 sts. Draw up and fasten securely.

Thumb: K the 14 sts that were left for thumb. Pick up and k 4 sts at base of thumb. Divide these 18 sts onto 3 needles. K 16 rnds.
Next Rnd: (K4, k2tog) 3 times.
Next Rnd: (K3, k2tog) 3 times.
Next Rnd: (K2, k2tog) 3 times.
Break yarn. Thread end through rem 9 sts. Draw up and fasten securely.

Left Glove: Work from ** to ** as given for Right Glove. **First Finger:** K first 8 sts. Slip all but last 4 sts onto a thread. Turn. Cast on 2 sts. Turn. K last 4 sts. Divide these 14 sts onto 3 needles. Join in rnd. K 20 rnds. Work remainder of Left Glove to match Right Glove.

HAT
Edging (worked sideways): With MC, cast on 17 sts.
Row 1 (WS): K3, work Row 1 of Cable Panel across next 11 sts, k3.
Row 2: K3, work Row 2 of Cable Panel across next 11 sts, k3.
Cable Panel is now in position. Cont in pat until Edging measures approx 19½" ending on Row 3 of Cable Panel. Bind off in pat.
With RS of Edging facing and MC, pick up and k 97 sts evenly across one long side of Edging. With MC, k 1 row on WS for garter st border. With A, k 1 row, p 1 row.
Proceed in Fair Isle pat as follows:
Row 1: With A, k1. * With MC, k2, with A, k2. Rep from * to end of row.
Row 2: With A, p.
Row 3: With B, k1. * With A, k2, with B, k2. Rep from * to end of row.
Row 4: With A, p.
Row 5: As Row 1.
Row 6: With A, p.
Row 7: With A, k.
Row 8: * With A, p1, with C, p1. Rep from * to last st, with A, p1.
Row 9: With C, k1, * k2tog, k6. Rep from * to end of row—85 sts.

Row 10: With A, p.
Row 11: * With MC, k1, with B, k1. Rep from * to last st, with MC, k1.
Row 12: With MC, p.
Row 13: * With B, k1, with MC, k2tog, (with B, k1, with MC, k1) twice. Rep from * to last st, with B, k1—73 sts.
Row 14: With A, p.
Row 15: With D, k.
Row 16: * With C, p1, with D, p1. Rep from * to last st, with C, p1.
Row 17: With D, k1, * k2tog, k4. Rep from * to end of row—61 sts.
Row 18: With A, p.
Row 19: As Row 11.
Row 20: With MC, p.
Row 21: * With B, k1, with MC, k2tog, with B, k1, with MC, k1. Rep from * to last st, with B, k1—49 sts.
Row 22: With A, p.
Row 23: With D, k.
Row 24: As Row 16.
Row 25: With D, k1, * k2tog, k2. Rep from * to end of row—37 sts.
Row 26: With A, p.
Row 27: As Row 11.
Row 28: With MC, p.
Row 29: * With B, k1, with MC, k2tog. Rep from * to last st, with B, k1—25 sts.
Row 30: With A, p.
Row 31: With D, k1, * k2tog. Rep from * to end of row—13 sts.
Row 32: As Row 16.
Row 33: With D, k1, (k2tog) 6 times. Break yarn, leaving a long end. Draw end through rem 7 sts and fasten securely. Sew center back seam.

Child's Colorful Pullover

photo on page 52

SKILL LEVEL: Intermediate

SIZES: Children's size 6 (8, 10, 12)
Note: *The pattern is written for the smallest size with changes for larger sizes in parentheses. When only one number is given, it applies to all sizes. For ease in working, before you begin, circle all numbers pertaining to the size you are knitting.*

FINISHED MEASUREMENTS:
Chest: 32 (34, 36, 38)"
Length: 16 (17, 18, 19)"

MATERIALS:
- Lion Brand Yarn's Cotton-Ease, 50% cotton/50% acrylic, worsted weight yarn (207 yards per skein): 1 (1, 2, 2) skein(s) of Orangeade (133) for Color A; 2 (2, 3, 3) skeins each of Cherry Red (113) for Color B and Pineapple (158) for Color C
- Size 7 (4.5mm) knitting needles or size needed to obtain gauge
- Size 6 (4.25mm) knitting needles
- Size 6 (4.25 mm) circular knitting needle
- Yarn needle

GAUGE:
In Colorful Pattern with larger needles, 17 sts and 24 rows = 4"/10 cm.
TAKE TIME TO CHECK YOUR GAUGE.

STITCHES USED:
K2 P2 Rib (a multiple of 4 sts + 2 sts; a rep of 2 rows)
Row 1 (RS): * K2, p2. Rep from * across, ending row with k2.
Row 2: * P2, k2. Rep from * across, ending row with p2.
Repeat Rows 1–2.

INSTRUCTIONS:
BACK
Beg at lower edge, with smaller needles and Color A, cast on 70 (74, 78, 82) sts. Change to Color B. Work K2 P2 Rib, using B only, to approx 1½ (2, 2, 2)" from beg, ending after WS row.

Body Pattern
Change to larger needles, beg Colorful Pattern, and work even to approx 16 (17, 18, 19)" from beg, ending after a WS row.
Shoulder Shaping
Bind off 8 (8, 9, 9) sts at beg of next 4 rows. Bind off 7 (9, 8, 10) sts at beg of next 2 rows. Bind off rem 24 (24, 26, 26) sts.

FRONT
Work as for Back until piece measures approx 15 (16, 17, 18)" from beg, ending after WS row.

KEY

☒	A - Orangeade
☐	B - Cherry Red
◎	C - Pineapple

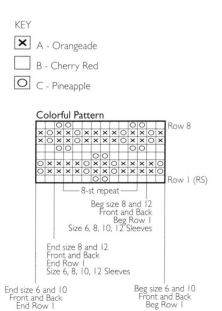

Colorful Pattern

Row 8
Row 1 (RS)

8-st repeat

Beg size 8 and 12
Front and Back
Beg Row 1
Size 6, 8, 10, 12 Sleeves

End size 8 and 12
Front and Back
End Row 1
Size 6, 8, 10, 12 Sleeves

End size 6 and 10
Front and Back
End Row 1

Beg size 6 and 10
Front and Back
Beg Row 1

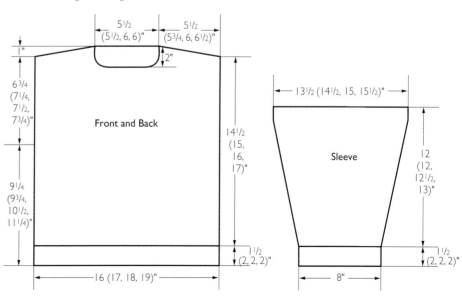

5½ (5½, 6, 6)"   5½ (5¾, 6, 6½)"

1"   2"

6¾ (7¼, 7½, 7¾)"

Front and Back

14½ (15, 16, 17)"

9¼ (9¾, 10½, 11¼)"

1½ (2, 2, 2)"

16 (17, 18, 19)"

13½ (14½, 15, 15½)"

Sleeve

12 (12, 12½, 13)"

1½ (2, 2, 2)"

8"

Casual Stripes

photo on page 53

SKILL LEVEL: Easy

SIZES: XS (S MEDIUM, L, XL)
Note: *The pattern is written for the smallest size with changes for larger sizes in parentheses. When only one number is given, it applies to all sizes. For ease in working, before you begin, circle all numbers pertaining to the size you are knitting.*

FINISHED MEASUREMENTS:
Bust: 36 (38, 40, 42, 46)"
Length: 18¾ (19¼, 19¾, 20¼, 20¾)"

MATERIALS:
- Muench's Samoa, 50% cotton/50% acrylic, worsted weight yarn (104 yards/95m per ball): 2 (3, 3, 4, 4) balls of Gold (72) for Color A; 4 (5, 5, 6, 6) balls of Magenta (37) for Color B; and 3 (4, 4, 5, 5) balls of Purple (76) for Color C
- Size 7 (4.5mm) knitting needles or size needed to obtain gauge
- Size 6 (4.25mm) knitting needles
- Size 6 (4.25 mm) circular knitting needle
- 7" zipper
- Safety pin
- Yarn needle

Neck Shaping
Work in pattern across first 29 (31, 32, 34) sts; join new strands and bind off center 12 (12, 14, 14) sts; work to end of row. Work both sides at once with separate strands of yarn and bind off 3 sts each neck edge once, then bind off 2 sts each neck edge once. Dec 1 st each neck edge once— 23 (25, 26, 28) sts rem. Complete as for Back.

SLEEVES (make two)
Beg at lower edge, with smaller needles and color A, cast on 30 sts.
Change to color B.
Work K2 P2 Rib, using B only, to approx 1½ (2, 2, 2)" from beg, ending after WS row, inc 4 sts evenly across last row—34 sts.

Body Pattern
Change to larger needles, and beg Colorful Pattern for 2 rows. Beg with next RS row, including new sts into pattern as they accumulate, inc at each edge every 4th row 3 (9, 11, 13) times, then every 6th row 9 (5, 4, 3) times—58 (62, 64, 66) sts. Work even to approx 13½ (14, 14½, 15)" from beg, ending after WS row. Bind off.

FINISHING
Join shoulder seams.
Neckband
With RS facing, circular needle, and B, pick up and k 64 (64, 68, 68) sts around neckline. Work rnds of K2 P2 Rib until band measures approx 1" from beg. Change to A and work one more rnd as you bind off in rib. Place markers 6¾ (7¼, 7½, 7¾)" down from shoulders. Set in sleeves between markers.
Sew underarm and side seams.

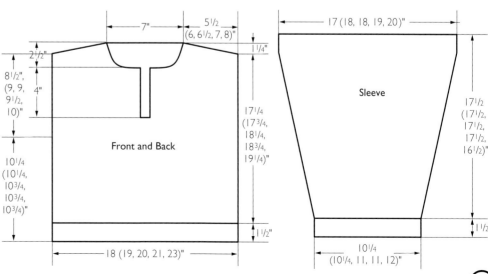

Casual Stripes

continued from page 81

GAUGE:
In St st with larger needles, 18 sts and 26 rows = 4"/10 cm.
TAKE TIME TO CHECK YOUR GAUGE.

STITCHES USED:
K2 P2 Rib (a multiple of 4 sts + 2 sts; a rep of 2 rows)
Row 1 (RS): * K2, p2. Rep from * across, ending row with k2.
Row 2: * P2, k2. Rep from * across, ending row with p2.
Repeat Rows 1 and 2.

St st (Any number of sts or rows)
Row 1 (RS): K across.
Row 2: P across.
Repeat Rows 1 and 2.

St st Striping Pattern * 2 rows A, 8 rows C, 2 rows A, 8 rows B. Rep from * for pattern.

INSTRUCTIONS:
BACK
Beg at lower edge with smaller needles and Color A, cast on 78 (82, 86, 94, 102) sts. Change to Color B. Work K2 P2 Rib, using B only, to approx 1½" from beg ending after WS row, inc 3 (3, 3, 1, 1) st(s) evenly across last row—81 (85, 89, 95, 103) sts.
Body Pattern
Change to larger needles, beg St st Striping Pattern, and work even to approx 18¾ (19¼, 19¾, 20¼, 20¾)" from beg, ending after a WS row.
Shoulder Shaping
Bind off 6 (7, 7, 8, 9) sts at beg of next six rows. Bind off 7 (6, 8, 8, 9) sts at beg of next two rows. Bind off rem 31 sts.

FRONT
Work as for Back until piece measures approx 13½ (14, 14½, 15, 15½)" from beg, ending after WS row.
Divide for Zipper Opening
K 39 (41, 43, 46, 50) sts; slip middle 3 sts onto safety pin; join new strand and work to end of row. Work both sides at once with separate balls of yarn until piece measures approx 17½ (18, 18½, 19, 19½)" from beg, ending after WS row.

Neck Shaping
Bind off 6 sts each neck edge once, bind off 4 sts each neck edge once, then bind off 2 sts each neck edge once. Dec 1 st each neck edge every row twice—25 (27, 29, 32, 36) sts rem. Complete as for Back.

SLEEVES (make two)
Beg at lower edge, with smaller needles and Color A, cast on 46 (46, 50, 50, 54) sts. Change to Color B. Work K2 P2 Rib, using B only, to approx 1½" from beg, ending after WS row.
Body Pattern
Change to larger needles, and beg St st Striping Pattern. Beg with next RS row, inc each edge every 4th row 0 (0, 0, 0, 4) times, then every 6th row 6 (18, 10, 18, 14) times, then every 8th row 9 (0, 6, 0, 0) times—76 (82, 82, 86, 90) sts. Work even to approx 19 (19, 19, 19, 18)" from beg, ending after WS row. Bind off.

FINISHING
Join shoulder seams.
Neckband
With RS facing, circular needle, and B, pick up and k 74 sts around neckline. Work rows of K2 P2 Rib. When neckband measures approx 3" from beg, change to A and bind off in rib.

Zipper Facing
With RS facing, circular needle, and A, pick up and k 34 sts along left side of center front opening, pick up and k 3 sts from safety pin, pick up and k 34 sts along right side of center front opening—71 sts total.
Next Row: Bind off knitwise. Sew in zipper. Place markers 8½ (9, 9, 9½, 10)" down from shoulders. Set in sleeves between markers. Sew underarm and side seams.

Peruvian Raglan and Cap

photos on pages 54–55

SKILL LEVEL: Advanced

SIZES: S (MEDIUM, L, XL)
Note: The pattern is written for the smallest size with changes for larger sizes in parentheses. When only one number is given, it applies to all sizes. For ease in working, before you begin, circle all numbers pertaining to the size you are knitting.

FINISHED MEASUREMENTS:
Bust: 40 (43, 46, 48)"
Length: 25½ (26, 26½, 26½)"

MATERIALS:
- Patons Classic Merino Wool, 100% wool, worsted weight yarn (223 yards per skein): 6 (7, 7, 7) skeins of Aran (202) for MC and 2 (2, 3, 3) skeins of Black (226) for Color A for Pullover. 1 skein each of Aran (202) for MC and Black (226) for Color A for Cap
- Size 7 (4.5mm) knitting needles or size needed to obtain gauge
- Sizes 6 (4.25mm) knitting needles
- Size H/8 (5mm) crochet hook for Hat edging
- 4 stitch holders
- Yarn needle

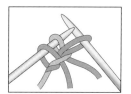

Two-Needle
Cast On Diagram

GAUGE:

In St st and color patterns with larger needles, 20 sts and 26 rows = 4"/10cm.
TAKE TIME TO CHECK YOUR GAUGE.

ABBREVIATIONS:

Ssk (slip, slip, knit): Slip next 2 sts knitwise, one at a time to right-hand needle, insert tip of left-hand needle into fronts of these 2 sts and k tog.
P2togb (p two together through the back loops): Turn work slightly, insert right-hand needle into 2nd and then first sts from left to right; p the 2 sts together.

Note: The lower border is worked in St st from Chart 1. Loosely carry unused strand along WS of fabric. When working Chart 2, use separate strands or bobbins for each color section and do not work partial diamond motifs while shaping the raglans. To change color, bring new strand from under present strand for a twist to prevent holes. Read charts from right to left for RS rows, and from left to right for RS rows.

INSTRUCTIONS:
BACK

Beg at lower edge with smaller needles and using 2-needle cast on method (see diagrams, *opposite*), * with MC, cast on 1 st, with A cast on 1 st. Rep from * 49 (52, 56, 58) times more—100 (106, 114, 118) sts. Change to larger needles.
Row 1 (RS): With MC, k.
Row 2: With MC, p inc 5 sts evenly across—105 (111, 119, 123) sts. Work Rows 1–10 of Chart 1 in St st (beg and ending at your size), reading k rows from right to left and p rows from left to right, noting 7 st rep will be worked 15 (15, 17, 17) times. With MC, work 2 rows St st, dec 5 sts evenly across last row—100 (106, 114, 118) sts.

KEY

☒ Black (Color A)
☐ Aran (MC)

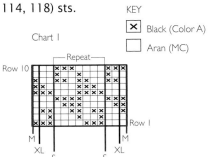

Chart 1

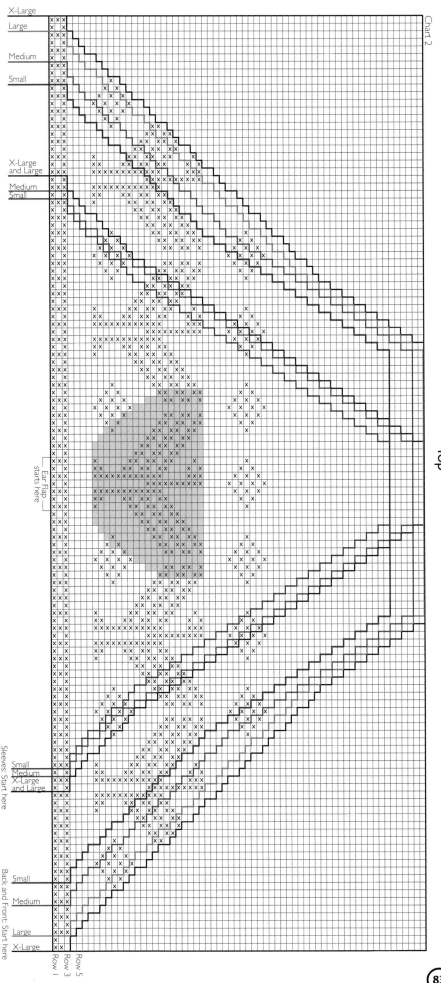

Chart 2

Top

83

Peruvian Raglan and Cap
continued from page 83

Body Pattern

Row 1 (RS): With A, k.

Row 2: * With MC, p1, with A, p1. Rep from * to end of row.

Row 3: With A, k.

Rows 4–18: With MC, work 15 rows St st.

These 18 rows form Body Pattern.

Cont in est pat until work from beg measures approx 16½" ending on an 18th row of pat and inc 5 sts evenly across last row—105 (111, 119, 123) sts.

Work Chart 2 in St st, reading k rows from right to left and p rows from left to right, noting raglan decs are worked as follows:

Rows 3 and 4 of Chart: Bind off 2 sts, work chart to end of row.

Row 5 of Chart (RS row dec): With MC, k1, ssk. Work chart to last 3 sts. With MC, k2tog, k1.

Row 6 of Chart (WS row dec): With MC, p1, p2tog. Work chart to last 3 sts. With MC, p2togb, p1.

Cont working chart using est raglan dec until there are 35 (35, 35, 37) sts. Leave rem sts on a st holder.

FRONT

Rep as for Back until there are 51 (51, 51, 53) sts rem on Chart 2, ending with a WS row.

Neck Shaping

Row 1 (RS): With MC, k1, ssk. Work chart across next 14 sts. Leave rem sts on a spare needle.

Row 2: P2tog. Work chart to end of row.

Row 3: With MC, k1, ssk. Work chart to last 2 sts. K2tog.

Rows 4–5: Rep Rows 2 and 3.

Row 6: Work chart to end of row.

Row 7: Rep Row 3.

Rep last 2 rows twice more—4 sts rem.

Next Row: With MC, p4.

Next Row: K1, ssk, k1.

Next Row: P3.

Next Row: K1, ssk.

Next Row: P2.

Next Row: Ssk. Fasten off.

With RS facing, slip center 17 (17, 17, 19) sts onto a st holder. Rejoin yarn to rem 17 sts and work to correspond to other side.

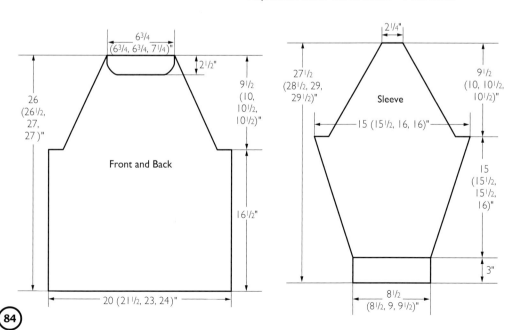

SLEEVES (make two)

Beg at lower edge with smaller needles and MC, cast on 39 (39, 45, 45) sts.

Ribbing

Row 1 (RS): * K3, p3, rep from * to last 3 sts, k3.

Row 2: * P3, k3, rep from * to last 3 sts, p3.

Rep last 2 rows until Sleeve measures approx 3" from beg, ending with a WS row and inc 4 (4, 0, 0) sts evenly across last row—43 (43, 45, 45) sts. With larger needles and MC, work 2 rows St st.

Next Row: With A, k.

Next Row: * With A, p1, with MC, p1. Rep from * to last st. With A, p1.

Next Row: With A, k.

Next Row: With MC, p.

With MC, cont in St st, shaping sides by inc 1 st each edge on next and every 4th row 16 (17, 18, 18) total times—75 (77, 81, 81) sts. Work even to approx 18 (18½, 18½, 19)" from beg, ending with a WS row. Work Chart 2 in St st, reading k rows from right to left and p rows from left to right, noting raglan decs are worked as for Back and Front. When 11 sts rem, place on a st holder.

FINISHING

Join raglan seams, leaving left back raglan open.

Collar

With RS facing using smaller needles and MC, k11 from Left Sleeve st holder and dec 2 sts evenly across, pick up and k14 sts down Left Front neck edge, k17 (17, 17, 19) from center front st holder dec 2 (2, 2, 0) sts evenly across, pick up and k14 sts up Right Front neck edge, k11 from Right Sleeve st holder and dec 2 sts evenly across, then k35 (35, 35, 37) from back st holder and dec 3 sts evenly across—93 (93, 93, 99) sts.

Row 1 (WS): With A, p.

Row 2: * With A, k1, With MC, k1. Rep from * to last st. With A, k1.

Row 3: With A, p.

Row 4: With MC, k.

Beg on a WS row, work Ribbing as for Sleeve until Collar measures approx 3½" from beg. Bind off in ribbing. Sew Collar and left back raglan seam. Sew side and sleeve seams.

CAP

First Ear Flap: With MC and larger needles, cast on 5 sts.

Row 1 (RS): K5.

Row 2: Inc 1 st in first st purlways (p into front and back loops of the stitch), p2, inc 1 st in next st purlwise, p1.

Row 3: Inc 1 st in first st knitwise, k4, inc 1 st in next st knitwise, k1.

Row 4: Inc 1 st in first st purlwise. P to last 2 sts, inc 1 st in next st purlwise, p1.

Row 5: Inc 1 st in first st knitwise, k1. Work Chart 2 across next 7 sts, inc 1 st in next st knitwise, k1.

Row 6: As Row 4 (keeping cont of chart).

Row 7: Inc 1 st in first st knitwise. K to last 2 sts (keeping cont of chart), inc 1 st in next st knitwise, k1.

Row 8: P, keeping cont of chart.

Rep last 2 rows 4 times more—25 sts. Cont working the charted bird through completion. With MC, work 3 rows even. Break yarn. Leave sts on a spare needle.

Second Ear Flap: Work as given for First Ear Flap, but do not break yarn. Proceed as follows.

Join Ear Flaps: Next Row: With MC, cast on 8 sts onto end of Second Ear Flap. K25 of Second Ear Flap. Cast on 27 sts. K25 of First Ear Flap. Cast on 8 sts—93 sts. P 1 row.

Next Row: With A, k.

Next Row: * With A, P1, with MC, p1. Rep from * to last st, with A, p1.

Next Row: With A, k.

Next Row: With MC, p.

Next Row: With MC, k inc 2 sts evenly across—95 sts.

Work rows 1 to 10 of Chart 1 in St st as given for size XL of pullover, reading p rows from left to right and k rows from right to left, noting 7 st rep will be worked 13 times.

With MC, work 2 rows St st, dec 2 sts evenly across last row—93 sts.

Next Row: With A, p.

Next Row: * With A, k1. With MC, k1. Rep from * to last st, with A, k1.

Next Row: With A, p.

Next Row: With MC, k.

Next Row: With MC, p.

Shape Top: Next Row: With MC, k2. * K2tog, k8. Rep from * to last st, k1— 84 sts. With MC, p 1 row.

Next Row: With MC, k2. * With A, k1, with MC, k3. Rep from * to last 2 sts, with A, k1, with MC, k1. With MC, p 1 row.

Next Row: With MC, K2. *K2tog, k7. Rep from * to last st, k1—75 sts. With MC, p 1 row.

Next Row: With MC, k.

Next Row: With MC, p2. * With A, p1, with MC, p3. Rep from * to last st, with A, p1.

Next Row: With MC, k2. * K2tog, k6. Rep from * to last st, k1—66 sts. Dot pat is now in position. Cont in dot pat, AT SAME TIME, dec 9 sts evenly across following 4th rows until there are 12 sts. Cont with MC only and work 3 rows in St st.

Next Row: (K2tog) 6 times. Leaving a long end, break the yarn. Draw end tightly through rem sts and fasten securely. Sew center back seam.

Edging: With crochet hook, join MC with sl st at center back seam. Ch1. Work 1 rnd of sc evenly around outer edge of Cap. Join with sl st to first sc.

Next Rnd: Working from left to right for reverse sc (instead of from right to left as usual), and changing colors by drawing through final 2 lps on hook of each sc as follows: With MC, ch1, work 1 sc in next sc; * with A, work 1 sc in next sc, with MC, work 1 sc in next sc. Rep from * around. Join with sl st to first sc. Fasten off.

Ties: Cut 12 strands of MC and 6 strands of A 24" long. Taking 6 strands of MC and 3 strands of A, draw strands through bottom of Ear Flap. Dividing into (6 strands of MC) twice and 6 strands of A, braid to make tie, leaving approx 1" open at end. Fasten securely. Repeat on rem Ear Flap.

Tassel: Using a piece of cardboard 3" wide x 5" deep, wind Color A 35 times around cardboard. Break yarn leaving a long end and thread end through a needle. Slip needle through all lps and tie tightly. Remove cardboard and wind yarn tightly around lps ¾" below fold. Fasten securely. Cut through rem lps and trim ends evenly. Attach to top of Cap.

Homespun Throw

continued from page 85

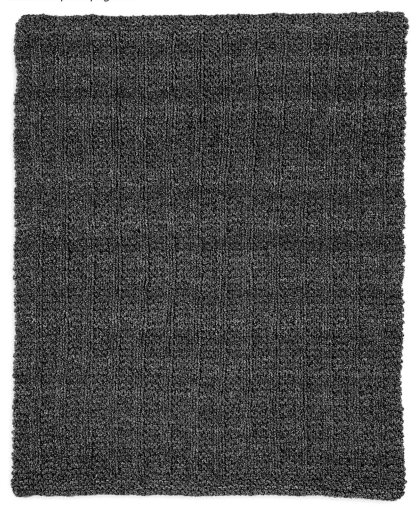

Back-to-Basics Sweater

photo on page 57

SKILL LEVEL: Beginner

SIZES: XS (S, MEDIUM, L, XL, XXL)
Note: *The pattern is written for the smallest size with changes for larger sizes in parentheses. When only one number is given, it applies to all sizes. For ease in working, before you begin, circle all numbers pertaining to the size you are knitting.*

FINISHED MEASUREMENTS:
Bust: 32 (36, 40, 44, 48, 52)"
Length: 22 (22½, 23, 23½, 24, 24½)"

MATERIALS:
- Lion Brand Yarn Company, Homespun, Article 790, 98% acrylic/2% polyester, bulky weight yarn (185 yards per skein): 3 (4, 4, 5, 5, 5) skeins of Seaspray (123)
- Size 10 (6mm) knitting needles or size needed to obtain gauge
- Size 8 (5mm) knitting needles
- Yarn needle

GAUGE:
In Stockinette stitch (k on right side, p on wrong side) with larger needles, 14 stitches and 20 rows = 4"/10cm.
TAKE TIME TO CHECK YOUR GAUGE.

INSTRUCTIONS:
BACK
Beg at the lower edge with smaller needles, CO 56 (63, 70, 77, 84, 91) sts. K 6 rows for Garter stitch band. Change to larger needles. Beg with a p row, work in St st (k 1 row, p 1 row) until piece measures approx 15 inches from beg, ending with a p row.
Armhole Shaping
At the beg of the next 2 rows, bind off 4 sts. Cont in St st on rem 48 (55, 62, 69, 76, 83) stitches to approx 21

Homespun Throw

photo on page 56

SKILL LEVEL: Beginner

SIZE: Approximately 45 x 50"

MATERIALS:
- Lion Brand Yarn Company, Homespun, Item #790, 98% acrylic/2% polyester, bulky weight yarn (185 yards per skein): 3 skeins each of Baroque (322) and Adirondack (319)
- Size 15 (12mm) circular knitting needle, 29-inch length, or size needed to obtain gauge

GAUGE:
Holding one strand of each yarn together, in Body Pattern, 10 stitches and 24 rows = 6"/15cm.

TAKE TIME TO CHECK YOUR GAUGE.

Note: *The entire afghan is worked back and forth on a circular needle with a double strand of yarn.*

INSTRUCTIONS:
With one strand of each yarn held together, cast on 75 stitches. K 7 rows for garter st border.

Body Pattern
Row 1 (RS): Knit.
Row 2: K4; (p2, k3) 13 times, p2, k4.
Repeat Rows 1–2 until Throw measures approx 49" from beginning, ending with a right side row.
K 7 rows for Garter stitch border.
Bind off.

sts. K 6 rows for border. Change to larger needles and p across next row. Working in St st, inc 1 stitch (k in front and in back of the same stitch) each edge now. Then inc 1 st each edge every 10th row 3 (2, 0, 0, 0, 0) times, every 8th row 5 (7, 8, 5, 2, 1) times, and every 6th row 0 (0, 2, 6, 10, 12) times. Work even on the 49 (52, 56, 59, 63, 66) sts to approx 18½ (19, 19½, 19½, 19½, 20) inches from beg, ending with a p row. Bind off loosely and knitwise.

FINISHING
Join shoulder seams. Set in sleeves, sewing bound off sts on body to sides of upper sleeves for square armholes. Join underarm and side seams. Weave in loose ends on WS of fabric.

Mittens (all)
photos on pages 58–61

Note: *Materials, gauge, and abbreviations below, apply to Stadium, Striped, Roarin' Good Times, and Knit Chex mittens.*

MATERIALS:
- Lion Brand Yarn Company, Wool-Ease Chunky, Article #630, 80% acrylic/20% wool yarn (153 yards per ball)
- Size 6 (4.25mm) knitting needles or size needed to obtain gauge
- Size 4 (3.5mm) knitting needles
- Yarn needle
- 2 ring-type stitch markers

GAUGE:
In St st (k RS rows, p WS rows) with larger needles, 16 sts and 23 rows = 4"/10cm. TAKE TIME TO CHECK YOUR GAUGE.

SPECIAL ABBREVIATIONS:
M1: To make 1 st, lift the horizontal bar between right and left needles onto the left needle, and k into back of this lp.
Ssk: Slip next 2 sts knitwise, one at a time to right-hand needle, insert tip of left-hand needle into fronts of these 2 sts and k tog.
Pm: Place a marker.

(21½, 22, 22½, 23, 23½)" from beg, ending with a k row.
Neckband
Row 1 (WS): P11 (14, 17, 20, 23, 26) sts, k26 (27, 28, 29, 30, 31) sts, p to end.
Row 2 and each following RS Row: K all sts.
Row 3: P10 (13, 16, 19, 22, 25), k28 (29, 30, 31, 32, 33) sts, p to end.
Row 5: P9 (12, 15, 18, 21, 24), k30 (31, 32, 33, 34, 35), p to end. RS facing, bind off knitwise and loosely.

FRONT
Work as for Back until piece measures approx 19 (19½, 20, 20½, 21, 21½) inches from beg, ending with a k row. Work Neckband Rows 1–5.

Neck Shaping
On the next RS row, k 13 (16, 19, 22, 25, 28) sts, bind off the center 22 (23, 24, 25, 26, 27) sts, k to end.
Right Shoulder: P9 (12, 15, 18, 21, 24), k4 sts. K across next row. Repeat last 2 rows until piece measures approx 22 (22½, 23, 23½, 24, 24½)" from beg ending with a WS row. Bind off knitwise and loosely.
Left Shoulder: With the WS facing, join yarn at neck edge. K4, p to end. K across next row. Rep last 2 rows to same length as Right Shoulder, ending with a WS row. Bind off knitwise and loosely.
SLEEVES (make two)
Beg at the lower edge with smaller needles, CO 31 (32, 34, 35, 37, 38)

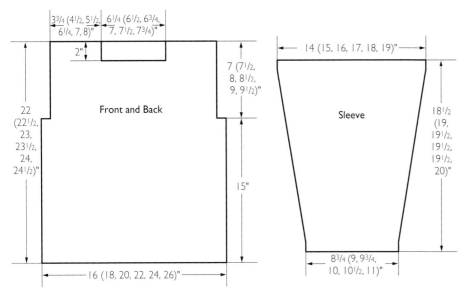

Stadium Mittens
photo on page 59

SKILL LEVEL: Easy

SIZE: Adult size S (MEDIUM, L)

FINISHED MEASUREMENTS:
Width: 3½ (4¼, 5)"
Length: 10½ (11¼, 12)"

Note: For detailed information regarding Materials, Gauge, and Abbreviations, please see basic mitten information on page 87.

MATERIALS:
- 1 ball each of Foliage (187) for MC and Evergreen (180) for Color A

STITCHES USED:
Body Pattern (a multiple of 2 sts + 1 st; a rep of 4 rows)
Row 1 (WS): Purl.
Row 2: * K1, p1; rep from * across, ending k1.
Rows 3: *P1, k1; rep from * across, ending p1.
Row 4: Knit.
Rows 1–4 for Body Pattern.

INSTRUCTIONS:
RIGHT MITTEN
For Cuff: With Color A and smaller needles, cast on 25 (31, 37) sts. K 1 row. * With MC, work Rows 1–4 of Body Pattern, with A, work Rows 1–4 of Body Pattern. Rep from * twice more.
Set Up for Body Pattern
With larger needles and MC, p.
Next Row: Work Body
Pattern on

first 13 (16, 19) sts, M1, k1, M1, k to end of row—27 (33, 39) sts. **Next Row:** P14 (17, 20), work Row 3 of Body Pattern to end. Pattern is now set. Work 2 (2, 4) more rows as est.
Thumb
Row 1 (RS): Work est pattern on first 13 (16, 19) sts, pm, M1, k1, M1, pm, pattern to end of row.
Row 2: Work pattern across.
Row 3: Work to marker, slip marker, M1, k to marker, M1, work to end of row. Rep Rows 2–3 until there are 13 (13, 15) sts between markers. Work 1 row even. **Next Row:** Work across, removing markers and placing thumb sts onto a spare strand of yarn. Cont in est patterns on the 26 (32, 38) sts until piece measures approx 9½ (10, 10½)" from beg, ending with a WS row and placing a marker after the 13th (16th, 19th) st.
Top Shaping
Row 1 (RS): Ssk, work to 2 sts before marker, k2tog, sl marker, ssk, work to last 2 sts, k2tog.
Row 2: Work pat across.
Rep last 2 rows until 18 (20, 22) sts rem. (K2tog) across—9 (10, 11) sts. Leaving a long tail, cut yarn.
Closure
Thread tail into yarn needle. Beg with the last st on needle, take yarn back through rem sts, twice. Pull up to close opening. Leave tail for joining sides.
Thumb
With RS facing, return sts to larger needle. Join MC and k 13 (13, 15).
Next Row: P 5 (5, 6), p2tog, p 6 (6, 7). Work 6 more St st rows on the 12 (12, 14) sts. (K2tog) across. Rep Closure as for Top. Join thumb seam. Darn opening. Weave in loose end on WS of fabric.

FINISHING
Join side seam.

LEFT MITTEN
Work Cuff as for Right Mitten.
Set Up for Body Pattern
With larger needles and MC, p.
Next Row: K11 (14, 17), pm. M1, k1, M1, pm, work Body Pattern to end— 27 (33, 39) sts. **Next Row:** Work Body Pattern Row 3 on 13 (16, 19) sts, p to end. Pattern is now set. Work 2 (2, 4) more rows as est. Complete as for Right Mitten.

Striped Mittens
photo on page 59

SKILL LEVEL: Easy

SIZES: Adult size S (MEDIUM, L)

FINISHED MEASUREMENTS:
Width: 3¾ (4¼, 5)"
Length: 10 (10½, 11¼)"

Note: For detailed information regarding Materials, Gauge, and Abbreviations, please see basic mitten information on page 87.

MATERIALS:
- 1 ball each of Huckleberry (139) for A, Concord (145) for B, Bluebell (107) for C, and Charcoal (152) for D

STITCHES USED:
Stripe Pattern (any multiple; a rep of 18 rows)
Row 1 (WS): P with A.
Row 2: K with A.
Rows 3–4: Rep Rows 1–2.
Row 5: Rep Row 1.
Row 6: K with D.
Rows 7–11: Rep Rows 1–5 with B.
Row 12: K with D.
Rows 13–17: Rep Rows 1–5 with C.
Row 18: K with D.
Rows 1–18 form Stripe Pattern.

INSTRUCTIONS:
FIRST MITTEN
With color A and larger needles, cast on 25 (29, 35) sts. Work Stripe Pattern Rows 1–5. Inc 1 st each edge now, and then every 4th row twice more—31 (35, 41) sts. Cont in est pattern to approx 2½ (3, 3½)" from beg, ending with a WS row.

Thumb (Cont in Stripe Pattern)
Row 1 (RS): K 15 (17, 20), pm, M1, k1, M1, pm, k 15 (17, 20).
Row 2: P across.
Row 3: K to marker, sl marker, M1, k to marker, M1, sl marker, k to end of row. Rep Rows 2–3 until there are 13 (13, 15) sts bet markers. P 1 row.
Next Row: K across, removing markers and placing thumb sts onto a spare strand of yarn. Cont in stripes on the 30 (34, 40) sts until piece measures approx 8½ (9, 9½)" from beg, ending with a WS row and pm after 15th (17th, 20th) st.
Top Shaping (Cont in Stripe Pattern)
Row 1 (RS): Ssk, k to 2 sts before marker, k2tog, sl marker, ssk, k to last 2 sts, k2tog.
Row 2: P across.
Rep Rows 1–2 until 18 (18, 20) sts rem. P across. (K2tog) across. P9 (9, 10). Leaving a long tail for sewing, cut yarn.

Closure
Thread tail into yarn needle. Beg with the last st on needle, take yarn back through rem sts, twice. Pull up to tightly close opening. Join sides tog.

Thumb (Cont in Stripe Pattern)
With RS facing, return sts to larger needle. Join correct yarn color and k13 (13, 15). **Next Row:** P5 (5, 7), p2tog, p6. Work 6 (6, 8) more rows in Stripe Pattern on the 12 (12, 14) sts. (K2tog) across. Cut yarn, leaving a 10" tail. Rep Closure as for Top. Join thumb seam. Darn opening. Weave in loose ends on WS of fabric.

SECOND MITTEN
Work as for First Mitten.

Knit Chex Mittens
photo on page 60

SKILL LEVEL: Intermediate

SIZES: Children's size 4–6 (8–10); Adult size Medium
FINISHED MEASUREMENTS:
Width: 3 (3½, 4¼)"
Length: 6 (7½, 9)"

Note: *For detailed information regarding Materials, Gauge, and Abbreviations, please see basic mitten information on* page 87.

MATERIALS:
- One ball each of Huckleberry (139) for A and Concord (145) for B
- Cable needle (cn)

ABBREVIATIONS:
C4B: Slip next 2 sts to cn and hold at back, k2 sts, k2 from cn.

STITCHES USED:
Checks (a multiple of 6 sts; over 9 rows)
Row 1 (WS): (P3-A, p3-B) across.
Row 2: (K3-B, k3-A) across.
Row 3: Rep Row 1.
Row 4: (K3-A, k3-B) across.
Row 5: (P3-B, p3-A) across.
Row 6: Rep Row 4.
Rows 7–9: Rep Rows 1–3.
Rows 1–9 form Checks.

Cable Panel (over 6 sts; a rep of 4 rows)
Row 1 (WS): K1, p4, k1.
Row 2: P1, k4, p1.
Row 3: Rep Row 1.
Row 4: P1, C4B, p1.
Rep Rows 1–4 for Cable Panel.

INSTRUCTIONS:
RIGHT MITTEN
Cuff: Leaving a long tail for joining the cuff, with smaller needles and A, cast on 24 (30, 36) sts. P 1 row. K 2 rows. Work Checks pattern, Rows 1–9. K 1 row with A. **Next Row (WS):** (K1-A, k1-B) across. Cut B, leaving a 12" tail.

Set Up for Body Pattern
Change to larger needles. With A, k3 (5, 6), p1, k4, p1, k to end of row.
Row 2: P the p sts and k the k sts.
Row 3: K3 (5, 6), p1, k4, p1, k3 (4, 6), M1, k to end—25 (31, 37).
Row 4: Rep Row 2.

Thumb
Row 1 (RS): K3 (5, 6) sts, work Row 4 of Cable Panel on next 6 sts, k3 (4, 6) sts; pm, M1, k1, M1, pm, k to end of row.
Row 2 and each following WS row: P the p sts and k the k sts.
Row 3: Work est pattern to marker, sl marker, M1, k to next marker, M1, sl marker, k to end of row.
Rep last 2 rows until there are 9 (11, 13) sts bet markers. **Next RS Row:** Work pat across, removing markers and placing sts bet markers onto a strand of yarn. Cont pat on the 24 (30, 36) sts until piece measures approx 5 (6, 7)" from beg, ending with a WS row and placing marker after 12th (15th, 18th) st.

Top Shaping
Row 1 (RS): Ssk, work to 2 sts before marker, k2tog, sl marker, ssk, work to last 2 sts, k2tog.
Row 2: Work est pat across.
Rep last 2 rows until 16 (18, 20) sts rem. (K2tog) across—8 (9, 10) sts. Leaving a 24" tail, cut yarn.

Closure
Thread tail into yarn needle. Beg with the last st on needle, take yarn back through rem sts, twice. Pull up to tightly close opening. Leave tail for joining sides.

Thumb
With RS facing, return sts to larger needle. Join A and k9 (11, 13). **Next Row:** P3 (4, 5), p2tog, p4 (5, 6). Work 2 (2, 6) more St st rows on the 8 (10, 12) sts. (K2tog) across. Rep Closure as for Top Shaping. Join thumb seam. Darn opening. Weave in loose ends on WS of fabric.

FINISHING
With tail from Top, join sides to cuff; with tail at lower edge, join cuff. Holding all of the saved tails tog, tie in an overhand knot next to the

Knit Chex Mittens
continued from page 89

fabric. Braid tails until piece measures approx 10" long. Tie an overhand knot at end. Tie another overhand knot next to first knot. Trim ends.

LEFT MITTEN
Work Cuff as for Right Mitten.
Set Up for Body Pattern
Change to larger needles. With A, k15 (19, 24), p1, k4, p1, k to end of row. **Row 2:** P the p sts and k the k sts. **Row 3:** K12 (15, 18), M1, k3 (4, 6), p1, k4, p1, k to end. **Row 4:** Rep Row 2.

Thumb
Row 1 (RS): K12 (15, 18), pm, M1, k1, M1, pm, k3 (4, 6), work Row 4 of Cable Panel on next 6 sts, k to end of row. Complete as for Right Thumb. Remainder of Left Mitten is worked as for Right Mitten.

Roarin' Good Time Mitts

photo on page 61
SKILL LEVEL: Easy

SIZES: Children's size 2 (4, 6, 8)

FINISHED MEASUREMENTS:
Width: 2¾ (3, 3¼, 3½)"
Length: 5 (6½, 7, 7½)"

Note: *For detailed information regarding Materials, Gauge, and Abbreviations, please see basic mitten information on* page 87.

MATERIALS:
- 1 ball each of Wheat (402) for MC and Foliage (187) for B.
- Size G/6 crochet hook

INSTRUCTIONS:
RIGHT MITTEN
Cuff: With MC and smaller needles, cast on 23 (25, 27, 29) sts.
Ribbing
Row 1 (WS): P1; (k1, p1) across.
Row 2: K1; (p1, k1) across.
Rep Ribbing Rows 1–2 to approx 1½ (2, 2½, 2½)" from beg, ending with a WS row. **Eyelets:** K1; (yo, k2tog) across. Change to larger needles. P 1 row. Work 0 (2, 4, 4) St st rows.

Thumb
Row 1 (RS): K11 (12, 13, 14), pm, M1, k1, M1, pm, k to end of row.
Row 2: P across.
Row 3: K to marker, sl marker, M1, k to marker, M1, k to end of row.
Rep Rows 2–3 until there are 9 (9, 11, 11) sts bet markers. P 1 row. **Next Row:** K across, removing markers and placing thumb sts onto a spare strand of yarn. Cont St st on the 22 (24, 26, 28) sts until piece measures approx 4 (5, 6, 6½)" from beg, ending with a WS row and placing a marker after the 11th (12th, 13th, 14th) st.

Top Shaping
Row 1 (RS): Ssk, k to 2 sts before marker, k2tog, sl marker, ssk, k to last 2 sts, k2tog.
Row 2: P across.
Rep last 2 rows until 14 (16, 18, 20) sts rem. (K2tog) across—7 (8, 9, 10) sts. Leaving a long tail, cut yarn.

Closure
Thread tail into yarn needle. Beg with the last st on needle, take yb through rem sts, twice. Pull up to tightly close opening. Leave tail for joining sides.
Thumb
With the RS facing, return sts to larger needle. Join MC and k9 (9, 11, 11).
Next Row: P3 (3, 4, 4), p2tog, p4 (4, 5, 5). Work 2 (2, 4, 4) more St st rows on the 8 (8, 10, 10) sts. (K2tog) across. Rep Closure as for Top Shaping. Join thumb seam. Darn opening closed. Weave in loose ends on WS.
Ears (make two)

Leaving an 8" tail at beg and end, with smaller needles and MC, cast on 5 sts. P 1 row. Ssk, k1, k2tog. P3. Sl 1 st purlwise and with yarn on WS, k2tog, pass slipped st over the k2tog. Fasten off.

FINISHING
Using saved tail from top closure, join side seam to same length as top of Thumb.
Mane
Cut 6" strands of Color B. * Fold one strand in half to form a lp. Beg at top of thumb and near the side edge, using crochet hook, take lp through one half of a st. Take ends through lp and pull up to form a knot. Rep from * around, adding a fringe in every other st so that sides correspond. Add two more rows of fringe. Trim. Place ears at top of head, 3 sts apart. Using saved tail, sew in place.
Facial Features
Referring to *page 61*, thread yarn needle with an 18" double strand of B. Locate center st and center row of the St st area of back. Mark st ½" below center. **For Nose:** * Take yarn needle from WS to RS into marked st. Take yarn needle from RS to WS ½" from first st. Rep from * 3 times more. **For Eyes:** Go up 2 sts from nose, take needle from WS to RS into sp next to center st. Skip 2 sts and take needle to WS in next st above. Make a corresponding eye on opposite side of nose. **For Mouth:** Take needle from WS to RS into sp below nose, skip 2 sts down and take needle to WS in space next to center st. Make a corresponding stitch for opposite side of mouth. Secure ends on WS. Cut 2 strands of B 5" long. Thread into needle and through space beneath nose. Fray ends. Complete side closing.

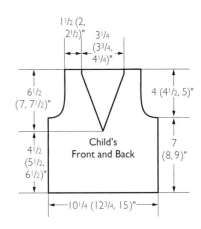

Matching Vests

photo on page 62-63

SKILL LEVEL: Easy

SIZES: Men's size S (MEDIUM, L, XL, XXL) or Children's 1 (2, 3)

Note: *The pattern is written for the smallest size with changes for larger sizes in parentheses. When only one number is given, it applies to all sizes. For ease in working, before you begin, circle all numbers pertaining to the size you are knitting.*

FINISHED MEASUREMENTS:

Men
Chest: 39½ (44, 49, 54)"
Length: 26 (26½, 27, 27½)"

Child
Chest: 20½ (25½, 30)"
Length: 11 (12½, 14)"

MATERIALS:

- Garnstudio, Alaska, 100% wool, worsted weight yarn (75 meters per ball): *For man,* 9 (10, 12, 13) balls of Charcoal Grey (05) for MC and 1 (1, 2, 2) ball(s) of Cranberry (11) for CC. *For child,* 2 (3, 3) balls of Cranberry for MC and 1 ball of Charcoal Grey for CC
- Size 9 (5.5mm) knitting needles or size needed to obtain gauge
- Size 7 (4.5mm) knitting needles
- Size 6 (4.25mm) circular needle, 16-inch length; yarn needle
- 1 ring-type stitch marker

GAUGE:

In Body Pattern with larger needles, 17 sts and 20 rows = 4"/10cm. TAKE TIME TO CHECK YOUR GAUGE.

STITCHES USED

Border (a multiple of 5 sts + 4 sts; a rep of 2 rows)
Row 1 (WS): With MC, p1; (k2, p1, k1, p1) across, ending k2, p1.
Row 2: With MC, (k4, p1) across, ending k4.
Rep Rows 1–2 for Border.

Body Pattern (a multiple of 10 sts + 4 sts; a rep of 32 rows)
Row 1 (RS): With MC, (k4, p1) across, ending k4.

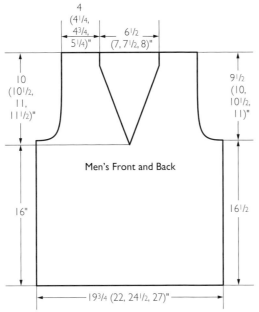

4
(4¼,
4¾,
5¼)"

6½
(7, 7½, 8)"

10
(10½,
11,
11½)"

9½
(10,
10½,
11)"

Men's Front and Back

16"

16½

19¾ (22, 24½, 27)"

Row 2: With MC, (p4, k1) across, ending p4.
Rows 3–4: Rep Rows 1–2.
Row 5: With MC, k4, p1; * k4–CC, with MC, p1, k4 **, p1; rep from * across, ending last rep at **.
Row 6: Rep Row 2.
Row 7: Rep Row 1.
Row 8: With MC, p4, k1; * p4–CC, with MC, k1, p4 **, k1; rep from * across, ending last rep at **.
Row 9: Rep Row 1.
Row 10: With MC, k5; (p4, k6) across, ending p4, k5.
Row 11: Rep Row 1.
Row 12: Rep Row 10.
Rows 13–20: Rep Rows 1–2.
Row 21: With CC, k4; * with MC, p1, k4 **, p1; rep from * across, ending last rep at **.
Row 22: Rep Row 2.

1½ (2, 2½)"

3¼
(3¾,
4¼)"

6½
(7, 7½)"

4 (4½, 5)"

Child's
Front and Back

4½
(5½,
6½)"

7
(8, 9)"

10¼ (12¾, 15)"

Matching Vests

continued from page 91

Row 23: Rep Row 1.
Row 24: With CC, p4; * with MC, k1, p4 **, k1; rep from * across, ending last rep at **.
Row 25: Rep Row 1.
Row 26: With MC, p4; (k6, p4) across.
Row 27: Rep Row 1.
Row 28: Rep Row 26.
Rows 29–32: Rep Rows 1–2.
Rep Rows 1–32 for Body Pattern.

Note: As you work the contrasting color rows, loosely carry color not in use along the WS of fabric. When changing color, bring next color from under present color for a twist to prevent holes.

INSTRUCTIONS:
MEN'S VEST—BACK

Beg at the lower edge with size 7 needles and MC, cast on 84 (94, 104, 114) sts. Work Border Rows 1–2 for 3 times; rep Row 1 again. Change to largest needles and work Body Pattern until piece measures approx 16½" from beg, ending with a WS row.

Armhole Shaping
Cont in pattern, bind off 6 sts at beg of next 2 rows, dec 1 st each edge every other row 5 (8, 10, 12) times—62 (66, 72, 78) sts. Work even to approx 26 (26½, 27, 27½)" from beg, ending with a WS row. Bind off with MC, loosely and knitwise.

FRONT

Work Border as for Back. Change to largest needles. Work Body Pattern Rows 17–32; rep Rows 1–32 for rem of Front. Work even to approx 16" from beg, ending with a WS row.

Neck Shaping
Work first 42 (47, 52, 57) sts in pat; join new strand(s) and work to end of row. Working sides separately and at the same time, dec 1 st each neck edge every other row 6 (7, 8, 9) times, then every 4th row 8 times. AT THE SAME TIME, when piece is approx 16½" from beg, shape armholes as for Back. Work even on rem 17 (18, 20, 22) sts for each shoulder to same length as Back, ending with a WS row. Bind off with MC, loosely and knitwise.

FINISHING

Join shoulder seams.

Armbands (make two)
With the RS facing using circular needle and MC, pick up and k 85 (89, 93, 97) sts evenly spaced around armhole.
Row 1 (WS): P1; (k1, p1) across.
Row 2: K1; (p1, k1) across.
Row 3: Rep Row 1. Bind off in ribbing.

Neckband
With the RS facing, using circular needle and MC, begin just past right shoulder seam on back and pick up and k 30 (32, 34, 36) sts evenly along back neck. Pick up and k 38 (40, 42, 44) sts evenly along each side of V-neck—106 (112, 118, 124) sts. Place a marker to indicate beg of rnd; join. Work k1, p1 rib around for 7 total rnds. Bind off loosely in rib. Turn ribbing to inside and whip st to pick up row. Join side seams. Weave in loose ends on WS.

CHILD'S VEST—BACK

Beg at the lower edge with size 7 needle and MC (cranberry), cast on 44 (54, 64) sts. Work Border Rows 1–2 for 3 times; rep Row 1 again. Change to largest needles and work Body Pattern until piece measures approx 7 (8, 9)" from beg, ending with a WS row.

Armhole Shaping
Cont in pattern, bind off 5 (6, 7) sts at beg of next 2 rows, dec 1 st each armhole edge every other row 3 (4, 5) times—28 (34, 40) sts. Work even to approx 11 (12½, 14)" from beg, ending with a WS row. Bind off loosely and knitwise with MC.

FRONT

Work Border as for Back. Change to largest needles and beg Body Pattern, working Rows 17–32 then rep Rows 1–32 to approx 4½ (5½, 6½)" from beg, ending with a WS row.

V-Neck Shaping
In pattern, work first 22 (27, 32) sts; join new strand(s) and work to end of row. Working sides separately and at the same time, dec 1 st each neck edge every other row 7 (8, 9) times. AT THE SAME TIME, when piece measures approx 7 (8, 9)" from beg,

shape armholes as for Back. Work even to same length as Back, ending with a WS row. Bind off rem 7 (9, 11) sts for each shoulder knitwise and loosely, using MC.

FINISHING

Join shoulder seam.

Armbands (make two)
With the RS facing, using circular needle and MC, pick up and k 43 (49, 55) sts evenly spaced along armhole edge.

Ribbing
Row 1 (WS): P1; (k1, p1) across.
Row 2: K1; (p1, k1) across.
Row 3: Rep Row 1. Bind off in ribbing.

Neckband
With the RS facing, using circular needle and MC, begin just past right shoulder seam to pick up and k 16 (18, 20) sts along back neck. Pick up and k 28 (30, 32) sts evenly spaced along each side of V-neck—72 (78, 84) sts. Place a marker to indicate beg of rnd; join. Work 7 rnds of k1, p1 rib. Bind off loosely in rib. Turn band to inside and whip st to pick up row. Join side seams. Weave in loose ends on WS.

Rodeo Drive for Lunch

photos on page 64–65

SKILL LEVEL: Intermediate

SIZES: S (MEDIUM, L, XL, XXL)
Note: The pattern is written for the smallest size with changes for larger sizes in parentheses. When only one number is given, it applies to all sizes. For ease in working, before you begin, circle all numbers pertaining to the size you are knitting.

FINISHED MEASUREMENTS:
Bust: 38 (42, 46, 50, 54)"
Length: 23½ (24, 24½, 25, 25½)"

MATERIALS:
- Brown Sheep Cotton Fleece, 80% Cotton/20% Merino Wool, DK weight yarn (215 yards per skein): 6 (7, 7, 8, 9) skeins of Antique Lace (150)

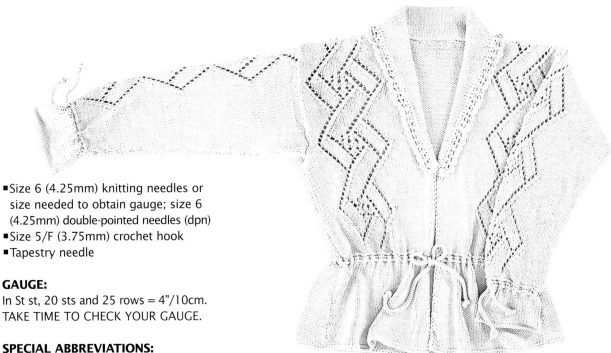

- Size 6 (4.25mm) knitting needles or size needed to obtain gauge; size 6 (4.25mm) double-pointed needles (dpn)
- Size 5/F (3.75mm) crochet hook
- Tapestry needle

GAUGE:
In St st, 20 sts and 25 rows = 4"/10cm.
TAKE TIME TO CHECK YOUR GAUGE.

SPECIAL ABBREVIATIONS:
Sl 1: Slip 1 st purlwise with yarn on WS of fabric.
Ssk (slip, slip, knit): Sl next 2 sts knitwise, one at a time to right-hand needle, insert tip of left-hand needle into fronts of these 2 sts and k tog.
K1b: K in back lp of next st.
Pm: Place marker.

STITCHES USED:
Lace Panel (over 25 sts; a rep of 32 rows)
Row 1 (WS): Purl.
Row 2: K8, k2tog, yo, k6, k2tog, yo, k7.
Row 3 and each following WS row: Purl.
Row 4: K7, k2tog, yo, k6, k2tog, yo, k8.
Row 6: (K6, k2tog, yo) twice, k9.
Row 8: K5, k2tog, yo, k6, k2tog, yo, k1b, yo, ssk, k7.
Row 10: K4, k2tog, yo, k6, k2tog, yo, k3, yo, ssk, k6.
Row 12: K3, k2tog, yo, k6, k2tog, yo, k5, yo, ssk, k5.
Row 14: K2, (k2tog, yo, k1b, yo, ssk, k3) twice, k1, yo, ssk, k4.
Row 16: (K1, k2tog, yo, k3, yo, ssk) twice, k4, yo, ssk, k3.
Row 18: K2tog, yo, k5, (yo, sl 1, k2tog, psso, yo, k1b) twice, yo, ssk, k4, yo, ssk, k2.
Row 20: K2, yo, ssk, k4, yo, ssk, k6, yo, ssk, k4, yo, ssk, k1.
Row 22: K3, yo, ssk, k4, yo, ssk, yo, sl 1, k2tog, psso, yo, k2tog, yo, k1b, yo, ssk, k4, yo, ssk.
Row 24: (K4, yo, ssk) twice, k2, k2tog, yo, k2, yo, ssk, k1, k2tog, yo, k2.
Row 26: K5, yo, ssk, k4, yo, k3tog, yo, k5, yo, k3tog, yo, k3.
Row 28: K6, yo, ssk, k3, k2tog, yo, k6, k2tog, yo, k4.
Row 30: K7, yo, ssk, k1, k2tog, yo, k6, k2tog, yo, k5.
Row 32: K8, yo, k3tog, yo, k6, k2tog, yo, k6.
Rep Rows 1–32 for Lace Panel.

I-Cord
On dpn, cast on 3 sts; k across. Do not turn work; rather, push sts to opposite end of needle and k across. Cont in this manner, without turning, until piece is required length.

INSTRUCTIONS:
BACK
Beg at lower edge, cast on 105 (115, 125, 135, 145) sts. Beg with a k row, work St st for 8 rows. * K across next row, dec 1 st each edge; work 7 more

Rodeo Drive for Lunch
continued from page 93

St st rows; rep from * 4 times more—95 (105, 115, 125, 135) sts. Work even to approx 6½" from beg, ending with a WS row.
Eyelets: K1; (yo, k2tog) across.
Garter Ridges: K 3 rows.

Set Up for Body Pattern
Row 1 (RS): K6 (8, 10, 12, 14); pm; k25; pm; k 33 (39, 45, 51, 57); pm; k25; pm; k 6 (8, 10, 12, 14). P across, slipping markers. Work Lace Panel over each 25-st section bet markers, beg with Row 2, keeping side and center sts in St st. Cont as est to approx 15½" from beg, ending with a WS row.

Armhole Shaping
Bind off 5 sts at beg of next 2 rows—85 (95, 105, 115, 125) sts. Cont est pattern to approx 22½ (23, 23½, 24, 24½)" from beg, ending with a WS row.

Neck Shaping
Work first 29 (33, 37, 41, 45) sts in pattern; join a new strand and bind off center 27 (29, 31, 33, 35) sts; work to end of row. Working sides separately and at the same time, dec 1 st each neck edge. Work even on 28 (32, 36, 40, 44) sts for each shoulder to approx 23½ (24, 24½, 25, 25½)" from beg, ending with a WS row. Bind off straight across and knitwise.

RIGHT FRONT
Beg at lower edge, cast on 50 (54, 60, 64, 70) sts. Beg with a k row, work St st for 8 rows. * K across next row, dec 1 st at side edge; work 7 more rows St st; rep from * 4 times more—45 (49, 55, 59, 65) sts. Work even to approx 6½" from beg, ending with a WS row. Work Eyelets as for Back, then k 3 rows for Garter Ridges.

Set Up for Body Pattern
Row 1 (RS): K14 (16, 20, 22, 26); pm, k25; pm, k6 (8, 10, 12, 14). P across, slipping markers. Working sts outside markers in St st, begin with Row 2 to work Lace Panel over 25 sts bet markers. Work even to approx 12½ (13, 13½, 14, 14½)" from beg, ending with a WS row.

Neck Shaping
Dec 1 st at neck edge now and then every 4th row 4 (6, 10, 13, 15) times, every 6th row 7 (5, 3, 0, 0) times. AT THE SAME TIME, when piece measures approx 15½" from beg, end with a RS row. Bind off 5 sts at armhole edge. Work even to same length as Back, ending with a WS row. Bind off rem 28 (32, 36, 40, 44) sts loosely and knitwise.

LEFT FRONT
Work as for Right Front to Body Pattern.

Set Up for Body Pattern
Row 1 (RS): K 6 (8, 10, 12, 14); pm, k25; pm, k 14 (16, 20, 22, 26). P across, slipping markers. Working sts outside markers in St st, begin with Row 2 to work Lace Panel over 25 sts bet markers. Cont as for Right Front, reversing neck and armhole shaping.

SLEEVES (make two)
Beg at lower edge, cast on 51 (53, 55, 57, 59) sts. Beg with a k row, work St st to approx 3" from beg, ending with a WS row. Work Eyelets as for Back; k 3 rows for Garter Ridges.

Set Up for Body Pattern
Row 1 (RS): K13 (14, 15, 16, 17); pm; k25; pm; k13 (14, 15, 16, 17). P across, slipping markers. Working sts outside markers in St st, begin with Row 2 to work Lace Panel over 25 sts bet markers. **Next RS Row:** Inc 1 st each edge now, and then every 6th row 6 (11, 9, 7, 1) time(s), every 4th row 0 (0, 6, 10, 17) times, then every 8th row 6 (3, 0, 0, 0) times. Work even on 77 (83, 87, 93, 97) sts to approx 20 (20, 19½, 19, 18½)" from beg, ending with a WS row. Bind off knitwise and loosely.

COLLAR
Cast on 27 (29, 31, 33, 35) sts. P 1 row. Working St st, cast on 3 sts at the beg of next 36 rows—135 (137, 139, 141, 143) sts. K 1 row. P 1 row. Bind off loosely and knitwise.

I-Cords (make two for sleeves)
With dpn, cast on 3 sts. Work I-cord until piece measures approx 25" from beg. Bind off.

I-Cord Drawstring
Work as for sleeves to approx 60 (60, 65, 70, 75)" from beg. Bind off.

FINISHING
Join shoulder seams. Set in sleeves, joining sides to bound off sts for square armholes. Join underarm and side seams. Placing RS of collar (the jagged edge) to WS of cardigan, pin in

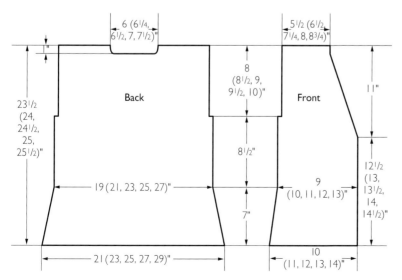

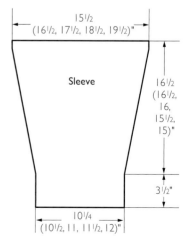

place starting and ending at first V-neck shaping row. Use crochet hook to sl st in place.
With the RS facing using crochet hook, sc in each of the 135 (137, 139, 141, 143) sts; turn. **Row 2:** Ch 1, sc in first sc; * ch 2, sk 1 sc, sc in next sc; rep from * across; turn. **Row 3:** Rep Row 2 again. **Row 4:** Sl st in first sc; * in ch2 sp (sc, hdc, sc), sl st in next sc; rep from * across. At end, fasten off.

Body Edging

With crochet hook, beg below collar, work sc along front edge, 3 sc in corner, sc evenly along lower edge, working 3 sc in corner, sc along opposite front edge; turn. Sl st in each sc around and fasten off. Trim sleeve edges as for body or let roll naturally as shown in the photo. Fold collar to outside, placing first sc row of collar onto the ridge formed by the sl st joining. With tapestry needle and yarn, baste the sc row to the ridge. Join ends of Body Edging to collar near the fold. Thread I-cords through eyelets, tying ends in overhand knots. Weave in loose ends on WS of fabric.

Red Hat, Scarf, and Bag

photos on page 66–67

SKILL LEVEL: Experienced

SIZES: Scarf: 7×52"; Hat (22" circumference) for average size; Bag: 6×8"

MATERIALS:

- Patons Classic Merino Wool, 100% wool, worsted weight yarn (223 yards per ball): Russet (206): Scarf 3 balls; Hat 1 ball; Bag 2 balls
- Size 10 (6mm) knitting needles or size needed to obtain gauge
- Size 9 (5.5 mm) knitting needles
- Cable needle (cn)
- Yarn needle

GAUGE:

16 sts and 20 rows = 4"/10cm in St st with 2 strands of yarn and larger needles. TAKE TIME TO CHECK GAUGE.

SPECIAL ABBREVIATIONS:

C4F: Slip next 2 sts onto a cn and leave at front of work, k2, then k2 from cn.

C7F: Slip next 3 sts onto a cn and leave at front of work. (K3, p1), then k3 from cn.

C7B: Slip next 4 sts onto a cn and leave at back of work. K3, then (p1, k3) from cn.

Sl 1: Slip next st purlwise and with yarn on WS.

STITCHES USED:

Panel A (worked over 17 sts; a rep of 28 rows).
Row 1 (RS): P1, (k3, p1) 4 times.
Row 2 and all WS rows: K1, (p3, k1) 4 times.
Rows 3 and 5: As Row 1.
Row 7: P1, k3, p1, C7F, p1, k3, p1.
Rows 9 and 11: As Row 1.
Row 13: As Row 7.
Rows 15, 17, and 19: As Row 1.
Row 21: P1, C7B, p1, C7F, p1.
Rows 23 and 25: As Row 1.
Row 27: As Row 21.
Row 28: As Row 2.
Rep Rows 1–28 for Panel A.

Panel B (worked over 6 sts; a rep of 8 rows).
Row 1 (RS): P1, k4, p1.
Row 2 and all WS rows: K1, p4, k1.

Row 3: P1, C4F, p1.
Rows 5 and 7: As Row 1.
Row 8: As Row 2.
Rep Rows 1–8 for Panel B.

Note: *Hat and purse are worked from side to side.*

INSTRUCTIONS:

HAT

With 2 strands of yarn and larger needles, cast on 43 sts.
** **Row 1 (RS):** K2, (p1, k1, p1 for Irish Moss); work Row 1 of Panel A; (p1, k1, p1 for Irish Moss); work Row 1 of Panel B; k12.
Row 2: P12, work Row 2 of Panel B, (k1, p1, k1 for Irish Moss), work Row 2 of Panel A, (k1, p1, k1 for Irish Moss), p2.
Row 3: K2, (k1, p1, k1 for Irish Moss), work Row 3 of Panel A, (k1, p1, k1 for Irish Moss), work Row 3 of Panel B, k to last 2 sts. Turn. Leave rem sts unworked.
Row 4: Sl 1, p9, work Row 4 of Panel B, (p1, k1, p1 for Irish Moss), work Row 4 of Panel A, (p1, k1, p1 for Irish Moss), p2.
Panels A and B are now in position. Rows 1–4 form Irish Moss pat. Cont in pat, keeping cont of Panels and Irish Moss st pat, proceed as follows:
Row 5: Pat to last 4 sts. Turn. Leave rem sts unworked.

Red Hat, Scarf, and Bag

continued from page 95

Row 6 and alt rows: Sl 1. Pat to end of row.
Row 7: Pat to last 5 sts. Turn. Leave rem sts unworked.
Row 9: Pat to last 6 sts. Turn. Leave rem sts unworked.
Row 11: Pat to last 7 sts. Turn. Leave rem sts unworked.
Row 13: Pat to last 8 sts. Turn. Leave rem sts unworked.
Row 15: Pat to last 9 sts. Turn. Leave rem sts unworked.
Row 17: Pat to last 10 sts. Turn. Leave rem sts unworked.
Row 19: Pat to last 11 sts. Turn. Leave rem sts unworked.
Row 21: Pat to last 12 sts. Turn. Leave rem sts unworked.
Row 23: Pat across all sts.
Row 24: Pat across all sts **.
Rep from ** to ** 3 times more working appropriate rows of Panels A and B. Bind off in pat. Sew back seam.

SCARF

With 2 strands of yarn and larger needles, cast on 31 sts.
Row 1 (RS): (K1, p1) 3 times, k1, work Row 1 of Panel A, (k1, p1) 3 times, k1.
Row 2: (P1, k1) 3 times, p1, work Row 2 of Panel A, (p1, k1) 3 times, p1.
Row 3: (P1, k1) 3 times, p1, work Row 3 of Panel A, (p1, k1) 3 times, p1.
Row 4: (K1, p1) 3 times, k1, work Row 4 of Panel A, (k1, p1) 3 times, k1.
Panel Pat A is now in position. Rows 1–4 form Irish Moss pat. Cont in pat, keeping cont of Panel Pat A and Irish Moss pat until work from beg measures approx 50", ending with a WS row; bind off.

BAG

With 2 strands of yarn and smaller needles, cast on 31 sts.
Row 1 (RS): K1, work Row 1 of Panel A, [(k1, p1) 6 times, k1 for Irish Moss].
Row 2: [P1, (k1, p1) 6 times for Irish Moss], work Row 2 of Panel A, p1.
Row 3: K1, work Row 3 of Panel A, [(p1, k1) 6 times, p1 for Irish Moss].
Row 4: [K1, (p1, k1) 6 times for Irish

Moss], work Row 4 of Panel A, p1. Panel A is now in position. Rows 1–4 form Irish Moss pat. Cont in pat, keeping cont of Panel A and Irish Moss pat until work from beg measures approx 2", ending with a WS row. Form eyelets for the tie as follows.
** **Next Row:** Pat 21 sts, yo, work k2tog, pat to end of row. Place marker at end of row. Work 3 rows even in pat.
Next Row: Pat 21 sts, yo, work k2tog, pat to end of row. Work even in pat until work from marked row measures approx 4", ending with a WS row **. Rep from ** to ** twice more, ending with a WS row.
Next Row: Pat 21 sts, yo, work k2tog, pat to end of row. Place marker at end of row. Work 3 rows even in pat.
Next Row: Pat 21 sts, yo, work k2tog, pat to end of row. Work even in pat until work from marked row measures approx 2", ending with a WS row. Bind off.
Bottom: With RS of work facing, pick up and k65 sts along bottom of bag. Beg with a p row, work 3 rows even in St st. Place marker at end of last row. **Shape bottom, Row 1:** K1, * k6, k2tog, rep from * to end of row— 57 sts.
Row 2 and alt rows: Purl.
Row 3: K1; * k5, k2tog, rep from * to end of row—49 sts.
Cont in same manner, dec 8 sts on every RS row until 17 sts rem. Break yarn, leaving a long end. Thread yarn into yarn needle and through rem sts; tighten securely. Sew bottom and side seam. With WS of work facing, sew marked row and pick up row tog to create a ridge on RS.

Handle: With 2 strands of yarn and smaller needles, CO 5 sts.
Row 1: (K1, p1) twice, k1.
Row 2: (P1, k1) twice, p1.
Row 3: As Row 2.
Row 4: As Row 1.
Rep last 4 rows until Handle measures approx 42", ending with a WS row. Bind off. Sew Handle inside of Bag 1" from top edge.
Twisted Cord: Cut 6 strands of yarn 78" long. With both strands tog, hold one end and with someone holding

other end, twist strands to the right until they begin to curl. Fold the 2 ends tog and tie in a knot so they will not unravel. The strands will now twist themselves tog. Adjust length if desired. Thread cord through the eyelet holes.

Tassel (make 2):. Wind yarn around a plastic card 20 times. Break yarn, leaving a long end, and thread end through a needle. Slip needle through all lps and tie tightly. Remove card and wind another strand of yarn tightly around lps 5¾" below fold. Fasten securely. Cut through rem lps and trim ends evenly. Sew tassels to ends of cord.

Christmas Stockings

photos on pages 68–69
SKILL LEVEL: Easy

SIZE: Approximately 18½" from top of cuff to toe

MATERIALS:
- Red Heart Classic, Article E267, 100% acrylic, worsted weight yarn (3.5 ounces per skein): 2 skeins of Off-White (3); 1 skein of Cherry Red (912)
- Red Heart Kids, Article E711, 100% acrylic, worsted weight yarn (5 ounces per skein): 1 skein of Lime (2652)
- Size 9 (5.5mm) straight knitting needles or size needed to obtain gauge
- 1 set of size 9 (5.5mm) double-pointed knitting needles (dpn)
- Yarn needle
- 2 stitch holders

GAUGE:
In Body Pattern, 16 sts and 22 rows = 4"/10cm.
TAKE TIME TO CHECK YOUR GAUGE.

SPECIAL ABBREVIATIONS:
Ssk (slip, slip, knit): Slip next 2 sts knitwise, one at a time to right-hand needle, insert tip of left-hand needle into fronts of these 2 sts and k tog.

Rnd 5: K7, k2tog, k2, ssk, k10, k2tog, k2, ssk, k7.
Rnd 6: K32.
Rnd 7: K6, k2tog, k2, ssk, k8, k2tog, k2, ssk, k6.
Rnd 8: K28.
Rnd 9: K5, k2tog, k2, ssk, k6, k2tog, k2, ssk, k5.
Rnd 10: K24. Break yarn, leaving a long tail. Thread tail into yarn needle and back through rem 24 sts. Pull up to close opening and secure in place.

FINISHING
Join back seam.

I-Cord: Using dpn and Cherry, cast on 3 sts. * Push sts to opposite end of needle, k3; rep from * until cord measures 40" long. Bind off. Make a Lime cord of same length.

Mock Cables
Insert green cord from back to front into first lower eyelet to the left of back seam at cuff; skip first top eyelet, take cord through next top eyelet from front to back; skip next lower eyelet, take cord through next lower eyelet from back to front. Cont weaving the green cord as est to the seam; take cord through top eyelet closest to seam then through first skipped top eyelet so cord is outside of cuff. With red, beg with first skipped lower eyelet, weave cord as est, ending so cord is right of seam and outside the cuff.

Hanging Loop
Holding cords tog, tie an overhand knot 1" from one end. Tie a second overhand knot 2" from first knot.

Bow and Ties
With Cherry make a 10" I-Cord; change to Lime and work even for 10"; bind off. With Cherry make a 6" I-Cord; change to Lime and work even for 6"; bind off. Weave in loose ends. Form longer cord into a bow; place shorter cord across center; use ends from mock cables cords to tie into place at cuff back.

Sl1p: Sl 1 st purlwise with yarn on WS of fabric.
Sl1k: Sl 1 st knitwise with yarn on WS of fabric.

INSTRUCTIONS:
OFF-WHITE STOCKING WITH CHERRY AND LIME STRIPES
Beg at the cuff, use straight needles and Off-White, cast on 53 sts. K 6 rows. **Eyelets:** K1, (yo, k2tog) across. K 1 row. Rep Eyelets. K 6 rows.
Stocking Body
Beginning with a p row, work 7 rows St st.
Row 1 (RS): K across with Lime.
Row 2: Rep Row 1.
Row 3: With Off-White, k across.
Row 4: With Off-White, p across.
Rows 5–10: Rep Rows 3–4.
Row 11: K across with Cherry.
Row 12: Rep Row 11.
Rows 13–20: Rep Rows 3–10.
Rep Rows 1–20 for Body Pattern until stocking measures approx 11½" from beg, ending with Row 4. Break yarn.

HEEL
With the RS facing, sl first 13 sts onto a holder; sl next 27 sts onto a holder; join Off-White and k the last 13 sts, then k13 sts from first holder. Beginning with a p row, work 9 rows of St st on the 26 heel sts.
To Turn Heel: K16, ssk, k1; turn.

Row 2: Sl1p, p7, p2tog, p1; turn.
Row 3: Sl1k, k7, ssk, k1; turn.
Rep Rows 2–3 until 10 sts rem, ending with Row 2. K10. Break yarn.

GUSSET (Note: *Change to dpns and work in rounds. When changing colors, twist strands around each other on WS of fabric to prevent holes).* With the RS facing and Off-White, pick up and k5 sts evenly spaced along left edge of heel, k27 sts from holder, pick up and k5 sts evenly spaced along right edge of heel, k5 heel sts, place a marker to indicate beg of rnd, k5 heel sts = 47 sts. K 5 rnds.

SOLE PATTERN
Rnd 1: With Cherry, k.
Rnd 2: With Cherry, p.
Rnds 3-10: With Off-White, k.
Rnd 11: With Lime, k.
Rnd 12: With Lime, p.
Rnds 13–20: Rep Rnds 3–10, dec 3 sts evenly spaced on Rnd 10—44 sts.
Rnds 21–22: Rep Rnds 1–2.

TOE
Change to Off-White for rem of stocking and work as follows:
Rnd 1: K9, k2tog, k2, ssk, k14, k2tog, k2, ssk, k9.
Rnd 2: K40.
Rnd 3: K8, k2tog, k2, ssk, k12, k2tog, k2, ssk, k8.
Rnd 4: K36.

CHERRY AND LIME STRIPE STOCKING WITH OFF-WHITE RIDGES

Beginning at the cuff using the straight needles and Cherry, cast on 11 sts.

Rows 1, 2, 3: Knit.
Row 4: K5, yo, k2tog, k4.
Rows 5–6: Knit.
* Change to Lime and rep Rows 1–6 **; change to Cherry and rep rows 1–6; rep from * 8 times then rep from * to ** once. Bind off straight across.

Stocking Body

With RS facing using straight needles and Lime, pick up and k54 sts evenly spaced along cuff edge (3 sts in each stripe). P 1 row, dec 1 st in center—53 sts. K 1 row, p 1 row. **Eyelets:** K1; (yo, k2tog) across. Beg with a k row, work 4 rows St st.

Body Pattern

Row 1 (RS): With Off-White, k.
Row 2: Rep Row 1.
Row 3: With Cherry, k.
Row 4: With Cherry, p.
Rows 5–6: Rep Rows 3–4.
Rows 7–8: Rep rows 1–2.
Rows 9–12: With Lime, rep Rows 3–6. Rep Rows 1–12 for Body Pattern until stocking measures approx 11½" from beg, ending with Row 8. Break yarn. Work Heel as for Off-White Stocking. Using Lime, work Gusset as for Off-White Stocking; knitting 3 rnds instead of 5 rnds.

SOLE PATTERN

Rnd 1: With Off-White, k.
Rnd 2: With Off-White, p.

Rnds 3–6: With Cherry, k.
Rnds 7–8: Rep Rnds 1-2.
Rnds 9–12: With Lime, k.
Rnds 13–18: Rep Rnds 1–6, dec 3 sts evenly spaced on Rnd 6 = 44 sts.
Rnds 19–20: Rep Rnds 1–2.

TOE

Work as for First Stocking.

FINISHING

Join back and cuff seams.
I-Cords (make 5)
Referring to I-Cord from Off-White Stocking, with Off-White, work 21 rows and bind off. Make one 50-row off-white cord. Fold long cord in half and tie into an overhand knot with approx 1" loop for hanging. With the knot at WS of stocking cuff, insert ends into eyelets on both sides of cuff seam, outside the cuff; tie. * Working from right to left, skip one cuff eyelet, tie short cord over next two cuff eyelets; rep from * around.

Men's Argyle Sweater

photos on pages 70–71

SKILL LEVEL: Intermediate

SIZES: S (MEDIUM, L, XL, 2XL)
Note: *The pattern is written for the smallest size with changes for larger sizes in parentheses. When only one number is given, it applies to all sizes. For ease in working, before you begin, circle all numbers pertaining to the size you are knitting.*

FINISHED MEASUREMENTS:
Chest: 43 (46, 48, 51, 56½)"
Length: 25½ (26¾, 27½, 28¼, 28½)"

MATERIALS:
- Patons Décor, 75% acrylic/25% wool, worsted weight yarn (210 yards per ball): 6 (7, 7, 8, 8) balls of Grey Heather (1672) for MC; 2 balls of Pale Grey Heather (1671) for Color A; 2 balls of Winter White (1614) for Color B
- Size 7 (4.5mm) knitting needles or size needed to obtain gauge
- Size 6 (4.25mm) knitting needles
- 2 stitch markers
- Yarn needle

GAUGE
In St st with larger needles, 20 sts and 24 rows = 4"/10 cm.
TAKE TIME TO CHECK YOUR GAUGE.

SPECIAL ABBREVIATIONS:
Sl 1: Slip 1 st purlwise and with yarn on WS of fabric.
P2togb: Turn work slightly, insert right-hand needle from left to right into 2nd and first sts and p these 2 sts together.

Notes: *Front only is worked from the chart. The chart is worked in St st except for the squares that are marked with a dash (–). Wind small balls of the colors to be used, one for each separate area of color in the design. Start new colors at appropriate points. To change colors, twist the two colors around each other where they meet, on WS, to avoid a hole.*

INSTRUCTIONS:
BACK
** With smaller needles and A, cast on 102 (110, 118, 122, 134) sts.
Row 1 (RS): With MC, k2; * p2, k2. Rep from * to end of row.
Row 2: P2, * k2, p2. Rep from * to end of row.
Rep last 2 rows of (k2, p2) ribbing for approx 2½", inc 6 (6, 4, 6, 8) sts evenly across last WS row—108 (116, 122, 128, 142) sts **. Change to

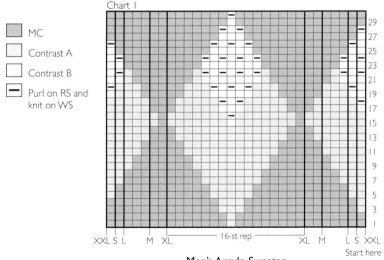

Chart I

MC
Contrast A
Contrast B
Purl on RS and knit on WS

29 27 25 23 21 19 17 15 13 11 9 7 5 3 1

XXL S L   M XL ⊢16-st rep⊣ XL M L S XXL

Start here

Men's Argyle Sweater

larger needles and proceed in St st, beg with a k row, until work from beg measures approx 16½ (17½, 18, 18½, 18½)". Place markers at each end of needle.

Armhole Shaping: Bind off 9 (10, 11, 12, 12) sts beg next 2 rows—90 (96, 100, 104, 118) sts. **Next Row:** K2, sl 1, k1, psso, k to last 4 sts, k2tog, k2.

Next Row: Purl. Rep last 2 rows 4 (4, 4, 5, 5) times more—80 (86, 90, 92, 106) sts. Cont in pat until armhole measures approx 8½ (8¾, 9, 9¼, 9½)", ending with a WS row.

Neck and Shoulder Shaping

K25 (27, 28, 29, 34), k2tog (neck edge). Turn. Leave rem sts on spare needle.

Next Row: P2tog, p to end of row.

Next Row: Bind off 12 (13, 13, 14, 16) sts, k to last 2 sts, k2tog.

Next Row: Purl. Bind off rem 12 (13, 14, 14, 17) sts. With RS of work facing, slip next 26 (28, 30, 30, 34) sts from spare needle onto a st holder. Join MC to rem sts and proceed as follows: Sl 1, k1, psso, k to end of row.

Next Row: Bind off 12 (13, 13, 14, 16) sts, p to last 2 sts, p2togb.
Next Row: Sl 1, k1, psso, k to end of row. Bind off rem 12 (13, 14, 14, 17) sts.

FRONT

Work from ** to ** as given for Back. Change to larger needles and Chart I *(page 98)* beg with a k row. Read k rows from right to left and p rows from left to right, noting 16-st rep will be worked 6 (7, 7, 8, 8) times. Rows 1–30 of chart form pat. Cont in pat until work from beg measures same length as Back.

Place markers at each end of needle.

Armhole Shaping

Keeping cont of Chart, bind off 9 (10, 11, 12, 12) sts beg next 2 rows—90 (96, 100, 104, 118) sts. **Next Row:** K2, sl 1, k1, psso, pat to last 4 sts, k2tog, k2.

Next Row: Work even in pat. Rep last 2 rows 4 (4, 4, 5, 5) times more—80 (86, 90, 92, 106) sts. Cont even in pat until armhole measures approx 5½ (5¾, 6, 6, 6½)" ending with a WS row.

Neck Shaping Pat 31 (33, 34, 35, 40) sts across (neck edge). Turn. Leave rem sts on spare needle. Dec 1 st at neck edge on next 4 rows, then

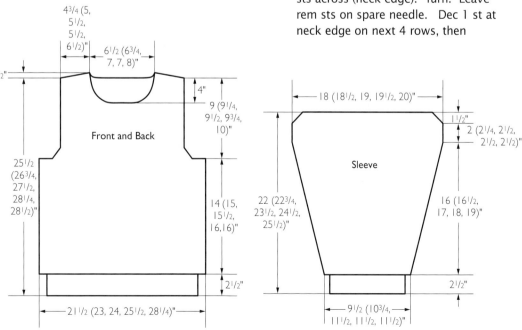

4¾ (5, 5½, 5½, 6½)"

6½ (6¾, 7, 7, 8)"

½"

4"

9 (9¼, 9½, 9¾, 10)"

Front and Back

25½ (26¾, 27½, 28¼, 28½)"

14 (15, 15½, 16,16)"

2½"

21½ (23, 24, 25½, 28¼)"

18 (18½, 19, 19½, 20)"

1½"

2 (2¼, 2½, 2½, 2½)"

Sleeve

22 (22¾, 23½, 24½, 25½)"

16 (16½, 17, 18, 19)"

2½"

9½ (10¾, 11½, 11½, 11½)"

Men's Argyle Sweater

continued from page 99

following alt rows 3 times—24 (26, 27, 28, 33) sts. Cont even in pat until work from beg measures same length as Back to beg of shoulder shaping ending with a WS row.

Shoulder Shaping

Bind off 12 (13, 13, 14, 16) sts. Work 1 row even. Bind off rem 12 (13, 14, 14, 17) sts. With RS of work facing, slip next 18 (20, 22, 22, 26) sts from spare needle onto a st holder. Join yarn to rem sts and work to correspond to other side, ending with a RS row.

SLEEVES (make two)

With smaller needles and A, cast on 42 (46, 50, 50, 50) sts. With MC, work in (k2, p2) ribbing as given for Back for approx 2½", inc 6 (8, 8, 8, 8) sts evenly across last WS row—48 (54, 58, 58, 58) sts. Change to larger needles and St st (beg with a k row), inc 1 st each end of needle on 3rd and every following 4th row until there are 90 (92, 96, 98, 100) sts. Cont even in St st until work from beg measures approx 18½ (19, 19½, 20½, 21½)", ending with a WS row. Place markers at each end of needle. Work 12 (14, 16, 16, 16) rows even, ending with a WS row. **Next Row:** K2, sl 1, k1,

psso, k to last 4 sts, k2tog, k2. **Next Row:** Purl. Rep last 2 rows 4 (4, 4, 5, 5) times more ending with a WS row—80 (82, 86, 86, 88) sts. Bind off.

FINISHING

Sew right shoulder seam.
Neckband: With RS of work facing, MC and smaller needles pick up and k26 (26, 26, 30, 30) down left front neck edge. K18 (20, 22, 22, 26) from front st holder. Pick up and k26 (26, 26, 30, 30) sts up right front neck edge. Pick up and k3 sts down right back neck edge. K 26 (28, 30, 30, 34) sts from back st holder. Pick up and k 3 sts up left back neck edge—102

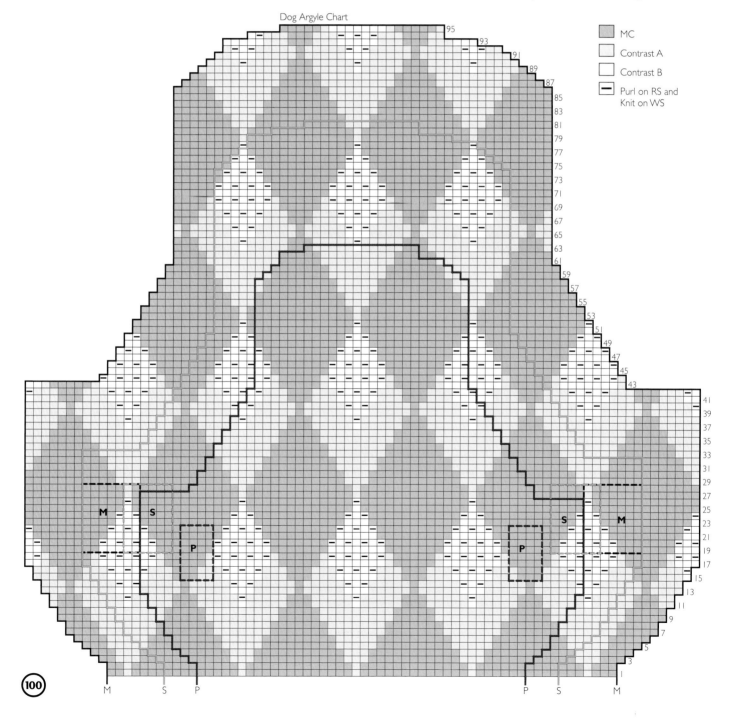

Dog Argyle Chart

MC
Contrast A
Contrast B
— Purl on RS and Knit on WS

(106, 110, 118, 126) sts. Work 8 rows in (k2 p2) ribbing as given for Back. With A, work 10 rows in (K2 P2) ribbing. Bind off loosely in ribbing. Sew left shoulder. Fold neckband in half to WS and sew in position. Sew in Sleeves matching underarm markers. Sew side and sleeve seams.

Dog Argyle
photo on page 70

SKILL LEVEL: Intermediate

MEASUREMENTS: Petite 10", Small 13", Medium 16"

Note: The pattern is written for the smallest size with changes for larger sizes in parentheses. When only one number is given, it applies to all sizes. For ease in working, before you begin, circle all numbers pertaining to the size you are knitting.

MATERIALS:
- Patons Décor, 75% acrylic/25% wool, worsted weight yarn (210 yards per ball): 1 ball of Grey Heather (1672) for MC; 1 ball of Pale Grey Heather (1671) for Color A; 1 ball of Winter White (1614) for Color B
- Size 7 (4.5mm) straight knitting needles or size needed to obtain gauge
- Size 6 (4.25mm) straight knitting needles
- Size 6 (4.25mm) circular needle 16-inch length and set of four size 6 (4.25mm) double-pointed needles.
- Yarn needle
- Markers

GAUGE:
With larger needles in St st, 20 sts and 24 rows = 4"/10cm TAKE TIME TO CHECK YOUR GAUGE.

Note: When working from chart, wind small balls of the colors to be used, one for each color in the design. Start new colors at appropriate points. To change colors, on WS twist the two colors around each other where they meet.

INSTRUCTIONS:
Beg at neck edge, with smaller needles and MC, cast on 39 (47, 61) sts.
Row 1 (RS): K1; * p1, k1. Rep from * to end of row.
Row 2: P1; * k1, p1. Rep from * to end of row.
Rep these 2 rows (k1, p1) ribbing for approx 1 (1½, 1½)", ending on a 2nd row and inc 1 st in center of last row—40 (48, 62) sts. Break MC. Change to larger needles and proceed in Chart, *opposite,* reading k rows from right to left and p rows from left to right, inc 1 st each end of needle on 3rd and next 2 (4, 4) rows—46 (58, 72) sts. Cont in Chart, inc 1 st each end of needle on following alt rows until Row 14 (18, 18) of Chart is completed—54 (68, 82) sts.
Leg Openings: Row 1 (RS): Work 5 (5, 7) Chart sts. Bind off next 4 (6, 6) sts. Work 36 (46, 56) Chart sts (including st on needle after bind off). Bind off next 4 (6, 6) sts. Work in Chart to end of row.
Note: All Leg Sections are worked at the same time using a separate ball of yarn for each section.
Beg with a p row, work Chart until Row 22 (28, 28) of Chart is completed.
Next Row (RS): Work k 5 (5, 7) Chart sts. Turn and cast on 4 (6, 6) sts. Turn and work in Chart pat on 36 (46, 56) sts. Turn and cast on 4 (6, 6) sts. Turn and work in Chart pat to end of row—54 (68, 82) sts.
Cont even in Chart until Row 26 (32, 42) of Chart is completed. Place a marker at each end of row.

Back Shaping: Cont in Chart, bind off 6 (7, 9) sts at beg of next 2 rows—

42 (54, 64) sts. Cont in Chart, dec 1 st each end of needle on next and every alt row until there are 26 (36, 46) sts. Cont even in Chart until Row 58 (74, 86) of Chart is complete. Dec 1 st each end of needle on next and every alt row until there are 20 (28, 34) sts. Bind off 3 sts beg next 2 rows, then 0 (4, 4) sts beg next 2 rows. Leave rem 14 (14, 20) sts on a spare needle.

Back Edging: With RS facing, MC and circular needle, pick up and k42 (51, 67) sts along body from marker to back. K14 (14, 20) from spare needle, dec 1 st at center. Pick up and k42 (51, 67) sts along opposite side of body to marker—97 (115, 153) sts. Work in (k1, p1) ribbing as given above for approx 1 (1, 1½)", ending with a WS row. Bind off in ribbing. Sew Neck and Body seam.

Leg Ribbing: With first dpn and A, pick up and k8 (8, 10) sts around leg opening. [With next dpn pick up and k7 (9, 10) sts] twice—22 (26, 30) total sts. Join in rnd and place a marker on first st, work approx 1 (1½, 2)" in (k1, p1) ribbing. Bind off loosely in ribbing. Repeat for 2nd leg opening.

Button-Up Jacket and Hat
photo on page 72
SKILL LEVEL: Easy

SIZES: XS (SMALL, M, L, XL)
Note: The pattern is written for the smallest size with changes for larger sizes in parentheses. When only one number is given, it applies to all sizes. For ease in working, before you begin, circle all numbers pertaining to the size you are knitting.

FINISHED MEASUREMENTS:
Bust (buttoned): 39 (41, 43, 46, 48)"
Length: 24 (24½, 25, 25½, 25½)"

MATERIALS:
- Patons Shetland Chunky, 75% acrylic/25% wool, chunky weight yarn (148 yards per skein): 7 (8, 8,

Button-Up Jacket and Hat

continued from page 101

9, 9) skeins of Aran (03008) and 1 skein of Contrast Taupe (03022) for embroidery for Jacket. 1 skein each of Aran (MC) (03008), Color A Steel Blue (03105) and Color B Taupe (03022) for Hat

- Size 10 (6mm) knitting needles or size needed to obtain gauge
- Size 9 (5.5mm) knitting needles
- Five ⅞-inch-diameter buttons
- Yarn needle

GAUGE:

In St st (k RS rows, p WS rows) on larger needles, 15 sts and 20 rows = 4"/10cm.   In Seed st on larger needles, 14 sts and 24 rows = 4"/10cm. TAKE TIME TO CHECK YOUR GAUGE.

STITCHES USED:

Seed St (worked over an odd number of sts; a rep of 1 row)
Row 1 (RS): * K1, p1; rep from * to last st, k1.
This row forms Seed St pat.

Rib Pat (worked over multiple of 6 sts plus 3; a rep of 2 rows).
Row 1 (RS): K3; * p3, k3; rep from * to end of row.
Row 2: P3; * k3, p3; rep from * to end of row.
These 2 rows form Rib Pat.

INSTRUCTIONS:
JACKET—BACK
Beg at lower edge with larger needles cast on 69 (71, 75, 81, 85) sts.

Work in Seed St pat until Back measures approx 15 (15, 15½, 15½, 15½)" from beg, ending with a WS row.
Armhole Shaping
At the beg of the next 2 rows, bind off 5 (6, 6, 7, 7) sts—59 (59, 63, 67, 71) sts.
Work even in Seed St pat to approx 24 (24½, 25, 25½, 25½)" from beg, ending with a WS row.
Shoulder Shaping
Bind off 9 (9, 9, 10, 11) sts beg next 2 rows, then 9 (9, 10, 10, 11) sts on the following 2 rows. Leave rem 23 (23, 25, 27, 27) sts on a spare needle.

LEFT FRONT
Beg at lower edge with larger needles, cast on 33 (35, 37, 39, 41) sts.
Work in Seed St pat until Left Front measures approx 15 (15, 15½, 15½, 15½)" from beg, ending with a WS row.
Armhole Shaping
At the beg of the next row, bind off 5 (6, 6, 7, 7) sts—28 (29, 31, 32, 34) sts.
Work even in Seed St to approx 21½ (22, 22, 22½, 22½)" from beg, ending with a RS row.
Neck Shaping
Bind off 5 (6, 6, 7, 7) sts beg next row. Dec 1 st at neck edge on next and following alt rows until there are 18 (18, 19, 20, 22) sts.
Work even in Seed St to approx 24 (24½, 25, 25½, 25½)" from beg, ending with a WS row.
Shoulder Shaping
Bind off 9 (9, 9, 10, 11) sts beg next row. Work 1 row even. Bind off rem 9 (9, 10, 10, 11) sts.

RIGHT FRONT
Beg at lower edge with larger needles, cast on 33 (35, 37, 39, 41) sts.
Work in Seed St pat until Right Front measures approx 15 (15, 15½, 15½, 15½)" from beg, ending with a RS row.
Armhole Shaping
At the beg of the next row, bind off 5 (6, 6, 7, 7) sts—28 (29, 31, 32, 34) sts.
Work even in Seed St pat to approx 21½ (22, 22, 22½, 22½)" from beg, ending with a WS row.
Neck Shaping
Bind off 5 (6, 6, 7, 7) sts beg next row.
Work 1 row even in Seed St pat.
Dec 1 st at neck edge on next and following alt rows until there are 18 (18, 19, 20, 22) sts.
Work even in Seed St pat to approx 24 (24½, 25, 25½, 25½)" from beg, ending with a RS row.
Shoulder Shaping
Bind off 9 (9, 9, 10, 11) sts beg next row. Work 1 row even. Bind off rem 9 (9, 10, 10, 11) sts.

SLEEVES (make two)
Beg at lower edge, with larger needles, cast on 39 (39, 39, 45, 45) sts.
Work approx 4½" in Rib Pat, ending with a WS row.
Cont in est pat, shaping sides by inc 1 st each edge on next and every 4th row 12 (14, 14, 7, 7) times more then every 6th row 0 (0, 0, 6, 6) times—65 (69, 69, 73, 73) sts, taking inc sts into Rib Pat.

All Sizes: Work even in Rib Pat to approx 19 (19½, 19½, 20, 20)" from beg, ending with a WS row.

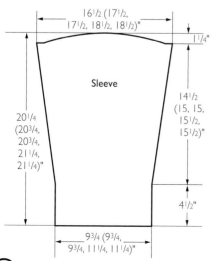

Sleeve

16½ (17½, 17½, 18½, 18½)"

1¼"

14½ (15, 15, 15½, 15½)"

20¼ (20¾, 20¾, 21¼, 21¼)"

4½"

9¾ (9¾, 9¾, 11¼, 11¼)"

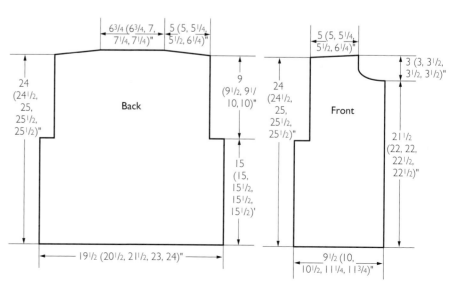

Back

6¾ (6¾, 7, 7¼, 7¼)"

5 (5, 5¼, 5½, 6¼)"

24 (24½, 25, 25½, 25½)"

9 (9½, 9½, 10, 10)"

15 (15, 15½, 15½, 15½)"

19½ (20½, 21½, 23, 24)"

Front

5 (5, 5¼, 5½, 6¼)"

3 (3, 3½, 3½, 3½)"

24 (24½, 25, 25½, 25½)"

21½ (22, 22, 22½, 22½)"

9½ (10, 10½, 11¼, 11¾)"

Indention near lower edge of sleeve indicates the fold for cuffs.

Shape Cap

Keeping cont of est pat, bind off 9 (9, 9, 10, 10) sts beg next 6 rows. Bind off rem 11 (15, 15, 13, 13) sts. Place markers on sides of sleeves 1½ (1¾, 1¾, 2, 2)" down from cast off edge.

POCKETS (make two)

Beg at lower edge, with larger needles, cast on 15 sts.
Work 2 rows in St st, beg with a k row.
Row 3 (RS): Inc 1 st in first st. K to last 2 sts. Inc 1 st in next st. K1.
Row 4: Purl.
Rep last 2 rows 3 times more—23 sts. Cont even until Pocket measures approx 5¼" from beg, ending with a RS row. K 2 rows for garter st. Bind off knitwise on WS.
With Taupe, work blanket stitch around the outer edges of each pocket, skipping the garter st border. Center each pocket onto a front 2½" from lower edge. Sew in place, leaving garter st edge free.

Blanket Stitch

FINISHING

Sew shoulder seams.
Neckband: With RS facing, using smaller needles, pick up and k17 (17, 17, 19, 19) sts up Right Front neck edge. K23 (23, 25, 27, 27) from Back spare needle. Pick up and k17 (17, 17, 19, 19) sts down Left Front neck edge—57 (57, 59, 65, 65) sts. K 2 rows for garter st. Bind off knitwise on WS.

Buttonhole Band

With RS facing and using smaller needles, pick up and k78 (80, 80, 82, 82) sts evenly spaced from lower edge to top of neckband along Right Front edge. K 1 row.
Row 2 (Buttonholes–RS): K2 (3, 3, 2, 2) sts. * Bind off 2 sts. K16 (16, 16, 17, 17) (including st on needle after bind off). Rep from * 3 times more. Bind off 2 sts. K to end of row.
Row 3: K, casting on 2 sts over bound off sts.
Row 4: Knit.
Bind off knitwise on WS.

Button Band

With RS facing and using smaller needles, pick up and k78 (80, 80, 82, 82) sts evenly spaced from top of neck band to lower edge along Left Front edge. K 4 rows for garter st. Bind off knitwise on WS.
Sew in Sleeves, placing rows above markers on side edges along cast off sts of Front and Back armholes to form square armholes. Sew side and sleeve seams reversing final 2½" of sleeve seam for cuff fold and leaving 3" open for side slits. Sew buttons opposite buttonholes.

HAT (20" circumference)
First Ear Flap

With MC and larger needles, cast on 3 sts.
Proceed in seed st pat, inc 1 st each end of row on 2nd and next row, then on following alt rows until there are 19 sts.
Work 7 rows even in seed st pat. Break yarn. Leave sts on a spare needle.

Second Ear Flap Work as given for First Ear Flap, but do not break yarn. Proceed as follows: **Join Ear Flaps:**
Next Row: With MC, cast on 6 sts onto end of Second Ear Flap and work seed st pat across these 6 sts. Seed St pat across 19 sts of Second Ear Flap. Cast on 21 sts. Seed St across 19 sts of First Ear Flap. Cast on 6 sts. 71 sts. Work 1 row seed st pat across all sts.
Work Rows 1–13 of Chart 1 (page 104) in St st, reading k rows from right to left and p rows from left to right, noting 10-st rep will be worked 7 times. With MC, work 2 rows St st.
Work Rows 1–5 of Chart 2 in St st, reading p rows from left to right and k rows from right to left, noting 6 st rep will be worked 11 times. With MC, work 2 rows St st.
Work 2 rows in Seed St pat.

Button Up Hat

Chart 1

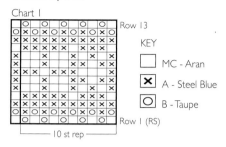

Row 13

Row 1 (RS)

10 st rep

KEY

☐ MC - Aran

☒ A - Steel Blue

◯ B - Taupe

Chart 2

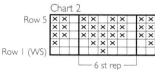

Row 5

Row 1 (WS)

6 st rep

Note: *When instructed to sl 1, sl the st purlwise with yarn on WS of fabric.*

Shape Top

K1, p1; * sl 1, k2tog, psso, (p1, k1) twice, p1. Rep from * to last 5 sts. Sl 1, k2tog, psso, p1, k1—53 sts.
Work 3 rows even in Seed St pat.
Next Row: K1, p1; * sl 1, k2tog, psso, p1, k1, p1. Rep from * to last 3 sts, k1, p1, k1—37 sts.
Work 3 rows even in Seed St pat.
Next Row: K1, p1; * sl 1, k2tog, psso, p1. Rep from * to last 3 sts, k1, p1, k1—21 sts.
Work 3 rows even in Seed St pat.
Next Row: K1, p1; * sl 1, k2tog, psso. Rep from * to last st, p1—9 sts.
Next Row: P, dec 1 st at center—8 sts.
Work 3 rows even in St st.
Next Row: (K2tog) 4 times. Break yarn, leaving a long end. Draw end tightly through rem sts and fasten securely. Sew center back seam. Using color B (Taupe), work blanket st around outside edges of Hat.

Tassel

Using a piece of cardboard 3" wide x 5" deep, wind Color B 35 times around cardboard. Break yarn, leaving a long end, and thread end through a needle. Slip needle through all lps and tie tightly. Remove cardboard and wind yarn tightly around lps ¾" below fold. Fasten

---

securely. Cut through rem lps and trim ends evenly. Attach to top of Hat.

Snowflake Pullover

photo on page 73

SKILL LEVEL: Intermediate

SIZES: Men's S (M, LARGE, XL)
Note: *The pattern is written for the smallest size with changes for larger sizes in parentheses. When only one number is given, it applies to all sizes. For ease in working, before you begin, circle all numbers pertaining to the size you are knitting.*

FINISHED MEASUREMENTS:
Chest: 41 (45½, 50, 54½)"
Length: 24¾ (25¾, 26¼, 26¾)"

MATERIALS:
- Brown Sheep's Naturespun Worsted, 100% wool, worsted weight yarn (245 yards per skein): 1 skein of Sunburst Gold (308) for Color A; 7 (8, 9, 10) skeins of Burnt Sienna (101) for Color B; 1 skein each of Enchanted Forest (N25) for Color C and Monument Green (N27) for Color D
- Size 7 (4.5mm) knitting needles or size needed to obtain gauge

---

- Size 6 (4.25mm) knitting needles
- Size 6 (4.25 mm) circular knitting needle, 16-inch length
- Yarn needle

GAUGE:
In Textured Pattern with larger needles, 32 sts and 39 rows = 6"/15.25cm.
TAKE TIME TO CHECK YOUR GAUGE.

STITCHES USED:
(K1 P1) Rib (a multiple of 2 sts + 1 st; a rep of 2 rows)
Row 1 (RS): * K1, p1; rep from * across, ending k1.
Row 2: * P1, k1; rep from * across, ending p1.
Rep Rows 1 and 2 for (K1 P1) Rib.

Textured Pattern (a multiple of 6 sts + 7 sts; a rep of 8 rows)
Row 1 (RS): Knit.
Row 2: P2, k1, p1, k1; * p3, k1, p1, k1; rep from * across, ending p2.
Row 3: K2; * p3, k3; rep from * across, ending p3, k2.
Row 4: Rep Row 2.
Row 5: Knit.
Row 6: P5; * k1, p1, k1, p3; rep from * across, ending p5 rather than p3.
Row 7: K2; * k3, p3; rep from * across, ending k5.
Row 8: Rep Row 6.
Repeat Rows 1–8 for Textured Pattern.

Chart 1

Row 8

Row 1 (RS)

6-st repeat

End　Beg

Textured Pattern

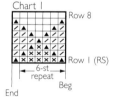

Row 8

Row 1(RS)

KEY

☐ K on RS, p on WS

━ P on RS, k on WS

Chart 3

Row 7

Row 1 (RS)

6-st repeat

End　Beg

Chart 2

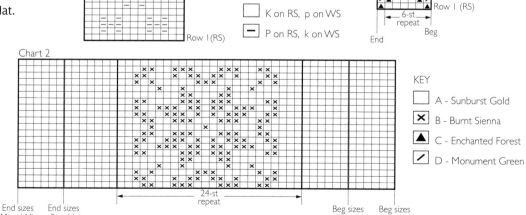

End sizes M and XL　End sizes S and L

24-st repeat

Beg sizes S and L　Beg sizes M and XL

Snowflake Pullover

KEY

☐ A - Sunburst Gold

☒ B - Burnt Sienna

▲ C - Enchanted Forest

◿ D - Monument Green

FRONT

Work same as for Back until piece measures approx 23 (24, 24½, 25)" from beg, ending after WS row.

Neck Shaping

Work in pat across first 45 (51, 57, 63) sts; join new strands and bind off center 19 sts; work to end of row. Work both sides at once with separate skeins of yarn, and bind off 3 sts each neck edge once, then bind off 2 sts each neck edge twice. Dec 1 st each neck edge every row 5 times—33 (39, 45, 51) sts rem. Complete as for Back.

SLEEVES (make two)

Beg at lower edge, with smaller needles and Color A, cast on 55 (55, 55, 61) sts. Change to Color B. Work (K1 P1) Rib, using B only, to approx 3" from beg ending after WS row.

Body Pattern

Change to larger needles, and Textured Pattern, working Rows 1–2. Beg with next RS row, including new sts into pat as they accumulate, inc each edge now, then every other row 0 (0, 5, 1) time(s), then every fourth row 18 (25, 23, 26) times, then every sixth row 5 (0, 0, 0) times—103 (107, 113, 117) sts. Work even to approx 20¼ (20, 20, 20½)" from beg, ending after WS row. Bind off.

FINISHING

Join shoulder seams.

Neckband

With RS facing, circular needle, and B, pick up and k106 sts around neckline. Work rnds of (K1 P1) Rib until band measures approx 1" from beg.

Change to A and work one more rnd as you bind off in rib. Place markers 9¾ (10, 10½, 11)" down from shoulders. Set in sleeves between markers. Sew underarm and side seams.

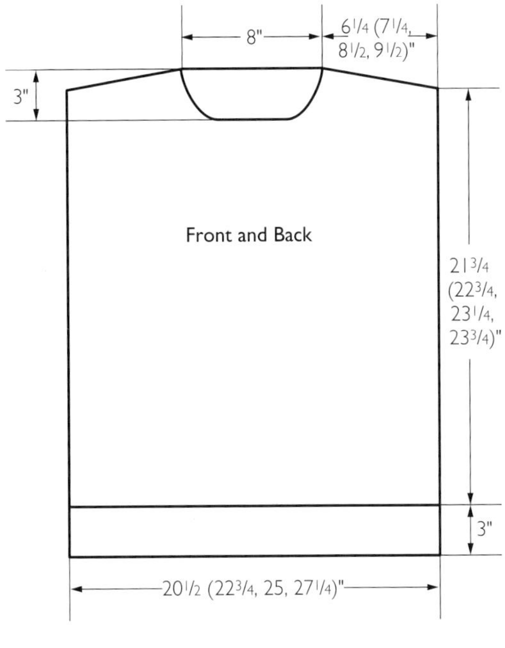

Note: The colorful yoke on front and back is worked in St st from a chart, reading from right to left for RS rows and from left to right for WS rows. Loosely carry color not in use along WS of fabric. When changing color, bring new strand from under present strand for a twist to prevent holes.

INSTRUCTIONS:
BACK

Beg at lower edge, with smaller needles and color A, cast on 109 (121, 133, 145) sts. Change to color B. Work (K1 P1) Rib, using B only, to approx 3" from beg ending after WS row.

Body Pattern

Change to larger needles, beg Textured Pattern, and work even to approx 13 (14, 14½, 15)" from beg, ending after a WS row.

Beg Fair Isle Stripe

Beg and end where indicated on chart, work Rows 1–8 of Chart 1, *opposite.* Work Rows 1–20 of Chart 2, *opposite,* noting 24 st rep will be worked 4 (4, 5, 5) times. Then work Rows 1–7 of Chart 3, *opposite.* With Color B, p across next row. Work in Textured Pattern to approx 24¾ (25¾, 26¼, 26¾)" from beg, ending after a WS row.

Shoulder Shaping

Bind off 8 (10, 11, 13) sts at beg of next 6 rows. Bind off 9 (9, 12, 12) sts at beg of next 2 rows. Bind off rem 43 sts.

8"

6¼ (7¼, 8½, 9½)"

3"

Front and Back

21¾ (22¾, 23¼, 23¾)"

3"

20½ (22¾, 25, 27¼)"

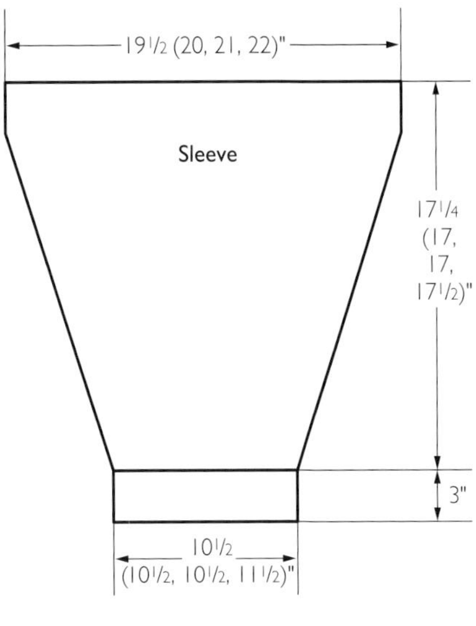

19½ (20, 21, 22)"

Sleeve

17¼ (17, 17, 17½)"

3"

10½ (10½, 10½, 11½)"

Christmastime Cape

photo on pages 74–75

SKILL LEVEL: Intermediate

SIZES: S (MEDIUM, L, XL, XXL)

Note: *The pattern is written for the smallest size with changes for larger sizes in parentheses. When only one number is given, it applies to all sizes. For ease in working, before you begin, circle all numbers pertaining to the size you are knitting.*

FINISHED MEASUREMENTS:
Bust 33 (37, 41, 45, 48)"
Length: 24½ (25½, 26½, 27½, 29)"

MATERIALS:
- White Buffalo 100% wool, 6-ply, 227g (8 oz): 4 (4, 4, 5, 5) cakes of White (9005)
- Size 13 (9mm) circular knitting needle, 29-inch length or size needed to obtain gauge
- Size 11 (8mm) circular knitting needle 29-inch length; one set of size 11 (8mm) double-pointed needles (dpn)
- Cable needle (cn)
- Markers

GAUGE:
In St St with larger needles, 9 sts and 13 rows = 4"/10cm.
TAKE TIME TO CHECK YOUR GAUGE.

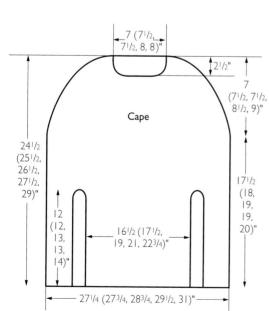

Cape

24½ (25½, 26½, 27½, 29)"

7 (7½, 7½, 8, 8)"

2½"

7 (7½, 7½, 8½, 9)"

17½ (18, 19, 19, 20)"

12 (12, 13, 13, 14)"

16½ (17½, 19, 21, 22¾)"

27¼ (27¾, 28¾, 29½, 31)"

SPECIAL ABBREVIATIONS:
C4F: Sl next 2 sts onto a cn and leave at front of work. K2, then k2 from cn.
C4B: Sl next 2 sts onto a cable needle and leave at back of work. K2, then k2 from cn.
Sl 1: Sl next st purlwise and with yarn on WS of fabric.
Sl 2, k2tog, p2sso: Sl next 2 sts purlwise and with yarn on WS of fabric, k2tog, pass the 2 slipped sts over the k2tog.

STITCHES USED:
Panel A (over 9 sts; a rep of 8 rows)
Row 1 (RS): K4, p1, k4.
Row 2 and alt rows: P4, k1, p4.
Row 3: C4B, p1, C4F.
Rows 5 and 7: As Row 1.
Row 8: P4, k1, p4.
These 8 rows form Panel A.

Note: *The cape is worked in two pieces. The Back, which also includes sts from sides, is worked back and forth to the top of the armhole vents and then the sts are saved for later. The center front panel is worked back and forth to the same length as the Back. Next,* the sts are combined and then worked in rnds to the neck.

INSTRUCTIONS:
BACK
Beg at lower edge, with smaller circular needle, cast on 79 (79, 79, 79, 81) sts.
Ribbing
Row 1 (RS): P1; (k1, p1) across.
Row 2: K1; (p1, k1) across.
Rep Ribbing Rows 1–2 once more and inc 1 st at center of last row—80 (80, 80, 80, 82) sts. With larger needle work in St st (k RS rows, p WS rows) to approx 12 (12, 13, 13, 14)" from beg, ending with a WS row. Slip all sts onto a spare needle.

FRONT
Beg at lower edge with smaller circular needle, cast on 37 (39, 43, 47, 51) sts.
Ribbing
Row 1 (RS): P1; (k1, p1) across.
Row 2: K1; (p1, k1) across.
Rep Ribbing Rows 1–2 once more.
Body Pattern
With larger needle proceed as follows:
Row 1 (RS): K14 (15, 17, 19, 21); Row 1 of Panel A over 9 sts; k14 (15, 17, 19, 21).
Row 2: P14 (15, 17, 19, 21); work

Row 2 of Panel A over 9 sts; p14 (15, 17, 19, 21). Panel A is now in position.

Rep pattern as est in first 2 rows to approx 12 (12, 13, 13, 14)" from beg, ending with a WS row.

Joining Row: Cast on 3 sts. Work in pat as est across 37 (39, 43, 47, 51) sts of Front. Cast on 3 sts. K80 (80, 80, 80, 82) sts across Back 123 (125, 129, 133, 139) sts. Join in rnd. K4 (5, 6, 8, 10), place marker on next st to mark beg of rnd. Cont in rnds, working Row 2 and alt rows of Panel A as k rows, cont in pat as established to approx 17½ (18, 19, 19, 20)" from beg.

Raglan Shaping

Rnd 1: K1, k2tog, work in pat across 29 (29, 31, 31, 31) sts, sl 1, k1, psso, k2, k2tog, k20 (21, 22, 24, 26), sl 1, k1, psso, k2, k2tog, k30 (30, 30, 30, 32), sl 1, k1, psso, k2, k2tog, k20 (21, 22, 24, 26), sl 1, k1, psso, k1. K 3 rnds even on 115 (117, 121, 125, 131) sts.

Rnd 5: K1, k2tog, work in pat across 27 (27, 29, 29, 29) sts, sl 1, k1, psso, k2, k2tog, k18 (19, 20, 22, 24), sl 1, k1, psso, k2, k2tog, k28 (28, 28, 28, 30), sl 1, k1, psso, k2, k2tog, k18 (19, 20, 22, 24), sl 1, k1, psso, k1. K 3 rnds even on 107 (109, 113, 117, 123) sts.

Next Rnd: K1, k2tog, work in pat across 25 (25, 27, 27, 27) sts, sl 1, k1, psso, k2, k2tog, k16 (17, 18, 20, 22), sl 1, k1, psso, k2, k2tog, k26 (26, 26, 26, 28), sl 1, k1, psso, k2, k2tog, k16 (17, 18, 20, 22), sl 1, k1, psso, k1. K1 (3, 3, 3, 3) rnd(s) even on 99 (101, 105, 109, 115) sts.

Next Rnd: K1, k2tog, work in pat across 23 (23, 25, 25, 25) sts, sl 1, k1, psso, k2, k2tog, k14 (15, 16, 18, 20), sl 1, k1, psso, k2, k2tog, k24 (24, 24, 24, 26), sl 1, k1, psso, k2, k2tog, k14 (15, 16, 18, 20), sl 1, k1, psso, k1. K1 (1, 1, 3, 3) rnd(s) even on 91 (93, 97, 101, 107) sts.

Next Rnd: K1, k2tog, work in pat across 21 (21, 23, 23, 23) sts, sl 1, k1, psso, k2, k2tog, k12 (13, 14, 16, 18), sl 1, k1, psso, k2, k2tog, k22 (22, 22, 22, 24), sl 1, k1, psso, k2, k2tog, k12 (13, 14, 16, 18), sl 1, k1, psso, k1. K1 (1, 1, 1, 3) rnd(s) even on 83 (85, 89, 93, 99) sts.

Neck Shaping

K8 (8, 9, 9, 8), sl next 9 (9, 11, 11, 11) sts onto a holder (neck edge). Rejoin yarn to rem sts and working back and forth across needle, proceed as follows:

Row 1: Sl 1, k1, psso, k3, sl 1, k1, psso, k2, k2tog, k10 (11, 12, 14, 16), sl 1, k1, psso, k2, k2tog, k20 (20, 20, 20, 22), sl 1, k1, psso, k2, k2tog, k10 (11, 12, 14, 16), sl 1, k1, psso, k2, k2tog, k3, k2tog—64 (66, 68, 72, 78) sts.

Row 2 and alt rows: Purl.

Row 3: Sl 1, k1, psso, k1, sl 1, k1, psso, k2, k2tog, k8 (9, 10, 12, 14), sl 1, k1, psso, k2, k2tog, k18 (18, 18, 18, 20), sl 1, k1, psso, k2, k2tog, k8 (9, 10, 12, 14), sl 1, k1, psso, k2, k2tog, k1, k2tog—54 (56, 58, 62, 68) sts.

Row 5: Sl 1, k2tog, psso, k2, k2tog, k 6 (7, 8, 10, 12), sl 1, k1, psso, k2, k2tog, k16 (16, 16, 16, 18), sl 1, k1, psso, k2, k2tog, k6 (7, 8, 10, 12), sl 1, k1, psso, k2, sl 1, k2tog, psso—44 (46, 48, 52, 58) sts.

Row 7: Sl 1, k1, psso, k1, k2tog, k4 (5, 6, 8, 10), sl 1, k1, psso, k2, k2tog, k14 (14, 14, 14, 16), sl 1, k1, psso, k2, k2tog, k4 (5, 6, 8, 10), sl 1, k1, psso, k1, k2tog—36 (38, 40, 44, 50) sts.

Row 9: Sl 2, k2tog, p2sso, k2 (3, 4, 6, 8), sl 1, k1, psso, k2, k2tog, k12 (12, 12, 12, 14), sl 1, k1, psso, k2, k2tog, k2 (3, 4, 6, 8), sl 2, k2tog, p2sso—26 (28, 30, 34, 40) sts.

Collar: With RS of work facing and set of four dpns, pick up and k9 sts down left front neck edge. Pat from front st holder across 9 (9, 11, 11, 11) sts. Pick up and k9 sts up right front neck edge. K across rem 26 (28, 30, 34, 40) sts—53 (55, 59, 63, 69) sts. Join in rnd, placing marker on first st to mark beg of rnd.

Rnd 1: K9 (9, 10, 10, 10). Pat across next 9 sts. K to end of rnd. Rep last rnd until collar from pick up row measures approx 3", dec 4 sts evenly across last rnd—49 (51, 55, 59, 65) sts.

Next Rnd: Purl.

Next Rnd: Knit. Then bind off purlwise.

FINISHING

With RS of work facing and smaller needle, pick up and k27 (27, 29, 29, 31) sts up along arm opening. Pick up and k3 sts along cast on edge, pick up and k27 (27, 29, 29, 31) sts down along arm opening—57 (57, 61, 61, 65) sts. Bind off knitwise (WS). Repeat for opposite arm opening.

Basketweave and Bobbles Jacket and Hat

photos on pages 76–77

SKILL LEVEL: Intermediate

SIZES: Girls' 4 (6, 8, 10)
Note: The pattern is written for the smallest size with changes for larger sizes in parentheses. When only one number is given, it applies to all sizes. For ease in working the pattern, before you begin, circle all numbers pertaining to the size you are knitting.

FINISHED MEASUREMENTS:
Chest (buttoned): 26½ (29, 31½, 34)"
Length: 15 (16, 17, 18)"

MATERIALS:
- *For Jacket:* Red Heart, TLC, Article E510 TLC, 100% acrylic, worsted weight yarn (5 ounces per skein): 3 (3, 4, 4) skeins of Grey Heather (5015) for MC; 1 skein each of Kiwi (5657) for Color A and Copper (5289) for Color B
- Size 8 (5mm) knitting needles or size needed to obtain gauge
- Size 6 (4.25mm) knitting needles
- Yarn needle
- Stitch holders
- 5 JHB International buttons (Capitol Dome #12680, Amber Topaz, size ¾-inch diameter)

GAUGE:
In Body Pattern with larger needles, 16 sts and 24 rows = 4"/10cm.
TAKE TIME TO CHECK YOUR GAUGE.

ABBREVIATIONS:
Ssk (slip, slip, knit): Slip next 2 sts knitwise, one at a time to right-hand needle, insert tip of left-hand needle into fronts of these 2 sts and k them tog.
P2tog-b: Turn work slightly and insert tip of needle from left to right and through 2nd and then first sts on

Basketweave and Bobbles Jacket and Hat
continued from page 107

left-hand needle; p the 2 sts tog.

Sl 1: Slip next st purlwise and with yarn on WS to right-hand needle.

STITCHES USED:

Basketweave [a multiple of 6 sts + 0 (4, 2, 0) sts; over 8 rows]

Row 1 (RS): K1 (3, 2, 1); (p4, k2) across, ending p4, k 1 (3, 2, 1).

Row 2: P1 (3, 2, 1); (k4, p2) across, ending k4, p1 (3, 2, 1).

Row 3: Rep Row 1.

Row 4: Purl.

Row 5: K1 (3, 2, 1), p1; (k2, p4) across, ending k2, p1, k1 (3, 2, 1).

Row 6: P1 (3, 2, 1), k1; (p2, k4) across, ending p2, k1, p1 (3, 2, 1).

Row 7: Rep Row 5.

Row 8: Purl.

Bumps I (a multiple of 10 sts + 2 sts; 5 rows)

Row 1 (RS): With color A, k3; * in next st [(k1, yo) 3 times, k1—7 sts made] **, k9; rep from * across, ending last rep at **, k8.

Row 2: With A, k.

Row 3: With MC, k2; * k2tog, k5, ssk, k7; rep from * across.

Row 4: With MC, p7; * p2tog-b, p1, sl 1, p1, p2tog **, p7; rep from * across, ending last rep at **, p2.

Row 5: With MC, k2; * k2tog, sl 1, ssk , k7; rep from * across.

Row 6: With MC, p.

Bumps II (a multiple of 10 sts + 2 sts; 5 rows)

Row 1 (RS): With color B, k8; * [(k1, yo) 3 times, k1—7 sts made] **, k9; rep from * across, ending last rep at **, k3.

Row 2: With B, k.

Row 3: With MC, k7; * k2tog, k5, ssk **, k7; rep from * across, ending last rep at **, k2.

Row 4: With MC, p2; * p2tog-b, p1, sl 1 wyif, p1, p2tog, p7; rep from * across.

Row 5: With MC, k7; * k2tog, sl 1

wyib, ssk **, k7; rep from * across, ending last rep at **, k2.

Row 6: With MC, p.

***Note:** The jacket is worked in one piece to the underarm.*

INSTRUCTIONS:
JACKET

Beg at the lower edge, with larger needles and MC, cast on 102 (112, 122, 132) sts. **For Body Pattern:** * Work Rows 1–8 of Basketweave, Rows 1–5 of Bumps I, Rows 1–8 of Basketweave, and Rows 1–5 of Bumps II; rep from * for pat. Work even to approx 9 (9½, 10, 10½)" from beg, ending with a WS row.

RIGHT FRONT

Work pat across first 25 (27, 30, 32) sts. Place rem sts onto a holder for later. Cont in est pat until piece measures approx 13 (14, 15, 16)" from beg, ending with a WS row.

Neck Shaping

At neck edge, bind off 6 sts once, 3 sts once, and 1 st 1 (1, 2, 2) time(s). Cont in pat on rem 15 (17, 19, 21) sts to approx 15 (16, 17, 18)" from beg, ending with a WS row. Bind off knitwise with MC.

BACK

With the RS facing, return 52 (58, 62, 68) sts to needle. Join yarn and work in est pat to approx 15 (16, 17, 18)" from beg, ending with a WS row. Bind off knitwise with MC.

LEFT FRONT

With the RS facing, return 25 (27, 30, 32) sts to needle. Reversing neck shaping, work as for Right Front.

SLEEVES (make two)

Beg at lower edge with larger needles and MC, cast on 32 sts. Keeping 1 st each edge St st on Basketweave only, work Rows 1–8 of Basketweave and Rows 1–5 of Bumps I. Including new sts into patterns as they accumulate, inc 1 st each edge now and every 4th row 0 (1, 4, 7) time(s) more, then every 6th row 7 (8, 7, 6) times. Work even in pat on 48 (52, 56, 60) sts to approx 12 (13, 14, 15)" from beg, ending with a WS row. Bind off knitwise with MC.

FINISHING

Join shoulder and sleeve seams. Set in sleeves.

Neckband

With the RS facing using smaller needles and MC, pick up and k53 (55, 59, 61) sts evenly spaced around neck.

Ribbing

Row 1 (WS): P1; (k1, p1) across.

Row 2: K1; (p1, k1) across.
Rep Ribbing Rows 1–2 again, then rep Row 1. Bind off in ribbing.

Left Front Band

With the RS facing using smaller needles and MC, pick up and k69 (73, 79, 83) sts evenly spaced along edge. Work Ribbing as for Neckband for 5 total rows. Bind off in ribbing.

Right Front Band

Pick up and k as for Left Band. Work 1 row of ribbing. **Row 2:** Rib 5 (5, 7, 7) sts; * yo, work 2 tog, rib 13 (14, 15, 16) more sts—14 (15, 16, 17) sts between buttonholes. Rep from * across for 5 buttonholes, ending rib to end. **Next Row:** Work est Rib Pat across. Rib 2 more rows. Bind off in ribbing. Sew buttons opposite buttonholes.

CAP (19½" circumference)

This project requires 1 ball of Grey Heather TLC; small amounts of Kiwi and Copper TLC; sizes 8 (5mm) and 6 (4.25mm) knitting needles; yarn needle. Gauge is same as for jacket, *opposite.*

With smaller needles and MC, cast on 77 sts.

Note: *When working Basketweave Rows 1–8, between each stripe of bumps, follow directions for first size, having a multiple of 6 sts.*

Ribbing: Work as for Cardigan Neckband to approx 3" from beg, ending with a WS row and inc 1 st— 78 sts. Change to larger needles and work Basketweave Rows 1–8.

Next Row (RS): K11; (ssk, k2tog, k22) twice, ssk, k2tog, k11. P72. Work Bumps I; k 1 row, p 1 row;

Basketweave Rows 1–8; k 1 row, p 1 row. Work Bumps II.

Next Row (RS): K10, (ssk, k2tog, k20) twice, ssk, k2tog, k10. P66. Work Basketweave Rows 1–8.

Next Row (RS): K9, (ssk, k2tog, k18) twice, ssk, k2tog, k9. P60.

Bumps I, Row 1 (RS): With Color A, k7; rep from * as before, ending last rep at **, k2.

Row 2: With A, k.

Row 3: With MC, k6; rep from * across, ending last rep at **, k1.

Row 4: With MC, p1; rep from * across, ending last rep at **, k6.

Row 5: With MC, k6; rep from * across, ending k1.

Row 6: With MC, p.

Next Row (RS): K8, (ssk, k2tog, k16) twice, ssk, k2tog, k8. P54. Work Basketweave Rows 1-8.

Next Row (RS): K7, (ssk, k2tog, k14) twice, ssk, k2tog, k7. P48.

Bumps II, Row 1 (RS): With Color B, k8; rep from * as before, ending last rep at **, k9.

Row 2: With B, k.

Row 3: With MC, k7; rep from * across, ending last rep at **, k8.

Row 4: With MC, p8; rep from * across, ending last rep at **, p7.

Row 5: With MC, k7; rep from * across, ending k8.

Row 6: With MC, p.

Next Row (RS): K6 (ssk, k2tog, k12) twice, ssk, k2tog, k6. P42. Work Basketweave Rows 1–8. **Next Row (RS):** K5, (ssk, k2tog, k10) twice, ssk, k2tog, k5. P36.

Bumps I, Row 1 (RS): With Color A, k8; rep from * across, ending last rep at **, k7.

Row 2: With A, k.

Row 3: With MC, k7; rep from * across, ending last rep at **, k6.

Row 4: With MC, p6; rep from * across, ending last rep at **, p7.

Row 5: With MC, k7; rep from * across, ending last rep at **, k6.

Row 6: With MC, p.

Next Row (RS): K4, (ssk, k2tog, k8) twice, ssk, k2tog, k4. P30. Work Basketweave Rows 1–8. **Next Row (RS):** K3, (ssk, k2tog, k6) twice, ssk, k2tog, k3. P24. **Next Row (RS):** K2, (ssk, k2tog, k4) twice, ssk, k2tog, k2. P18. **Next Row (RS):** K1, (ssk, k2tog, k2) twice, ssk, k2tog, k1. P12. **Next Row (RS):** (Ssk, k2tog) 3 times. P6. Cut yarn leaving a long tail. Thread tail into yarn needle and back through rem sts. Pull up to close opening. With same tail, join sides.

Pom-pom

Wrap color B around a plastic card 50 times. Remove from card and tie a separate strand tightly around center. Trim ends. Attach to tip of Cap.

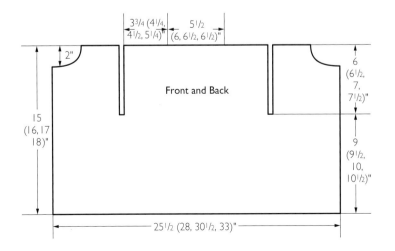

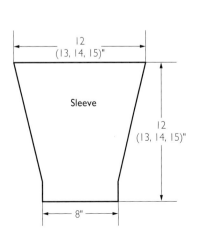

Like a breath of fresh spring air, this chapter is packed with inspiration for your knitting passion. You'll see babies wrapped in pink lacy bobbles and blue head-to-toe cables. You'll discover throws with whimsical stripes and pom-poms. You'll fall in love with the sweaters, hats, and home decor accessories—all designed to celebrate...

Spring

PRETTY PINK BABY SET
Any mother would be thrilled
to see her tiny girl wearing this
adorable dress, cap, and
matching sweater. A keyhole
back opening in the dress
allows for easy over-the-head
dressing. Instructions begin on
page 130.

baby cakes

KISSES AND HUGS
Baby will enjoy wearing this soft set of pants and hooded pullover. The pull-on pants have a drawstring for easy size adjusting. Instructions, written for newborns to 18 months, begin on page 133.

POM-POM THROW Any child will love to cuddle under the I-cords and bright pom-poms that embellish this colorful afghan. For boys, change the main color to green, yellow, or orange. Instructions begin on page 135.

lullaby

BALLET INSPIRED TOP
An adorable crop top, this
sweater features center cables,
raglan shaping, and a slight
scoop neckline. Youthful and fun,
crocheted chains border the
sleeves and lower edge.
Instructions begin on page 136.

SPRING FLING This cotton
sweater sprinkled with color
makes a great spring-weight
top. The main attraction of
the sweater is a center
pattern of bobbles and twists.
Instructions begin on
page 138.

front and center

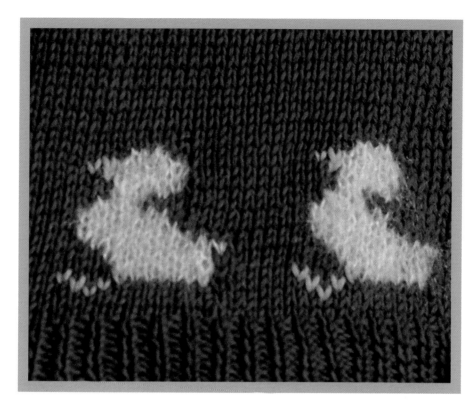

RUBBER DUCKY PULLOVER

You'll look just ducky in this crewneck with set-in cap sleeves and a short, fitted style. The entire sweater is worked in stockinette stitch with ribbed borders. Duplicate-stitch embroidery is used to add the features on each duck. For best results, use a single strand of yarn for each color while working the duck motifs. Instructions begin on page 139.

just ducky

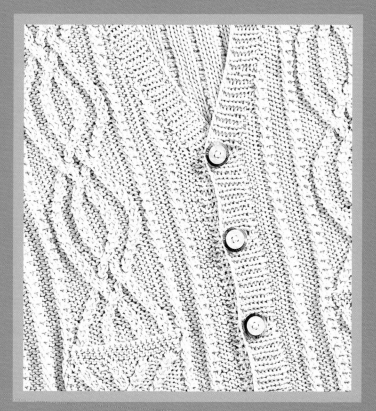

CASUAL FRIDAY
SLEEVELESS CARDIGAN

Ruggedly handsome, this cabled vest is a great fit for casual office days. Front pockets make this vest a favorite. Although the pattern is recommended for experienced knitters, after the stitches become familiar, they are not difficult. Instructions begin on page 141.

tea time

PILLOWS IN STRIPES AND CHECKS Easily adaptable to fit any decorating palette, this trio of pillows is a perfect project for beginners and experienced knitters. Each pillow has a double strand of yarn for cushy comfort and durability. Instructions begin on page 143.

VARIEGATED PLACE MATS Easy and fast to knit, these garter-stitch place mats add drama to your dining table. Choose and combine two colors to complement your dishes or decor. Instructions begin on page 145.

sit a spell

DRAWSTRING SHOULDER BAG, CELL PHONE CASE, AND HAT Perfect for a sweet teen, these projects are made with a double strand of yarn and stockinette stitch. The knitting is easy with interesting shaping and I-cord drawstrings. The three matching pieces are a much appreciated gift. Instructions begin on page 147.

chitchat

OCEAN STRIPES Long and hooded, this striking sweater is adorable over a dress or a pair of pants. The 3×3 striped ribs add flare to the lower portion of this cardigan. The sleeves, bodice, and hood are worked in 1×3 striped ribs. Instructions begin on page 149.

bold beauty

EASY STRIPES AND CHECKS TOP with set-in cap sleeves, a scooped neck, and a mid-hip length, this fresh sweater is attractive alone or under a jacket. Instructions begin on page 150.

get the scoop

Pretty Pink Baby Set

photo on pages 112–113

SKILL LEVEL: Advanced

SIZES: Infants 6 (12, 18) months

Note: *The pattern is written for the smallest size with changes for larger sizes in parentheses. When only one number is given, it applies to all sizes. For ease in working, before you begin, circle all numbers pertaining to the size you are knitting.*

FINISHED MEASUREMENTS:
Cardigan Chest (buttoned): 23 (25, 27)"
Cardigan Length: 11 (12, 13)"
Dress Chest: 20 (20½, 22)"
Dress Length: 16¼ (18, 20¾)"
Cap: One size 16" circumference

MATERIALS:
- Patons Bumblebee Baby Cotton, 100% cotton, double knitting (DK) weight yarn (123 yards per skein): 4 (4, 5) skeins of Apple Blossom (2421) for Cardigan; 6 (6, 7) skeins of Apple Blossom (2421) for Dress; and 1 skein Apple Blossom (2421) for Cap
- Sizes 6 (4mm) and 3 (3.25mm) circular knitting needle 36" long and pair of sizes 3 (3.25mm) and 6 (4mm) straight knitting needles or size needed to obtain gauge
- Five ½-inch buttons for Cardigan; 1 button for Dress
- Yarn needle
- Stitch holder
- Size D/3 (3.25mm) crochet hook

GAUGE:
In St st on larger needles, 22 sts and 30 rows = 4"/10cm.
TAKE TIME TO CHECK YOUR GAUGE.

ABBREVIATIONS:
Ssk (slip, slip, knit): Slip next 2 sts knitwise, one at a time to right-hand needle, insert tip of left-hand needle into fronts of these 2 sts and k2tog.
MBA: Knit next 2 sts tog but do not slip sts off needle. (Yo, knit same 2 sts tog again) twice. Slip sts onto right-hand needle. Slip fourth, third, second, and first sts separately over fifth st—1 st remains.
MB: (K1, yo, k1, yo, k1) all in next st. Turn; k5. Turn; p5. Turn; k1, sl 1, k2tog, psso, k1. Turn; p3tog—1 st remains.
Sl 1: Sl 1 stitch purlwise and with yarn on WS of fabric.
P2togb: Turn work slightly, insert right-hand needle from left to right into 2nd and then first sts and p them tog.

STITCHES USED:
Climbing Vine Lace Pattern (a multiple of 11 sts; a rep of 20 rows).
Row 1 (RS): * K1, MB, k2, yo, k1, yo, k4, k2tog. Rep from * across.
Rows 2, 4, 6, 8, and 10: * P2tog, p10. Rep from * across.
Row 3: * K5, yo, k1, yo, k3, k2tog. Rep from * across.
Row 5: * K6, yo, k1, yo, k2, k2tog. Rep from * across.
Row 7: * K7, (yo, k1) twice, k2tog. Rep from * across.
Row 9: * K8, yo, k1, yo, k2tog. Rep from * across.
Row 11: * Ssk, k4, yo, k1, yo, k2, MB, k1. Rep from * across.
Rows 12, 14, 16, and 18: * P10, p2togb. Rep from * across.
Row 13: * Ssk, k3, yo, k1, yo, k5. Rep from * across.
Row 15: * Ssk, k2, yo, k1, yo, k6. Rep from * across.
Row 17: * Ssk, (k1, yo) twice, k7. Rep from * across.
Row 19: * Ssk, yo, k1, yo, k8. Rep from * across.
Row 20: As Row 12.
These 20 rows form Climbing Vine Lace Pattern.

INSTRUCTIONS:
DRESS—FRONT
** Beg at lower edge, with smaller circular needle, cast on 110 (120, 130) sts. Do not join. Work back and forth across needle in rows as follows:
Edging Pattern
Row 1 (WS): Knit.
Rows 2–3: Knit.
Row 4: K1; * yo, MBA. Rep from * to last st, k1.
Rows 5–6: Knit.
Row 7: Knit, inc 2 (3, 4) sts evenly across last row—112 (123, 134) sts.
With larger circular needle, work 2 rows in garter st, then work in Climbing Vine Lace Pat (working first and last st of each row in St st) until Front measures approx 10½ (11½, 13½)" from beg, ending with a WS row. Change to larger pair of straight needles.
Next Row: * K2tog. Rep from * to last 0 (1, 0) st(s). K0 (1, 0)—56 (62, 67) sts.
Next Row: Knit, dec 6 (10, 11) sts evenly across—50 (52, 56) sts.
Work a further 9 rows in garter st.

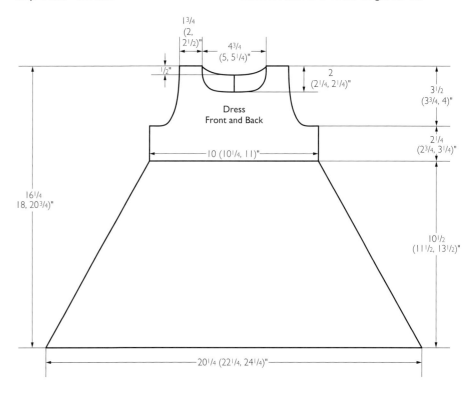

Dress
Front and Back

1¾
(2,
2½)"

4¾
(5, 5¼)"

½"

2
(2¼, 2¼)"

3½
(3¾, 4)"

2¼
(2¾, 3¼)"

10 (10¼, 11)"

16¼
18, 20¾)"

10½
(11½, 13½)"

20¼ (22¼, 24¼)"

Next Row (WS): Knit, inc 5 sts evenly across—55 (57, 61) sts.

Body Pattern

Row 1 (RS): K5 (3, 2); * yo, ssk, k5. Rep from * to last 8 (5, 3) sts, yo, ssk, k6 (3, 1).

Rows 2–4: Work 3 rows even in St st.

Row 5: K1 (6, 5); * yo, ssk, k5. Rep from * to last 5 (2, 7) sts, (yo, ssk) 1 (0, 1) time(s), k3 (2, 5).

Rows 6–8: Work 3 rows St st. Last 8 rows form Body Pattern. Work a further 2 (4, 6) rows even in est pat.

Armhole Shaping

Keeping cont of est pat, bind off 3 sts beg next 2 rows—49 (51, 55) sts. Dec 1 st each end of row on next and following alt rows until there are 45 (49, 49) sts **.

Work 3 (5, 7) rows even in pat, ending with a WS row.

Neck Shaping

Next Row: Pat across 17 (19, 19) sts (neck edge). Turn. Leave rem sts on a spare needle. Work 1 row even in pat. Dec 1 st at neck edge on next and following alt rows until there are 9 (11, 11) sts. Work 1 row even in pat. Bind off. With RS facing, slip center 11 sts onto a st holder. Rejoin yarn to rem sts and work to correspond to other side.

BACK

Work as for Front from ** to **. Work 3 (5, 7) rows even in pat, ending with a WS row.

Back Opening

Next Row: Pat across 22 (24, 24) sts. bind off center st. Pat to end of row. Working on Right Back, work 11 rows even in pat.

Neck Shaping

Next Row (RS): Bind off 8 sts (neck edge). Pat to end of row. Dec 1 st at neck edge on next 5 rows—9 (11, 11) sts. Work 1 row even in pat. Bind off. With WS facing, rejoin yarn to Left Back sts and work to correspond to Right Back, reversing all shapings.

FINISHING

Armbands: Sew shoulder seams. With RS facing and smaller needles, pick up and k40 (44, 48) sts along armhole edge. K 2 rows. Bind off knitwise (WS).

Back Edging

With RS facing and smaller needles, pick up and k9 sts down Right Back edge of back opening, 1 st at center and 9 sts up Left Back edge of back opening. 19 sts. Bind off knitwise (WS).

Neckband

With RS facing and smaller needles, pick up and k13 sts up Left Back neck edge, 14 sts down Left Front neck edge. K11 from Front st holder, dec 1 st at center. Pick up and k14 sts up Right Front neck edge and 13 sts down Right Back neck edge—64 sts. K 3 rows. **Next Row:** K1, * yo, MBA. Rep from * to last st, k1. K 2 rows. Bind off knitwise (WS). Sew side seams. To make button lp: with crochet hook, join yarn with a sl st in corner of right back neck. Ch 6, slip stitch at base of garter st border; turn. Sc over ch-6 lp10 times. Fasten off. Sew button to correspond to lp.

CAP (16" circumference)

With smaller needles, cast on 86 sts. Work 7 rows of Edging Pat as for Front of Dress, inc 2 sts evenly across last row—88 sts. Work 2 rows St st, then

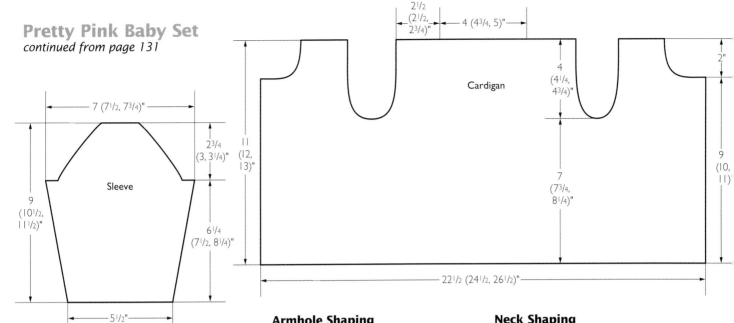

work 20 rows of Climbing Vine Lace Pat. Work 2 rows St st.

Top Shaping

Row 1 (RS): * K2tog, k9; rep from * to end of row—80 sts.

Row 2 and alt rows: Purl.

Row 3: * K2tog, k8; rep from * to end of row—72 sts.

Row 5: * K2tog, k7; rep from * to end of row—64 sts.

Cont in this manner, dec 8 sts evenly across every following alt row until there are 16 sts. **Next WS Row:** (P2tog) 8 times. Break yarn, leaving a long end. Draw end tightly through rem sts and fasten securely. Sew center back seam.

CARDIGAN

BODY (worked in one piece to armholes)

Beg at lower edge, with smaller circular needle, cast on 120 (130, 140) sts. Do not join. Work back and forth across needle in rows. Rep Rows 1–6 of Edging Pattern as for Dress Front.

Row 7: Knit, inc 5 (6, 7) sts evenly across—125 (136, 147) sts. With larger circular needle, work 2 rows in St st, then work in Climbing Vine Lace Pat (working first and last 2 sts of each row in St st) until Body measures approx 7 (7¾, 8¼)" from beg, ending with a WS row.

Armhole Shaping

Next Row: Pat across 27 (30, 32) sts. Bind off next 8 (8, 9) sts. Pat across 55 (60, 65) sts (including st on needle after bind off). Bind off next 8 (8, 9) sts. Pat to end of row.

Working on Left Front, work 1 row even in pat, then dec 1 st at the beg of the next and following alt rows 2 (3, 4) times more—24 (26, 27) sts. Work even in pat to approx 9 (10, 11)" from beg, ending with a RS row.

Neck Shaping

Bind off 6 sts beg next row. Dec 1 st at neck edge on next and following alt rows until there are 13 (13, 14) sts. Work even in pat to approx 11 (12, 13)" from beg, ending with a WS row. Bind off.

BACK

With WS of work facing, rejoin yarn to center 55 (60, 65) sts. Work 1 row even in pat, then dec 1 st at each end of the next and following alt rows 2 (3, 4) times more—49 (52, 55) sts. Work even in pat to approx 11 (12, 13)" from beg, ending with a WS row. Bind off.

RIGHT FRONT

With WS of work facing, rejoin yarn to last 27 (30, 32) sts. Work 1 row even in pat, then dec 1 st at end of the next and following alt rows 2 (3, 4) times more—24 (26, 27) sts. Work even in pat to approx 9 (10, 11)" from beg, ending with a WS row.

Neck Shaping

Bind off 6 sts beg next row. Work 1 row even in pat, then dec 1 st at neck edge on next and following alt rows until there are 13 (13, 14) sts. Work even in pat to approx 11 (12, 13)" from beg, ending with a WS row. Bind off.

SLEEVES (make two)

Beg at lower edge, with pair of smaller needles, cast on 30 sts. Work 7 rows of Edging Pat as for Front of Dress, inc 1 st in center of last row—31 sts. Change to larger needles.

Body Pattern

Row 1 (RS): K4; * yo, ssk, k5. Rep from * to last 6 sts, yo, ssk, k4.

Rows 2–4: Work 3 rows even in St st.

Row 5: K7; * yo, ssk, k5. Rep from * to last 3 sts, yo, ssk, k1.

Rows 6–8: Work 3 rows in St st.

Last 8 rows form Body Pattern. Cont in est pat, shaping sides by inc 1 st each edge on next and every 8th row 4 (5, 6) total times—39 (41, 43) sts. Work even to approx 6¼ (7½, 8¼)" from beg, ending with a WS row.

Cap Shaping

Keeping cont of est pat, bind off 2 sts beg next 2 rows, then dec 1 st each end of next and every alt row until there are 19 sts. Dec 1 st each end of every row until there are 13 sts. Bind off.

FINISHING

Sew shoulder and sleeve seams.

Buttonhole Band

With RS facing, using smaller needles, pick up and k46 (50, 56) sts evenly spaced from lower edge to neck edge along Right Front edge. K 1 row.

Row 2 (Buttonholes–RS): K2 (2, 3) sts. * Bind off 2 sts. K8 (9, 10) sts (including st on needle after bind off). Rep from * 3 times more. Bind off 2 sts. Knit to end of row.

Row 3: Knit, casting on 2 sts over bound off sts.

Rows 4–5: Knit.
Bind off knitwise on WS.

Left Front Band

With RS facing and using smaller needles, pick up and k46 (50, 56) sts evenly spaced from neck edge to lower edge along Left Front edge. Work 5 rows in garter st (knit every row). Bind off knitwise (WS).

Collar

With RS facing and using smaller needles, pick up and k18 (20, 20) sts up Right Front neck edge (beg at center of side edge of Buttonhole Band). Pick up and k22 (24, 26) sts across center Back neck edge, then 18 (20, 20) sts down Left Front neck edge (ending at center of side edge of Button Band)—58 (64, 66) sts. Work approx 2 (2¼, 2¼)" in garter st, ending with a WS row.

Next Row (RS of Collar/WS of Cardigan): K1; * yo, MBA. Rep from * to last st, k1. K 2 rows. Bind off knitwise (WS of Collar).

Sew in Sleeves. Sew buttons opposite buttonholes.

Kisses and Hugs
photo on page 114

SKILL LEVEL: Intermediate

SIZES: 3–6 (6–12, 12–18) months

Note: *The pattern is written for the smallest size with changes for larger sizes in parentheses. When only one number is given, it applies to all sizes. For ease in working, before you begin, circle all numbers pertaining to the size you are knitting.*

FINISHED MEASUREMENTS:
Sweater Chest: 22 (24½, 27)"
Sweater Length: 10½ (11, 12)"
Pants Waist: 17½ (18, 20½)"
Pants Length: 14 (16, 18)"

MATERIALS:
- Sandnes (Swedish Yarn Imports) Lanett Superwash, 100% merino wool, fingering weight yarn (215 yards per ball): 5 (5, 6) balls of light blue (5904) for MC

- Size 3 (3.25mm) knitting needles or size needed to obtain gauge
- Size 2 (2.75mm) knitting needles
- Cable needle (cn)
- 3 stitch holders
- Tapestry needle

GAUGE:
In St st with larger needles, 24 sts and 38 rows = 4"/10cm.
TAKE TIME TO CHECK YOUR GAUGE.

SPECIAL ABBREVIATIONS:
K1B: Insert needle through center of st below next stitch on needle and k this in the usual way, slipping the st above off needle at the same time.
C4B: Slip 2 sts to cn and hold at back, k2; k2 from cn.
C4F: Slip 2 sts to cn and hold at front, k2; k2 from cn.
Sssk: Slip next 3 sts singly and knitwise to right-hand needle, insert tip of left-hand needle into fronts of these 3 sts and knit them together.

Kisses and Hugs
continued from page 133

STITCHES USED:
Pattern A
Rib Stitch (over 17 sts; a rep of 2 rows)
Row 1 (RS): P1, k2, p1, k3, p1, k2, p1, k3, p1, k2.
Row 2: P2, K1B, p3, K1B, p2, K1B, p3, K1B, p2, K1B.
Rep Rows 1–2 for Pattern A.

Pattern B
OXOX Cable (panel of 12 sts; a rep of 22 rows)
Row 1 (RS): P2, C4B, C4F, p2.
Row 2 and all WS rows: K the k sts and p the p sts.
Rows 3, 5, 7: P2, k8, p2.
Row 9: P2, C4F, C4B, p2.
Row 11: P2, k8, p2.
Row 13: Rep Row 9.
Rows 15 and 17: P2, k8, p2.
Row 19: Rep Row 1.
Row 21: P2, k8, p2.

Row 22: Rep Row 2.
Rep Rows 1–22 for Pattern B.

Pattern C
Rib Stitch (over 17 sts; a rep of 2 rows)
Row 1 (RS): K2, p1, k3, p1, k2, p1, k3, p1, k2, p1.
Row 2: K1B, p2, K1B, p3, K1B, p2, K1B, p3, K1B, p2.
Rep Rows 1–2 for Pattern C.

Pattern D
Rib Stitch (over 12 sts; a rep of 2 rows)
Row 1 (RS): P1, k3, p1, k2, p1, k3, p1.
Row 2: K1B, p3, K1B, p2, K1B, p3, K1B.
Rep Rows 1–2 for Pattern C.

INSTRUCTIONS:
SWEATER—BACK
Beg at lower edge, with smaller needles, cast on 66 (74, 82) sts.
Ribbing
Row 1 (WS): P2; (k2, p2) across.
Row 2: K2; (p2, k2) across.
Rep Ribbing Rows 1–2 to approx 1" from beg, ending with a RS row. Change to larger needles and p 1 row. K10 (14,18), work Pattern A over 17 sts, Pattern B over 12 sts, and Pattern C over 17 sts, k10 (14,18). Cont est patterns to approx 6 (6½, 7)" from beg, ending with a WS row.

Raglan Shaping
Bind off 6 sts at beg of next 2 rows—54 (62, 70) sts. **Dec Row (RS):** K2, k3tog, work pattern across to last 5 sts, sssk, k2. Rep Dec Row every 4th row 7 (9, 11) more times—22 sts rem. Place marker on each edge to note start of hood panel.

Back Hood Panel
Cont est pattern on rem sts for approx 9 (9, 10)", ending with a RS row. Rep Ribbing Rows 1–2 as for Sweater Back for approx 1", ending with a WS row. Bind off knitwise.

FRONT
Work as for Back to approx 8½ (10, 11)" from beg, ending with a WS row. Place markers on both sides of center 12 sts.

Neck Shaping
Work est pattern to marker, place 12 sts on holder, join second ball of yarn and work to end of row. Working sides separately and at the same time, dec 1 st each neck edge every other row 3 times. AT SAME TIME, work raglan shaping on following fourth rows as est until 2 sts rem. Cont in pattern on rem 2 sts to approx 9½ (11, 12¼)" from beg, ending with a WS row. Bind off.

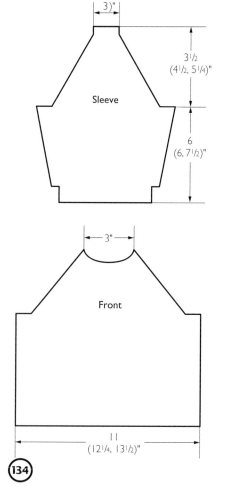

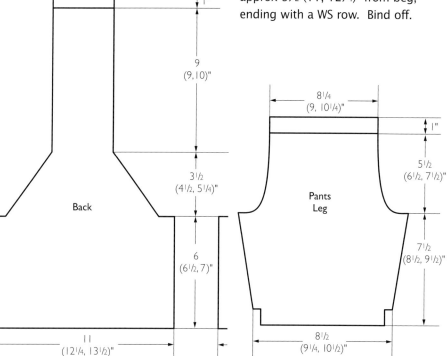

SLEEVES (make two)

Beg at lower edge, with smaller needles, cast on 34 (34, 42) sts. Rep Ribbing as for Back to approx 1" from beg, ending with a RS row and inc 6 sts evenly spaced across last row—40 (40, 48) sts. Change to larger needles and p 1 row. **Next Row:** K14 (14, 18), Pattern D on 12 sts, k14 (14, 18). Pat is now set. Including new sts into St st side panels, beg with the next RS row, inc 1 st each edge now and then every 6th row, 4 times more—50 (50, 58) sts. Work even to approx 6 (6, 7½)" from beg, ending with a WS row.

Raglan Shaping

Bind off 6 sts at beg of next 2 rows—38 (38, 46) sts. **Dec Row (RS):** K2, k3tog, work pat across to last 5 sts, sssk, k2. Rep Dec row every 4th row 3 (0, 0) times, every 6th row 3 (6, 3) times, every 8th row 0 (0, 3) times. Work even on rem 10 (10, 18) sts to approx 9½ (10½, 12¾)" from beg, ending with a WS row. Place sts on holder.

FINISHING

Join raglan sleeves to front and back. Join side seams.

Right Hood Side Panel

With the RS facing and larger needles, beg at center Front neck edge, pick up and k4 sts across center cable plus 9 more sts evenly spaced up right front neck edge, k across 10 (10, 18) sts from sleeve holder—23 (23, 31) total sts. **Next Row:** Purl. **Next Row:** P4, k to end. **Next Row:** Purl. **Next Row:** Knit. Rep last 4 rows for side panel, AT THE SAME TIME, inc 1 st at back edge every other row, 6 times—29 (29, 37) sts. Cont in est pat to approx 6 (6, 7)" from beg, ending with a WS row. Bind off loosely.

Left Hood Side Panel

K across 10 (10, 18) sts from sleeve holder, pick up and k13 sts evenly spaced along left front neck edge, ending with last 4 sts meeting at center front neck. Reversing shaping and front border trim, work as for Right Side Panel.

Join hood side panels to hood center. Without touching iron to fabric, steam lightly to finish.

PANT LEG (make two)

Beg at lower edge, with smallest needles, cast on 46 (50, 58) sts. Work 1" of Ribbing as for Sweater Back, ending with a RS row and inc 6 sts evenly spaced across last row—52 (56, 64) sts. Change to larger needles and p 1 row.

Body Pattern

Row 1 (RS): K3 (5, 9), Pattern A on 17 sts, Pattern B on 12 sts, Pattern C on 17 sts, k3 (5, 9). Pat is now set.

Next RS Row: Including new sts into St st, inc 1 st each edge now and then every 12th row 4 times more—62 (66, 74) sts. Work even to approx 7½ (8½, 9½)" from beg, ending with a WS row.

Crotch Shaping

Bind off 3 sts at beg of next 2 rows—56 (60, 68) sts. Dec 1 st each edge every other row 3 times—50 (54, 62) sts. Cont in pat to approx 13 (15, 17)" from beg, ending with a RS row.

Trim

Change to smaller needles and ribbing as follows:

Row 1 (WS): P2; (k2, p2) across.

Row 2: K2; (p2, k2) across.

Rep Ribbing Rows 1–2 to approx 14 (16, 18) " from beg, ending with a WS row. Bind off knitwise.

I-Cord Tie

With smaller needles, cast on 3 sts.

Row 1: K3.

Row 2: Sl 3 sts to left needle purlwise. With working yarn at left end of needle, take to back and k3. Rep Row 2 until tie measures approx 20 (22, 24)" from beg. Bind off. Join crotch and leg seams. Lace I-cord through center of waistband ribbing, and tie. Without touching iron to fabric, lightly steam to finish.

photo on page 115

Pom-Pom Throw

SKILL LEVEL: Intermediate

SIZE: Approximately 30×44" including trim

MATERIALS:

- Wendy, Velvet Touch, 100% nylon, sport weight yarn (115 yards per ball): 8 balls of Pink (1214) for MC
- Patons, Look At Me, 60% acrylic/ 40% nylon, sport weight yarn (152 yards per ball): 2 balls each of Hot Pink (6357) for CC1; Mango (6356) for CC2; Bright Lilac (6383) for CC3; and Green Apple (6362) for CC4; 1 ball Sunny Yellow (6366) for CC5
- Size 6 (4.25mm) circular knitting needle, 36-inch length, or size needed to obtain gauge
- Size 3 (3.25mm) double-pointed needles (dpns)
- Pom-pom maker—1½" size
- 9 small stitch holders
- Yarn needle

GAUGE:

In St st and color pattern with size 6 knitting needle, 20 sts and 28 rows = 4"/10cm.
TAKE TIME TO CHECK YOUR GAUGE.

Note: Use one ball of yarn for each vertical stripe. When changing color, bring next color from under present color for a twist to prevent holes.

INSTRUCTIONS:

Border

I-cord: Using 2 dpns and CC1, cast on 5 sts. * DO NOT TURN. Push sts to end of needle and k5; rep from * to approx 3" from beg. DO NOT CUT YARN. Place sts on holder. Make 8 more I-cords as est in colors CC2, CC3, CC4, CC5, CC4, CC3, CC2, and CC1.

Set Up Row: With size 6 needle, k5 CC1 sts; * cast on 13 MC sts, k5 CC2 sts; rep from * in color order listed above, ending cast on 13 MC sts, k5 CC1 sts—149 sts. In est color pat, purl across. In est color pat, knit across. Rep last 2 rows on the 149 sts to approx 38" from Set Up Row, ending with a WS row.

Second Border: Return 5 CC1 sts to dpn and work as for beg I-cord Border for approx 3". Bind off. Pull tail into center of I-cord for easy finishing. Bind off MC stripe with larger needle. Repeat as est for each I-cord and stripe across.

FINISHING
Wash blanket in cold water and lay flat to dry. Make pom-poms in the following colors: 2 of CC1, 4 of CC2, 4 of CC3, 4 of CC4, and 4 of CC5.

Attach a pom-pom to each I-cord as follows: CC1 cord to CC3, CC2 cord to CC4, CC3 cord to CC5, CC4 cord to CC2, and CC5 to CC1.

Ballet-Inspired Top
photo on page 116

SKILL LEVEL: Intermediate

SIZES: XS (S, MEDIUM, LG, XLG)
Note: *The pattern is written for the smallest size with changes for larger sizes in parentheses. When only one number is given, it applies to all sizes. For ease in working, before you begin circle all numbers pertaining to the size you are knitting.*

FINISHED MEASUREMENTS:
Bust: 32 (34½, 36, 38½, 40)"
Length: 13½ (13½, 13½, 14¼, 15)"

MATERIALS:
- Classic Elite Provence, 100% mercerized Egyptian cotton (256 yards per hank): 3 (3, 3, 4, 4) hanks of Clear Blue Sky (2607)
- Size 6 (4.25mm) knitting needles or size needed to obtain gauge
- Size 4 (3.5mm) circular needle, 16-inch length
- Size E/4 (3.5mm) aluminum crochet hook
- Cable needle (cn); 4 stitch holders
- 2 ring-type stitch markers
- Tapestry needle

GAUGE:
In St st with larger needles, 20 sts and 24 rows = 4"/10cm.
TAKE TIME TO CHECK YOUR GAUGE.

ABBREVIATIONS:
C4B (cable 4 back): Slip 2 sts to cn and hold at back, k2, k2 from cn.
C4F (cable 4 front): Slip 2 sts to cn and hold at front, k2, k2 from cn.
BC (back cross): Slip 2 sts to cn and hold at back, k2, p2 from cn.
FC (front cross): Slip 2 sts to cn and hold at front, p2, k2 from cn.
T3F (twist 3 front): Slip 2 sts to cn and hold at front, p1, k2 from cn.
T3B (twist 3 back): Slip 1 st to cn and hold at back, k2, p1 from cn.
Ssk: Slip next 2 sts knitwise, one at a time to right-hand needle, insert tip of left-hand needle into fronts of these 2 sts and knit them together.

STITCHES USED:

Cable Panel (over 26 sts; a rep of 32 rows)

Row 1 (WS): K11, p4, k11.

Row 2: P11, C4B, p11.

Row 3: Rep Row 1.

Row 4: P9, C4B, C4F, p9.

Row 5 and all WS rows: K the k sts and p the p sts.

Row 6: P7, BC, C4F, FC, p7.

Row 8: P5, BC, p2, k4, p2, FC, p5.

Row 10: P4, T3B, p4, C4F, p4, T3F, p4.

Row 12: P3, T3B, p3, C4B, C4F, p3, T3F, p3.

Row 14: P2, T3B, p2, BC, k4, FC, p2, T3F, p2.

Row 16: P2, k2, p1, BC, p2, C4B, p2, FC, p1, k2, p2.

Row 18: P2, k2, p1, k2, p4, k4, p4, k2, p1, k2, p2.

Row 20: P2, k2, p1, FC, p2, C4B, p2, BC, p1, k2, p2.

Row 22: P2, T3F, p2, FC, k4, BC, p2, T3B, p2.

Row 24: P3, T3F, p3, FC, BC, p3, T3B, p3.

Row 26: P4, T3F, p4, C4F, p4, T3B, p4.

Row 28: P5, FC, p2, k4, p2, BC, p5.

Row 30: P7, FC, C4F, BC, p7.

Row 32: P9, FC, BC, p9.

Rep Rows 1–32 for Cable Panel.

Left Cable (over 3 sts; a rep of 6 rows)

Row 1 (WS): P1, k1, p1.

Row 2: Slip 2 sts to cn and hold in back, k1, (p1, k1) from cn.

Row 3: Rep Row 1.

Row 4: K1, p1, k1.

Row 5: Rep Row 1.

Row 6: Rep Row 4.

Rep Rows 1–6 for Left Cable.

Right Cable (over 3 sts; a rep of 6 rows)

Row 1 (WS): P1, k1, p1.

Row 2: Slip 1 st to cn and hold in front, (k1, p1), k1 from cn.

Row 3: Rep Row 1.

Row 4: K1, p1, k1.

Row 5: Rep Row 1.

Row 6: Rep Row 4.

Rep Rows 1–6 for Right Cable.

Note: *The front and back of the sweater have different numbers of stitches.*

INSTRUCTIONS:

BACK

Beg at the lower edge and above the border, with larger needles, cast on 70 (76, 80, 86, 90) sts. Beg with a purl row, work 5 St st rows. Inc 1 st each edge now, then every 4th row for 4 times more—80 (86, 90, 96, 100) sts. Work even to approx 5½ (5¼, 5, 5½, 6)" from beg, ending with a WS row.

Raglan Shaping

Bind off 2 sts at beg of next 2 rows.

Dec Row: K1, ssk, k across to last 3 sts, k2tog, k1. P 1 row. Rep last 2 rows for 16 (17, 18, 19, 20) times more—42 (46, 48, 52, 54) sts rem. Place sts onto a holder.

FRONT

Beg at the lower edge and above the border, with larger needles, cast on 78 (84, 88, 94, 98) sts.

Set Up for Cable Panel

Row 1 (WS): P21 (24, 26, 29, 31), k2, p1, k1, p1, k11, p4, k11, p1, k1, p1, k2, p21 (24, 26, 29, 31).

Row 2: K21 (24, 26, 29, 31), p2, Left Cable Row 2 over 3 sts, p11, k4, p11, Right Cable Row 2 over 3 sts, p2, k21 (24, 26, 29, 31).

Row 3: Rep Row 1.

Row 4: K21 (24, 26, 29, 31), place a marker (pm), p2, k1, p1, k1, p11, k4, p11, k1, p1, k1, p2, pm, k21 (24, 26, 29, 31).

Row 5: Rep Row 1.

Row 6: Inc 1 st in first st, k to marker, p2, Left Cable Row 2 over 3 sts, Cable Panel Row 2 over 26 sts, Right Cable Row 2 over 3 sts, p2, sl marker, k to end, inc 1 st in last st.

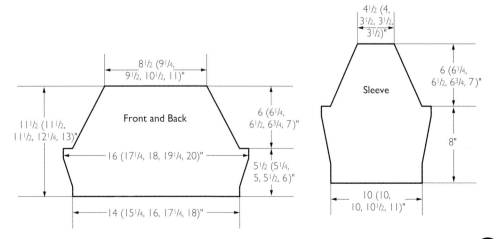

Front and Back

8½ (9¼, 9½, 10½, 11)"

11½ (11½, 11½, 12¼, 13)"

6 (6¼, 6½, 6¾, 7)"

5½ (5¼, 5, 5½, 6)"

16 (17¼, 18, 19¼, 20)"

14 (15¼, 16, 17¼, 18)"

Sleeve

4½ (4, 3½, 3½, 3½)"

6 (6¼, 6½, 6¾, 7)"

8"

10 (10, 10, 10½, 11)"

Ballet-Inspired Top
continued from page 137

Pat is now set. Inc 1 st each edge every 4th row 4 times more—88 (94, 98, 104, 108) sts. Work even to approx 5½ (5¼, 5, 5½, 6)" from beg, ending with a WS row. Shape Raglan as for Back—50 (54, 56, 60, 62) sts. Place sts onto a holder. ***Note:*** *For all sizes, after completing 2nd rep of Cable Panel, rep Rows 1-2 then work as follows: RS rows—p11, k4, p11. WS rows—k11, p4, k11. Work Left and Right Cables as est.*

SLEEVES (make two)
Beg at the lower edge and above the border, with larger needles, cast on 50 (50, 50, 52, 54) sts. Beg with a purl row, work 13 St st rows. Inc 1 st each edge now, then every 8th row 4 times more—60 (60, 60, 62, 64) sts. Work even to approx 8" from beg, ending with a WS row. Rep Raglan Shaping as for Back—22 (20, 18, 18, 18) sts rem. Place sts onto a holder.

FINISHING
With RS facing, return sts from holders to smaller circular needle as follows: sleeve, front, sleeve, back. Join yarn and k across sts for back and sleeve; on front, dec 8 sts evenly spaced—42 (46, 48, 52, 54) sts; k across next sleeve. K 4 more rows on the 128 (132, 132, 140, 144) sts. Join and place a marker to indicate beg of rnd. Work 4 rnds of k1, p1 rib. P 1 rnd. Bind off loosely and knitwise. Join raglans, underarms, and side seams.

Sleeve Trim
With RS facing, using crochet hook, join yarn with a sl st near seam. Ch 1, sc in each cast on st around. Sl st in first sc; (ch 15, sl st in next sc) around. At end, fasten off.

Lower Body Trim
With RS facing, using crochet hook, join yarn with a slip st near seam. Ch 1; * sc in 3 cast on sts, sk 1 st; rep from * around. Slip st in first sc; (ch 15, slip st in next sc) around. Fasten off.

Spring Fling
photo on page 117

SKILL LEVEL: Intermediate

SIZES: XS (S, MEDIUM, L, XL)
Note: *The pattern is written for the smallest size with changes for larger sizes in parentheses. When only one number is given, it applies to all sizes. For ease in working, before you begin, circle all numbers pertaining to the size you are knitting.*

FINISHED MEASUREMENTS:
Bust: 34 (36, 38, 40, 42)"
Length: 18 (19, 20, 21, 22)"

MATERIALS:
- Classic Elite Yarns, Flash, 100% cotton, DK weight yarn (93 yards per hank): 4 (4, 5, 5, 6) hanks of Lotus Blossom (6127)
- Size 6 (4.25mm) knitting needles or size needed to obtain gauge
- Size 4 (3.5mm) circular knitting needle, 22-inch length
- Tapestry needle
- 2 ring-type stitch markers

GAUGE:
In St st with larger needles,
20 sts and 28 rows = 4"/10cm.
TAKE TIME TO CHECK YOUR GAUGE.

SPECIAL ABBREVIATIONS:
RT (right twist): Pass needle in front of first st, knit 2nd st, knit first st and sl both sts off needle.
LT (left twist): Pass needle behind first st, k 2nd st through the back lp, knit first st and sl both sts off needle.
Sl 1: Slip 1 st purlwise and with yarn on WS of fabric.
MB (make bobble): In next st (k1, yo, k1, yo, k1); turn; p5; turn; k5; turn, p1, sl 1, p2tog, psso, p1; turn, k3tog.

STITCHES USED:
Center Panel (over 17 sts; a rep of 12 rows).
Row 1 and all WS rows: Yo, p2tog, p13, yo, p2tog.
Row 2: Yo, k2tog, k2, LT, k2, RT, k5, yo, k2tog.

Row 4: Yo, k2tog, k3, LT, RT, k6, yo, k2tog.
Row 6: Yo, k2tog, k4, LT, k4, MB, k2, yo, k2tog.
Row 8: Yo, k2tog, k5, LT, k2, RT, k2, yo, k2tog.
Row 10: Yo, k2tog, k6, LT, RT, k3, yo, k2tog.
Row 12: Yo, k2tog, k2, MB, k4, RT, k4, yo, k2tog.
Rep Rows 1–12 for Center Panel.

INSTRUCTIONS:
BACK
Beg at lower edge, with smaller circular needle, cast on 85 (89, 95, 99, 105) sts. Work back and forth across needle in rows.
Ribbing
Row 1 (WS): P1; (k1, p1) across.
Row 2: K1; (p1, k1) across.
Rep Rows 1–2 to approx 1" from beg, ending with Row 1. Change to larger needles.
Beg with a knit row, work St st to approx 9½ (10, 10½, 11, 11½)" from beg, ending with a WS row.
Armhole Shaping
Bind off 2 sts at the beg of next 2 rows, dec 1 st each edge every other row twice—77 (81, 87, 91, 97) sts. Work even to approx 15½ (16½, 17½, 18½, 19½)" from beg, ending with a WS row.
Neck Shaping
K28 (30, 32, 33, 36); join a new strand and bind off center 21 (21, 23, 25, 25) sts; work to end of row. Working sides separately and at the same time, bind off at each neck edge 3 sts twice, 2 sts twice, and 1 st 4 times. Work even on rem 14 (16, 18, 19, 22) sts for each shoulder to approx 18 (19, 20, 21, 22)" from beg, ending with a WS row. Bind off.

FRONT
Cast on and work Ribbing as for Back. Change to larger needles. **Next Row:** K34 (36, 39, 41, 44); place marker (pm); k17; pm; k to end. Keeping sts at side edges of markers in St st, work Center Panel over 17 sts. Cont as est, shaping armholes as for Back. When piece measures approx 15½ (16½, 17½, 18½, 19½)" from beg, end with a WS row.

Place a marker to indicate beg of rnd. Work 5 rnds of k1, p1 ribbing. Bind off in ribbing.

Rubber Ducky Pullover

photos on pages 118–119

SKILL LEVEL: Intermediate

SIZES: XS (S, MEDIUM, L, XL)
Note: *The pattern is written for the smallest size with changes for larger sizes in parentheses. When only one number is given, it applies to all sizes. For ease in working, before you begin, circle all numbers pertaining to the size you are knitting.*

FINISHED MEASUREMENTS:
Bust: 34 (37, 40, 43, 46)"
Length: 18½ (19, 19½, 20, 20½)"

MATERIALS:
- Garnstudio, Paris, 100% cotton, worsted weight yarn (75 meters per skein): 8 (9, 0, 11, 12) skeins of Royal Blue (09); 1 skein of Orange (13)
- Garnstudio, Vienna, 90% mohair/10% polyester, bulky weight yarn (95 meters per skein): 1 skein of Yellow (46)
- Size 8 (5mm) knitting needles or size needed to obtain gauge
- Size 6 (4.25mm) knitting needles
- Size 4 (3.5mm) circular knitting needle, 16-inch length
- Yarn needle
- 1 ring-type stitch marker

GAUGE:
In St st with larger needles, 17 sts and 21 rows = 4"/10cm.
TAKE TIME TO CHECK YOUR GAUGE.

Note: *The St st duck motifs are worked from a chart, reading from right to left for RS rows and from left to right for WS rows. Use bobbins or separate strands of yarn for each color section. When changing color, bring next strand from under present strand for a twist to prevent holes. Work ducks with*

Shape neck as for Back. Work even on rem 14 (16, 18, 19, 22) sts for each shoulder to same length as Back, ending with a WS row. Bind off.

SLEEVES (make two)
With smaller circular needle, cast on 69 (71, 75, 79, 83) sts. Work back and forth across needle in rows. Rep Ribbing Rows 1–2 as for Back. Change to larger needles, and k across, inc 1 st—70 (72, 76, 80, 84) sts. P 1 row. Cont St st, inc 1 st each edge every other row, twice—74 (76, 80, 84, 88) sts. Work even to approx 1½ (1¾, 2, 2¼, 2½)" from beg, ending with a WS row.

Sleeve Cap Shaping
Bind off 4 sts at beg of next 2 rows—66 (68, 72, 76, 80) sts. Bind off 2 sts at beg of next 2 rows 0 (1, 0, 0, 0, 1) time(s). Bind off 3 sts at beg of each row until 12 (16, 18, 22, 22) sts rem. Bind off rem sts.

FINISHING
Join shoulder seams. Set in sleeves. Join underarm and side seams.
Neckband
With the RS facing, using smaller needle, beg at right back shoulder seam, pick up and k68 (68, 70, 72, 72) sts evenly spaced along back neck to shoulder and 68 (68, 70, 72, 72) sts evenly spaced along front neck.

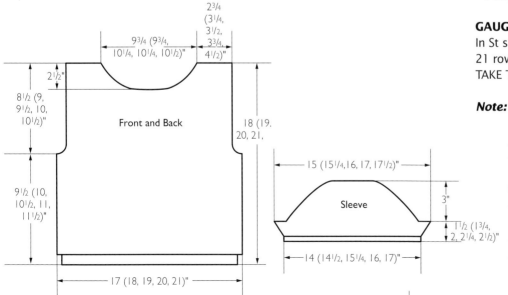

2¾ (3¼, 3½, 3¾, 4½)"

9¾ (9¾, 10¼, 10¼, 10½)"

2½"

8½ (9, 9½, 10, 10½)"

Front and Back

18 (19. 20, 21,

9½ (10, 10½, 11, 11½)"

17 (18, 19, 20, 21)"

15 (15¼, 16, 17, 17½)"

3"

Sleeve

1½ (1¾, 2, 2¼, 2½)"

14 (14½, 15¼, 16, 17)"

Rubber Ducky Pullover

continued from page 139

yellow mohair. After the knitting is complete, add duplicate stitch embroidery bills and feet with orange.

INSTRUCTIONS:
BACK
Beg at the lower edge with smaller straight needles and blue, cast on 73 (79, 85, 91, 97) sts.
Ribbing
Row 1 (WS): P1; (k1, p1) across.
Row 2: K1; (p1, k1) across.
Rep Rows 1–2 to approx 2" from beg, ending with a WS row. Change to larger straight needles. Beg with a knit row, work 4 St st rows. For Back Chart: Begin with Row 5 and work

C–D across, with blue k to end of row. After completing Row 17, cont in St st with blue until piece measures approx 11" from beg, ending with a WS row.
Armhole Shaping
At each armhole edge, bind off 5 sts. Dec 1 st each edge every other row 3 (3, 5, 5, 7) times. Cont in St st on rem 57 (63, 65, 71, 73) sts to approx 18½ (19, 19½, 20, 20½)" from beg, ending with a WS row.
Shoulder Shaping
Bind off 13 (15, 15, 17, 17) sts at the beg of the next 2 rows. Bind off rem 31 (33, 35, 37, 39) sts for back neck.

FRONT
Work as for Back to Chart.
Row 5: K 18 (24, 30, 36, 42) blue sts, then work A–B of Front Chart across. After completing Row 17 work remainder of front with blue, shaping armholes as for Back. Cont in St st to approx 16½ (17, 17½, 18, 18½)" from beg, ending with a WS row.
Neck Shaping
Work first 19 (21, 21, 23, 23) sts; join a new strand of blue and bind off the center 19 (21, 23, 25, 27) sts; work to end of row. Working sides separately and at the same time, bind off at each neck edge 3 sts once, 2 sts once, and 1 st once. When piece measures same as Back, ending with a WS row, bind off rem 13 (15, 15, 17, 17) sts for each shoulder.

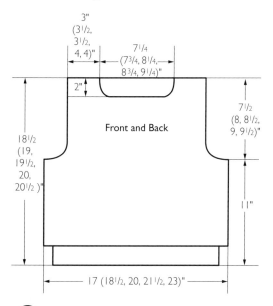

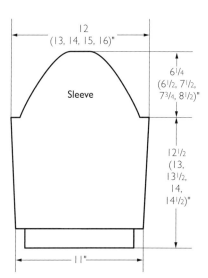

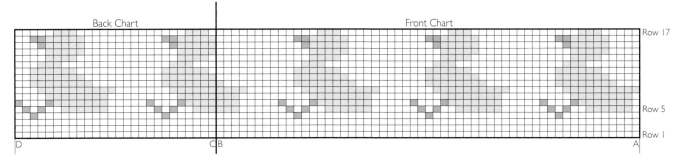

Back Chart   Front Chart   Row 17

Row 5

Row 1

D   CB   A

KEY

☐ Royal Blue

☐ Yellow Mohair

■ Orange

SLEEVES (make two)

Beg at the lower edge, with smaller needles and blue, cast on 41 sts. Work Ribbing as for Back to approx 2" from beg, ending with a WS row. Change to larger needles. K across next row, inc 6 (6, 6, 7, 7) sts evenly spaced—47 (47, 47, 48, 48) sts. Work 9 (9, 9, 3, 1) rows even. Inc 1 st each edge every 6th row 0 (0, 3, 6, 10) times and every 10th row 2 (4, 3, 2, 0) times—51 (55, 59, 64, 68) sts. When piece measures approx 12½ (13, 13½, 14, 14½)" from beg, end with a WS row.

Sleeve Cap Shaping

Bind off 5 sts at beg of next 2 rows. Dec 1 st each edge every other row 14 (15, 17, 18, 20) times. Bind off 2 (3, 3, 4, 4) sts at beg of next 2 rows. Bind off rem 9 (9, 9, 10, 10) sts.

FINISHING

Join shoulder seams. Set in sleeves. Join underarm and side seams.

Neckband

With the RS facing using circular needle and blue, begin at left shoulder seam to pick up and k72 (78, 84, 90, 96) sts evenly spaced around neck. Place a marker to indicate beg of rnd. K1, p1 around to approx 1" from beg. Bind off in ribbing.

Embroider feet and bill onto each duck using duplicate stitch and orange yarn.

Casual Friday Sleeveless Cardigan

photo on pages 120–121

SKILL LEVEL: Experienced

SIZES: S (MEDIUM, L, XL)
Note: The pattern is written for the smallest size with changes for larger sizes in parentheses. When only one number is given, it applies to all sizes. For ease in working the pattern, before you begin, circle all numbers pertaining to the size you are knitting.

FINISHED MEASUREMENTS:
Chest (buttoned): 42 (45½, 49¾, 54½)"
Length: 27 (27½, 28, 28½)"

MATERIALS:
- Classic Elite Yarns, Newport, 100% mercerized pima cotton, worsted weight yarn (70 yards per hank): 14 (15, 17, 19) hanks of Ecru (2016)
- Size 9 (5.50mm) knitting needles or size needed to obtain gauge
- Size 7 (4.50mm) knitting needles
- Cable needle (cn)
- 2 stitch holders
- Yarn needle
- Five 1-inch-diameter buttons

GAUGE:
In Body Pattern with larger needles, 27 sts and 32 rows = 6"/15.25cm.
TAKE TIME TO CHECK YOUR GAUGE.

ABBREVIATIONS:
MR (make ringlet): On the RS, p2, keeping yarn in front, sl these 2 sts back to left-hand needle; take yarn around (passing in front of the 2 sts) to back, slip the sts back to right-hand needle.

B2 (bind 2): On the WS, yo, p2, yb, pass the yo over the 2 purl sts.
T3F (twist 3 front): Slip 2 sts to cn and hold at front, p1, k2 from cn.
T3B (twist 3 back): Slip 1 st to cn and hold at back, k2, p1 from cn.
C4B (cable 4 back): Slip 2 sts to cn and hold at back, k2, k2 from cn.
C4F (cable 4 front): Slip 2 sts to cn and hold at front, k2, k2 from cn.

STITCHES USED:
Cable Panel (over 20 sts; a rep of 24 rows)
Row 1 (RS): P1, k2, p3, k2, p4, k2, p3, k2, p1.
Row 2: K1, B2, k3, B2, k4, B2, k3, B2, k1.
Row 3: P1, T3F, p2, T3F, (p2, T3B) twice, p1.
Row 4: K2, B2, k3, B2, k2, B2, k3, B2, k2.
Row 5: (P2, T3F) twice, (T3B, p2) twice.
Row 6: (K3, B2) twice, p2, k3, B2, k3.
Row 7: P3, T3F, p2, C4B, p2, T3B, p3.
Row 8: K4, B2, k2, (B2) twice, k2, B2, k4.
Row 9: P4, (T3F, T3B) twice, p4.
Row 10: K5, p2, B2, k2, p2, B2, k5.
Row 11: P5, C4F, p2, C4F, p5.
Row 12: K5, (B2) twice, k2, (B2) twice, k5.
Row 13: P4, (T3B, T3F) twice, p4.
Row 14: K4, B2, k2, B2, p2, k2, B2, k4.
Row 15: P3, T3B, p2, C4B, p2, T3F, p3.
Row 16: K3, B2, k3, (B2) twice, k3, B2, k3.
Row 17: P2, T3B, p2, T3B, T3F, p2, T3F, p2.
Row 18: Rep Row 4.
Row 19: P1, T3B, p2, T3B, (p2, T3F) twice, p1.
Row 20: Rep Row 2.
Row 21: Rep Row 1.
Row 22: Rep Row 2.

Row 23: Rep Row 1.
Row 24: Rep Row 2.
Rep Rows 1–24 for Cable Panel.

INSTRUCTIONS:
BACK
Beg at lower edge, with larger needles, cast on 94 (104, 114, 124) sts.
Set Up for Body Pattern
Row 1 (RS): K1, (p3, MR) 2 (3, 3, 4) times; rep Row 1 of Cable Panel across 20 sts; (MR, p3) 6 (6, 8, 8) times, MR; rep Row 1 of Cable Panel across 20 sts; (MR, p3) 2 (3, 3, 4) times, k1.
Row 2: P1, (k3, p2) 2 (3, 3, 4) times; rep Row 2 of Cable Panel across 20 sts; (p2, k3) 6 (6, 8, 8) times, p2; rep Row 2 of Cable Panel across 20 sts; (p2, k3) 2 (3, 3, 4) times, p1.
Pattern is now set. Cont as est to approx 17½" from beg, ending with a WS row.
Armhole Shaping
Bind off 6 (6, 8, 10) sts at beg of next 2 rows, dec 1 st each edge every other row 5 (7, 9, 10) times. Keeping 1 st each edge in St st for a selvege, work even on rem 72 (78, 80, 84) sts to approx 27 (27½, 28, 28½)" from beg, ending with a WS row. Bind off knitwise and loosely.

Pocket Linings (make two)
With larger needles, cast on 20 sts. Beg with a purl row, work St st for 6", ending with a purl row. Place sts onto a holder.

RIGHT FRONT
Beg at lower edge with larger needles, cast on 42 (47, 52, 57) sts.
Set Up for Body Pattern
Row 1 (RS): K1, (p3, MR) 2 (2, 3, 3) times; rep Row 1 of Cable Panel across 20 sts; (MR, p3) 2 (3, 3, 4) times, k1.
Row 2: P1, (k3, p2) 2 (3, 3, 4) times; rep Row 2 of Cable Panel across 20 sts; (p2, k3) 2 (2, 3, 3) times, p1.
Pattern is now set. Cont as est to approx 8½" from beg, ending with a WS row.

Pocket Opening

Next Row: Work est pattern across first 11 (11, 16, 16) sts; place next 20 sts onto a holder; work Cable Panel across 20 sts of Pocket Lining; work est pattern to end of row. Cont as est to approx 16½" from beg, ending with a WS row.

V-Neck Shaping

Dec 1 st at front edge now, then every 4th row 9 (9, 9, 11) times more. AT THE SAME TIME, when piece measures approx 17½" from beg, end with a RS row.

Armhole Shaping

Bind off 6 (6, 8, 10) sts at beg of next row, dec 1 st at armhole edge every other row 5 (7, 9, 10) times. Keeping 1 st each edge in St st for a selvage, work on rem 21 (24, 25, 25) sts to same length as Back, ending with a WS row. Bind off knitwise and loosely.

LEFT FRONT

Cast on as for Right Front.

Set Up for Body Pattern

Row 1 (RS): K1, (p3, MR) 2 (3, 3, 4) times; rep Row 1 of Cable Panel across 20 sts; (MR, p3) 2 (2, 3, 3) times, k1.

Row 2: P1, (k3, p2) 2 (2, 3, 3) times; rep Row 2 of Cable Panel across 20 sts; (MR, p3) 2 (3, 3, 4) times, p1. Pat is now set. Cont as est to approx 8½" from beg, ending with a WS row.

Pocket Opening

Work est pattern across first 11 (16, 16, 21) sts; place next 20 sts onto a holder, work Cable Panel across 20 sts

of Pocket Lining, work est pattern to end of row. Complete as for Right Front, reversing neck and armhole shaping.

FINISHING

Join shoulder seams.

Armbands (make two)

With RS facing, and smaller needles, pick up and k95 (99, 103, 109) sts evenly spaced along armhole opening.

Ribbing, Row 1 (WS): P1; (k1, p1) across.

Row 2: K1; (p1, k1) across.

Row 3: Rep Row 1.
Bind off in ribbing.

Pocket Trim (make two)

With the RS facing, return sts from holder to smaller needles. Join yarn and k 5 rows. Bind off knitwise on WS. Join sides of trim to sweater front. Sew pocket lining in place.

Left Neck and Front Band

With the RS facing and smaller needles, beg at center of back neck to pick up and k15 (15, 15, 17) sts evenly spaced to shoulder, 47 (49, 51, 53) sts along V-neck, and 63 sts from first shaping row to lower edge—125 (127, 129, 131) sts. Work Ribbing as for Armbands for 3 rows.

Buttonhole Row: Rib 63 (65, 67, 69) sts; * yo, k2tog, k12; rep from * 3 times more, yo, k2tog, k4. Work est rib pat for 3 more rows. Bind off in ribbing.

Right Neck and Front Band

With the RS facing and smaller needles, beg at lower edge to pick up

and k63 sts evenly spaced to first neck shaping row, 47 (49, 51, 53) sts to shoulder, and 15 (15, 15, 17) sts along back neck—125 (127, 129, 131) sts. Rib 7 rows; bind off in ribbing. Join bands together at back neck. Sew buttons opposite buttonholes.

Checked Pillow
photo on page 122

SKILL LEVEL: Easy

SIZE: Approximately 12" square with a ¾-inch welt

MATERIALS:

- Patons Grace, 100% mercerized cotton, sport weight yarn (136 yards per ball): 4 balls of Champagne (60011) for MC; 1 ball each of Ruby (60409) for Color A and Terra-Cotta (60011) for Color B
- Size 5 (3.75mm) knitting needles or size needed to obtain gauge
- Yarn needle
- 12" square pillow form

GAUGE:

In St st with a double strand of yarn, 22 sts and 30 rows = 4"/10cm.
TAKE TIME TO CHECK YOUR GAUGE.

Notes: *Use two strands of yarn held together throughout this project to give the knitted yarn a fabriclike quality. Each square within the design is 22 sts wide and 30 rows deep. Make a small ball of yarn, using two strands for each color. When starting a new color, tie new color around color in use with a slip knot. When changing yarn color within the design, twist new color around color in use.*

Schematic

Back: 27 (27½, 28, 28½)"
6¾ (6¾, 6¾, 7½)"
21 (23, 25¼, 27½)"

Front: 4¾ (5¼, 5½, 5½)"
9½ (10, 10½, 11)"
10½ (11, 11½, 12)"
17½"
16½"
9½ (10½, 11½, 12½)"

Checked Pillow

continued from page 143

INSTRUCTIONS:
FRONT
Using double strands throughout, with MC, cast on 74 sts. K 7 rows for garter St border.

Body Pattern
Row 1 (RS): K4-MC; k22-A, k22-B, k22-A, k4-MC.

Row 2: K4-MC, p22-A, p22-B, p22-A, k4-MC.

Rows 3–30: Rep last 2 rows 14 times more.

Striped Chex Pillow Key and Chart (instructions, *page 145*)

Row 31: K4-MC, k22-B, k22-MC, k22-B, k4-MC.

Row 32: K4-MC, p22-B, p22-MC, p22-B, k4-MC.

Rows 33–60: Rep Rows 31–32.

Rows 61–90: Rep Rows 1–2.
With MC, k 7 rows for second border. With one strand only, bind off.

BACK
With a double strand of MC, cast on 66 sts. Beg with a k row, work 90 rows of St st. Piece should measure approx 12" square. With one strand only, bind off.

FINISHING
Weave loose ends along WS of fabric, closing holes as necessary. Holding WS together, place base of back next to garter st welt. Using one strand of yarn, sew three sides tog along inside edge of welt (1 st per knitted st is best). Insert pillow form and sew rem side.

KEY

☐ MC

■ Color A – Night

☐ Color B – Snow

Center

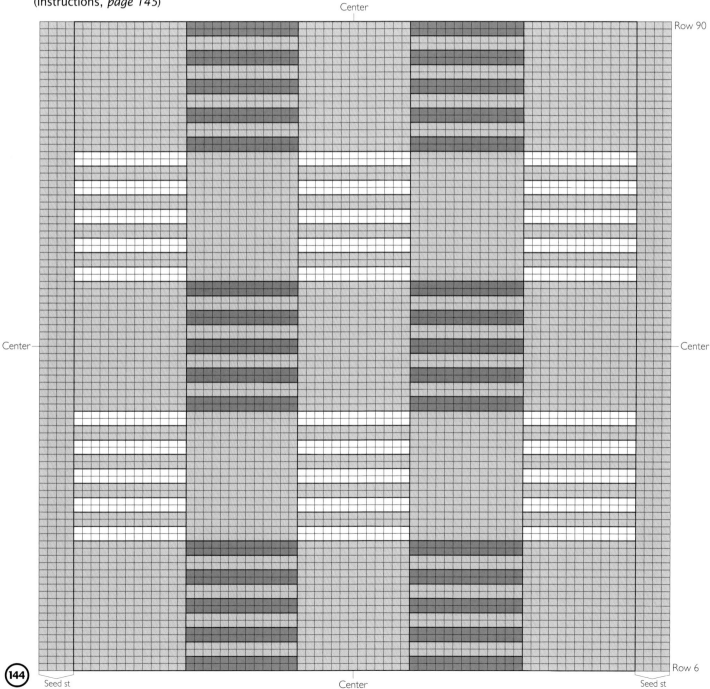

Row 90

Center — — Center

Seed st

Center

Seed st

Row 6

Striped Chex Pillow

photo on page 122

SKILL LEVEL: Intermediate

SIZE: Approximately 12" square with a ¾-inch welt

MATERIALS:
- Patons Grace, 100% mercerized cotton, sport weight yarn (136 yards per ball): 5 balls of Champagne (60011) for MC; 1 ball each of Night (60040) for Color A and Snow (60005) for Color B
- Size 5 (3.75mm) knitting needles or size needed to obtain gauge
- Yarn needle
- 12" square pillow form

GAUGE:
In St st with a double strand of yarn, 22 sts and 30 rows = 4"/10cm.
TAKE TIME TO CHECK YOUR GAUGE.

STITCHES USED:
Seed Stitch
Row 1 (WS): K1; (p1, k1) across.
Row 2: Knit the purl sts and purl the knit sts across.
Rep Rows 1–2 for seed st.

Note: Double strands of yarn are used for entire project. Each square within the design is 13 sts wide and 18 rows deep. Stripes are 2 rows deep. Make a small ball of yarn using two strands for each color. When starting a new color, tie new color around color in use with a slip knot. When changing yarn color within the design, twist new color around color in use.

INSTRUCTIONS:
FRONT
Using double strands throughout, with MC, cast on 73 sts. Work 5 rows of seed st.
First Chart Row (RS): With MC, work 4 seed sts; (k13-MC, k13-A) twice, k13-MC, with MC, work 4 seed sts. Pattern is now set. Follow chart through completion of Row 90. With MC, work 5 rows of seed st. Bind off using a single strand of MC.

BACK
With a double strand of MC, cast on 65 sts. Beg with a knit row, work 90 rows of St st. Piece should measure approx 12" square. Bind off using a single strand.

FINISHING
Weave loose ends along WS of fabric, closing holes as necessary. Holding WS tog, use a single strand of MC to join back to base of welt on 3 sides. Insert pillow form and close rem side.

Variegated Place Mats

photo on page 123

SKILL LEVEL: Beginner

SIZE: 12×16"

MATERIALS:
- Classic Elite's Provence, 100% mercerized cotton, DK (double knitting) weight (256 yards per hank): For 4 mats; 2 hanks each of Lemon (2612) for Color A and Hydrangea Blossom (2679) for Color B; OR Bright Chartreuse (2681) for Color A and Slate Blue (2648) for Color B
- Size 6 (3.75mm) knitting needles or size needed to obtain gauge
- Yarn needle

GAUGE:
In garter st (knit all rows), 20 stitches and 40 rows (20 ridges) = 4"/10cm.
TAKE TIME TO CHECK YOUR GAUGE.

INSTRUCTIONS:
With A, cast on 60 sts. K all rows changing color at beg of rows as follows (first row is RS):
12 ridges A, 1 ridge B
8 ridges A, 1 ridge B
6 ridges A, 1 ridge B
4 ridges A, 1 ridge B
2 ridges A, 1 ridge B
1 ridge A, 2 ridges B
1 ridge A, 4 ridges B
1 ridge A, 6 ridges B
1 ridge A, 8 ridges B
1 ridge A, 12 ridges B
Bind off.

FINISHING
Weave loose ends into WS of work.

Black Pillow with Stripes

Center

Row 89

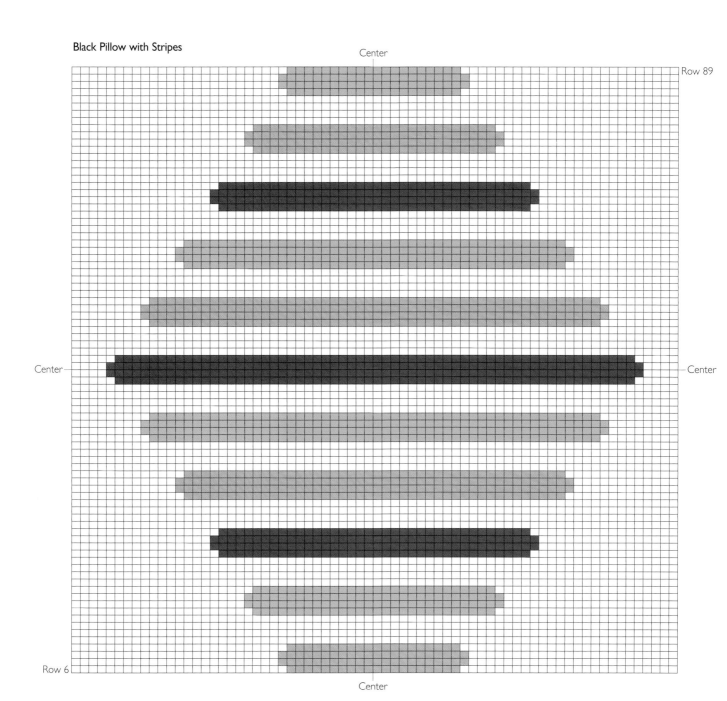

Center

Center

Row 6

Center

Black Pillow with Stripes

photo on page 122

SKILL LEVEL: Intermediate

SIZE: Approximately 12" square

MATERIALS:
- Patons Grace, 100% mercerized cotton, sport weight yarn (136 yards per ball): 5 balls of Night (60040) for MC; 1 ball each of Royal (60134) for

Color A, Lime (60712) for Color B, and Cardinal (60705) for Color C
- Size 5 (3.75mm) knitting needles or size needed to obtain gauge
- Yarn needle
- 12" square pillow form

GAUGE
Using a double strand of yarn in St st, 22 sts and 30 rows = 4"/10cm.
TAKE TIME TO CHECK YOUR GAUGE.

Notes: Make this pillow top in one piece. Use double strands of yarn are used throughout entire project. Make a small ball of yarn using two strands for each color. When starting a new color, tie new color around color in use with a slip knot. When changing color within the design, twist new color around color in use.

INSTRUCTIONS:
Using double strands throughout, with MC, cast on 70 sts. Beg with a k row, work 5 St st rows.
First Chart Row 6 (WS): P25-MC, p20-A, p25-MC. (See chart, *page 146*.) Chart pattern is now set. Follow chart through completion of Row 89. Beg with a purl row, work 8 St st rows with MC. Rep Chart Rows 6–89 once again. Beg with a purl row, work 5 St st rows with MC. Bind off with MC.

FINISHING
Fold pillow top in half RS tog. Using 1 strand of MC, sew two sides tog through 2 thicknesses, one st in from each edge; 1 st per knitted st is best. Weave loose ends along WS of fabric, closing holes as necessary. Turn RS out. Insert pillow form and close rem side.

Drawstring Shoulder Bag, Cell Phone Case, and Hat
photos on pages 124–125

SKILL LEVEL: Easy

SIZES:
Shoulder Bag: 8×10" high
Cell Phone Case: 3×7" high

Hat: Circumference 21" with drawstring to adjust fit.

MATERIALS:
- Patons Grace, 100% mercerized cotton, sport weight yarn (136 yards per skein): *Shoulder bag, Cell Phone Case, and Hat:* 5 skeins of Cardinal (60705) for MC; 2 skeins of Royal (60134) for Color A
- Size 5 (3.75mm) knitting needles or size needed to obtain gauge
- 2 double-pointed needles, size 5 (3.75mm), for I-cord bag strap
- Yarn needle

GAUGE:
In St st (knit RS rows, purl WS rows), using a double strand of yarn, 22 sts and 30 rows = 4"/10cm.
TAKE TIME TO CHECK YOUR GAUGE.

ABBREVIATIONS:
Rsl inc (Right slant increase): Insert left needle from back to front under horizontal "ladder" between 2 needle points. Knit this lifted strand through the front.
Lsl inc (Left slant increase): Insert left needle from front to back under

horizontal "ladder" between 2 needle points. Knit this lifted strand through the back.

Notes: Use two strands of yarn together throughout to give the knitted yarn a fabriclike quality. When changing yarn color, at beg of color-change row, tie new color around color in use with a slip knot. Shoulder bag and cell phone case have drawstring closures. Use an I-cord shoulder strap for the shoulder bag. Thread a drawstring around hat, adjust, and tie in a bow to fit.

INSTRUCTIONS:
SHOULDER BAG
Using two strands of MC and leaving a 36" tail of yarn for finishing, beg at lower edge, cast on 78 sts.
Row 1: K across.
Row 2: P across.
Row 3: K2, Lsl inc, k36, Rsl inc, k2, Lsl inc, k36, Rsl inc, k2.
Row 4: P82.
Row 5: K3, Lsl inc, k36, Rsl inc, k4, Lsl inc, k36, Rsl inc, k3.
Row 6: P86.

Drawstring Shoulder Bag, Cell Phone Case, and Hat

continued from page 147

Row 7: K4, Lsl inc, k36, Rsl inc, k6, Lsl inc, k36, Rsl inc, k4.
Row 8: P90.
Row 9: K5, Lsl inc, k36, Rsl inc, k8, Lsl inc, k36, Rsl inc, k5—94 sts. Work 3 more St st rows (ending with a p row). Cont in St st, changing color on k rows as follows: 2 rows A, 4 rows MC, 8 rows A, 4 rows MC, 2 rows A. Change to MC and cont until work measures approx 9½" from base of shoulder bag, ending with a p row. **Next Row** (make picot st holes for drawstrings): [K1, (yo, k2tog) across to last st, k1]. Work 7 St st rows then repeat bet [ ] above to form picot st edging. Work 5 St st rows. Leaving a 36" tail of yarn for finishing, thread all sts onto another 36" length of yarn.

FINISHING

With WS of bag tog and 1 strand of MC, sew sides tog through both thicknesses, one st in from each edge, working from top to base. With same tail, join base. Fold facing to inside along picot edging and with one strand of yarn, hem sts (that were saved on the waste yarn) in place above the drawstring holes. Remove thread as you work. Weave loose ends into WS of work. Turn RS out.

Shoulder Strap

With dpns and a double strand of A, cast on 4 sts and k 1 row. * Without turning work, push sts to other end of needle. **Next Row:** K, pulling yarn tight when working first st *. Rep between * until strap measures approx 36" from beg, bind off. Weave loose ends into WS of work. Thread strap through picot hole at side of bag from inside of bag; thread other end through picot hole at opposite side of bag, from outside. Make an overhand knot 1" from each end of strap.

Drawstring Closure (make 2)

Cut 4—84" lengths of yarn A. Knot 4 cut ends tog ½ inch from each end.

Loop one end over small door knob. Insert pencil through yarn at other knot, pull tight and twist as much as possible. Remove pencil. Fold twisted yarn in half. Remove from door knob. Knot 2 knotted ends tog to prevent unraveling. Thread other end through picot holes, beg at hole to right of the left end of shoulder strap. Weave through the holes going to the right to the opposite side of bag at the last hole. Knot both ends of drawstring tog, 1" from end, and trim. Repeat for opposite side with second drawstring.

CELL PHONE CASE

Using two strands of MC and leaving a 30" tail of yarn for finishing, beg at lower edge, cast on 26 sts.
Row 1: K across.
Row 2: P across.
Row 3: K2, Lsl inc, k10, Rsl inc, k2, Lsl inc, k10, Rsl inc, k2.
Row 4: P30.
Row 5: K3, Lsl inc, k10, Rsl inc, k4, Lsl inc, k10, Rsl inc, k3—34 sts. Work 3 more St st rows (ending with a p row). Cont in St st, changing color on k rows as follows: 2 rows A, 4 rows MC, 6 rows A, 4 rows MC, 2 rows A. Change to MC and cont until work measures approx 6" from base of case ending with a p row.
Next Row (make picot st holes for draw strings): [K1, (yo, k2tog) across to last st, k1]. Work 5 St st rows then repeat bet [ ] above to form picot edging. Work 3 St st rows. Leaving a 24" tail of yarn for finishing, thread all sts onto another length of yarn.

FINISHING

With WS of case tog and one strand of A, sew sides tog through both thicknesses, one st in from each edge and working from top to base. With same tail, join base. Fold facing toward you at picot edging and using one strand yarn, hem sts (from thread) in place and above the drawstring holes. Remove thread as you work. Weave loose ends into WS of work. Turn RS out.

Drawstring Closure

Cut 4—36" lengths of MC yarn and follow directions from Drawstring Closure for Shoulder Bag.

HAT

Using two strands of MC and leaving a 40" tail of yarn for finishing, beg at lower edge, cast on 116 sts.
Row 1: K across.
Row 2: P across.
Row 3: K8, (Lsl inc, k8) 13 times, ending Lsl inc, k4—130 sts.
Rows 4–6: Work 3 St st rows, beg p.
Row 7 (Picot Edge): K1, (yo, k2 tog) across to last st, k1.
Rows 8–12: Work 5 St st rows, beg p.
Row 13: K8, (k2tog, k7) 13 times, k2tog, k3—116 sts.
Row 14: P across.
Row 15 (Drawstring Holes): Rep row 7. Cont in St st to approx 3" from Row 13, ending with a p row. Beg stripes on next row as follows: 2 rows A, 4 rows MC, 6 rows A, 4 rows MC, 2 rows A.

Crown Shaping

Row 1: K1; (k2tog, k17) 6 times, k1—110 sts.
Rows 2–4: Work 3 St st rows, beg p.
Row 5: K1, (k2tog, k16) 6 times, k1—104 sts.
Row 6: Purl.
Cont as set, evenly dec 6 sts on knit rows—56 sts. Cont evenly dec 6 sts on each row—8 sts. Leaving a long tail, cut yarn. Thread tail into yarn needle and back through rem 8 sts. Pull up to close opening. Secure in place.

FINISHING

With RS tog and single strand of yarn, sew sides of hat tog from base to top, one st in from each edge. Fold bottom edge to inside along first picot row and hem just below second picot row, for picot border. Weave all loose ends into inside of work.

Drawstring Tie

Cut six 90" lengths of yarn A and follow directions for Shoulder Bag drawstrings. Thread drawstring through holes around hat; knot each end 1" from tip and trim. Tie with a bow to adjust fit.

Ocean Stripes

photos on pages 126–127

SKILL LEVEL: Easy

SIZES: Girls' 6 (8, 10)
Note: *The pattern is written for the smallest size with changes for larger sizes in parentheses. When only one number is given, it applies to all sizes. For ease in working the pattern, before you begin, circle all numbers pertaining to the size you are knitting.*

FINISHED MEASUREMENTS:
Chest (buttoned): 30 (34, 37¾)"
Length: 18 (19, 20)"

MATERIALS:
- Red Heart Super Saver, Article E300, 100% Acrylic, worsted weight yarn (8 ounces per skein): 1 skein of Delft Blue (885) for MC
- Red Heart Classic, Article E267, 100% acrylic, worsted weight yarn (3½ ounces per skein): 3 skeins of Skipper Blue (848) for Color A; 1 skein each of Parakeet (513) for Color B, and Mist Green (681) for Color C
- Red Heart Kids, Article E711, 100% acrylic, worsted weight yarn (5 ounces per skein): 1 skein of Lime (2652) for Color D
- Size 8 (5mm) knitting needles or size needed to obtain gauge
- Size 6 (4.25mm) knitting needles
- Yarn needle
- Five ⅝-inch-diameter buttons

GAUGE:
In Bodice Pattern with larger needles, 17 sts and 24 rows = 4"/10cm.
TAKE TIME TO CHECK YOUR GAUGE.

INSTRUCTIONS:
BACK
Beg at the lower edge, with larger needles and Color A, cast on 93 (105, 117) sts.

Lower Body Pattern
Row 1 (WS): With color A, p3; (k3, p3) across.
Row 2: With A, k3; (p3, k3) across.
Row 3: Rep Row 1.
Rows 4–5: With D, rep Rows 2–3.
Rows 6–7: With A, rep Rows 2–3.
Rows 8–9: With B, rep Rows 2–3.
Rows 10–11: With A, rep Rows 2–3.
Rows 12–13: With C, rep Rows 2–3.
Rows 14–15: With A, rep Rows 2–3.

Rows 16–21: With MC, rep Rows 2–3. Rep Rows 2–20 once more.
Decrease Row: With MC, p3; * sl 1, k2tog, psso, p3; rep from * across—63 (71, 79) sts. Piece should measure approx 7" from beg.

Upper Body Pattern
Row 1 (RS): With A, k3; (p1, k3) across.
Row 2: With A, p3; (k1, p3) across.
Rows 3–4: With D, rep Rows 1–2.

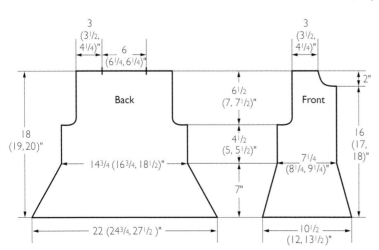

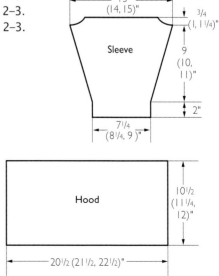

149

Ocean Stripes

continued from page 149

Rows 5–6: With A, rep Rows 1–2.
Rows 7–8: With B, rep Rows 1–2.
Rows 9–10: With A, rep Rows 1–2.
Rows 11–12: With C, rep Rows 1–2.
Rows 13–14: With A, rep Rows 1–2.
Rows 15–20: With MC, rep Rows 1–2.
Rep Rows 1–20 until piece measures approx 11½ (12, 12½)" from beg, ending with a WS row.

Armhole Shaping
Bind off 5 sts at beg of next 2 rows then dec 1 st each edge every other row 1 (2, 3) time(s)—51 (57, 63) sts. Keeping 1 st each edge in St st, cont pattern to approx 18 (19, 20)" from beg, ending with a WS row. Bind off straight across and knitwise using color from previous row.

RIGHT FRONT
Beg at lower edge, with larger needles and Color A, cast on 45 (51, 57) sts. Work Lower Body as for Back. After Decrease Row—31 (35, 39) sts. Work Upper Body Pattern as for Back until piece measures approx 11½ (12, 12½)" from beg, ending with a RS row.

Armhole Shaping
At armhole edge, bind off 5 sts once, then dec 1 st at armhole edge every other row 1 (2, 3) time(s)—25 (28, 31) sts. Keeping 1 st at armhole edge in St st, cont pat to approx 16 (17, 18)" from beg, ending with a WS row.

Neck Shaping
At neck edge, bind off 6 (7, 7) sts once, 3 sts once, 2 sts once, and 1 st once. Work even on rem 13 (15, 18) sts to same length as Back, ending with a WS row. Bind off knitwise using color from previous row.

LEFT FRONT
Work as for Right Front, reversing armhole and neck shaping.

SLEEVES (make two)
With larger needles and Color A, cast on 31 (35, 39) sts. With A, p3; (k1, p3) across for first WS row. Rep Rows 1–20 of Upper Body Pattern as for Back for entire sleeve. When piece measures approx 2" from beg, end with a WS row. Including new sts into pattern as they accumulate, inc 1 st

each edge every 4th row 10 (8, 5) times and every 6th row 2 (4, 7) times. Work even on 55 (59, 63) sts to approx 11 (12, 13)" from beg, ending with a WS row. Rep Armhole Shaping as for Back. On next RS row, bind off rem 43 (45, 47) sts knitwise using color from previous row.

Hood
With larger needles and Color A, cast on 87 (91, 95) sts. With A, p3; (k1, p3) across for first WS row. Rep Rows 1–20 of Upper Body Pattern as for Back until piece measures approx 10½ (11¼, 12)" from beg, ending with a WS row. Bind off knitwise using color from previous row.

FINISHING
Join shoulder seams. Set in sleeves. Join underarm and side seams. Fold hood in half lengthwise and join ends to form top seam. Holding RS tog, join hood to neck edge. With the RS facing, using smaller needles and Color A, pick up and k88 (92, 96) sts evenly spaced around hood. K 5 rows. Bind off loosely and knitwise.

Left Front Band
With the RS facing, using smaller needles and Color A, pick up and k69 (73, 77) sts evenly spaced along edge. K 5 rows. Bind off knitwise. Sew top of band to hood trim.

Right Front Band
Work as for Left Band through completion of first k row.
Row 2: K31 (35, 39); * (yo, k2tog, k6) 4 times, yo, k2tog, k4. K 3 more rows. Bind off knitwise. Sew top of band to hood trim. Sew buttons opposite buttonholes.

Easy Stripes and Checks Top
photos on pages 128–129

SKILL LEVEL: Easy

SIZES: XS (SMALL, M, L)
Note: *The pattern is written for the smallest size with changes for larger sizes in parentheses. When only one number is given, it applies to all sizes. For ease in working, before you begin, circle all numbers pertaining to the size you are knitting.*

FINISHED MEASUREMENTS:
Bust: 34½ (36, 38, 40)"
Length: 19 (20, 21, 22)"

MATERIALS:
- Berroco's Cotton Twist, 70% mercerized cotton/30% rayon, worsted weight yarn (85 yards per hank): 6 (7, 7, 8) hanks of Navy Blue (8325) for MC; 1 hank each of Kaboom (8340) for Color A and California Turquoise (8306) for Color B
- Size 8 (5mm) knitting needles or size needed to obtain gauge
- Size 6 (4.25mm) knitting needles; size 6 circular knitting needle, 24" length
- 1 ring-type stitch marker
- Tapestry needle

GAUGE:
In St st with larger needles, 19 sts and 28 rows = 4"/10cm.
TAKE TIME TO CHECK YOUR GAUGE.

STITCHES USED:
Ribbing (a multiple of 4 sts; over 17 rows)
Row 1 (WS): With MC, p1; (k2, p2) across, ending k2, p1.
Row 2: With MC, k1; (p2, k2) across, ending p2, k1.
Row 3: Rep Row 1.
Rows 4–5: With Color A, rep Rows 2–3.
Rows 6–7: With MC, rep Rows 2–3.
Rows 8–9: With Color B, rep Rows 2–3.
Rows 10–11: Rep Rows 6–7.
Rows 12–13: Rep Rows 4–5.
Rows 14–17: Rep Rows 6–7.

Checks (a multiple of 4 sts + 2 sts; a rep of 4 rows)
Row 1 (RS): * K2-B, k2-MC; rep from * across, ending k2-B.
Row 2: * P2-B, p2-MC; rep from * across, ending p2-B.
Row 3: * K2–MC, k2–A; rep from * across, ending k2–MC.
Row 4: * P2–MC, p2–A; rep from * across, ending p2–MC.
Rep Rows 1–4 for Checks.

Note: *When changing color while working the checks, bring new color from under present color for a twist to prevent holes.*

INSTRUCTIONS:
BACK
Beginning at the lower edge with smaller needles and MC, cast on 80 (84, 88, 92) sts. Work Ribbing Rows 1–17. Change to larger needles and knit across next row, inc 1 st each edge—82 (86, 90, 94) sts. Work St st (purl WS rows, knit RS rows) until piece measures approx 12 (12½, 13, 13½)" from beg, ending with a WS row.

Armhole Shaping
Bind off 5 sts at the beg of next 2 rows; dec 1 st each edge every other row 3 times. Work even on 66 (70, 74, 78) sts to approx 14 (15, 16, 17)" from beg, ending with a WS row. Work Checks to approx 15 (16, 17, 18)" from beg, ending with a WS row.
Neck Shaping
Cont in Checks, work first 21 (22, 23, 25) sts; join new strands and bind off center 24 (26, 28, 28) sts; work to end of row. Working sides separately and AT THE SAME TIME, bind off 3 sts at each neck edge once, 2 sts once,

and 1 st once. Cont in pattern on rem 15 (16, 17, 19) sts for each shoulder to approx 19 (20, 21, 22)" from beg, ending with a WS row. Bind off loosely with MC.

FRONT
Work as for Back.

SLEEVES (make two)
Beg at the lower edge with smaller needles and MC, cast on 52 (56, 62, 66) sts. K 2 rows. With larger needles work St st, beg with a knit row, until piece measures approx 1¾ (2, 2¼, 2½)" from beg, ending with a WS row.
Cap Shaping
Bind off 5 sts at beg of next 2 rows, dec 1 st each edge every other row 10 (12, 15, 17) times. Work on 22 sts until piece measures approx 5¼ (6, 6¾, 8)" from beg, ending with a WS row. Bind off 7 sts at beg of next 2 rows. Bind off rem 8 sts.

FINISHING
Join shoulder seams. Set in sleeves. Join underarm and side seams.
Neckband
With the RS facing, using circular needle and MC, beg at shoulder, pick up and k118 (122, 126, 126) sts evenly spaced around neck. Place a marker to indicate beg of rnd. Work k1, p1 ribbing for 5 rnds. Bind off in ribbing. Weave in loose ends on WS of fabric.

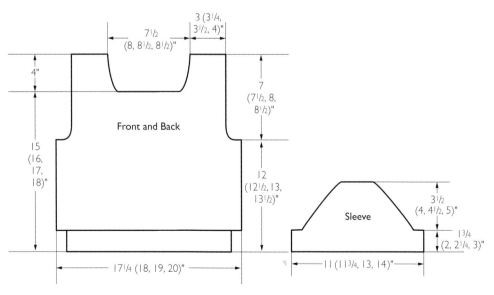

W herever you head—to the beach, out on a picnic, or off to work, this sampling of summer wear will have you smile with style. Just wait until you see the lovely stitches—pretty lace, cables, ruffles, plaid, and more. Plus there's an oh-so-sweet sweater and purse set for a little girl, and a subtle stars-and-stripes patterned throw to show your patriotism—all in this chapter devoted to...

Summer

SEA CAPS TOP This attractive top works up quickly in two easy pieces with ribbed straps. The elegant ribbon/yarn introduces luxury to summer evenings. For cooler days, just wear it over a colorful T-shirt. Instructions begin on page 168.

LACE AND CABLES CARDIGAN Zigzag eyelets mirror cable patterns on this soft summer cardigan. For intermediate knitters, this lightweight sweater will come in handy when the sun sets on a summer's eve. Instructions begin on page 169.

fun in the sun

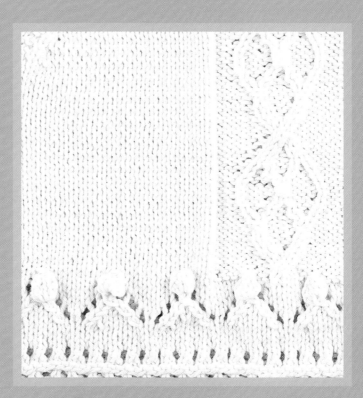

TINY TOP A bit of lace, bobbles, and a center cable on front and back make this project a joy to complete. The top is so quick to knit (and so cute!), you'll want to make it in a variety of colors. Instructions begin on page 171.

summer top

LINGERIE-INSPIRED TOP
A hot look during hot weather, this crochet-edged top shows off a ribbed pattern with knits worked in the back loops on the right side and the purls worked in the back loops on the wrong side. The lower edge adds swing to the fitted top. Instructions begin on page 174.

PLAID PULLOVER With directions for sizes XS to XXL, this pretty sweater style is becoming on many women. Square armholes and short sleeves, and a square mitered neckline add to the design. Instructions begin on page 173.

dressing delicate

FAUX CABLE TWIN SET
A short summer jacket rests over the easy-to-work mock turtleneck tank, making a great ensemble for an air-conditioned office. Simple Fair Isle patterns border the lower edges of the tank and the wrists of the cardigan. Instructions begin on page 176.

twin set

UNITED WE STAND PULLOVER

Show your colors in this vibrant sweater, complete with boat neck, dropped shoulders, and three-quarter sleeves. Stockinette-stitch stripes are set off with rows of eyelets. Instructions begin on page 178.

STARS & STRIPES THROW

A subtle flag pattern is worked into this 44×56-inch throw. Made with 20 separate blocks, this is a good project to carry along on summer trips. A single crochet border is worked around the edge after the blocks are joined together. Instructions begin on page 180.

stars & stripes

GARDEN PARTY SWEATER AND PURSE Dainty as a daisy, this sweet little number blooms with lazy daisies randomly placed among a sprinkling of eyelets. Crochet provides pretty borders at the neck and arm openings. The matching purse has chained handles and floral buttons. Instructions for the pair begin on page 180.

love me knots

FISH PLACE MAT The fun fish on this mat is worked from head to fin, making the knitting interesting and not terribly difficult. Easy seed stitches border the mat. A set of these swimmers would surely add a sea of fun to a patio table for any summertime get-together. Instructions begin on page 182.

SUMMER SUN TOP Knit in a cotton/acrylic blend, this top is an easy combination of knit and purl stitching to form lively chevrons along the bodice. Set-in cap sleeves, a straight style, and a feminine neck treatment make this a delightful sweater to wear. Instructions begin on page 183.

Sea Caps Top

photo on page 154

SKILL LEVEL: Intermediate

SIZE: S (MEDIUM, L, XL)
Note: *The pattern is written for the smallest size with changes for larger sizes in parentheses. When only one number is given, it applies to all sizes. For ease in working, before you begin, circle all numbers pertaining to the size you are knitting.*

FINISHED MEASUREMENTS:
Bust: 32 (36, 40, 44)"
Length: 17½ (17½, 18, 18½)"

MATERIALS:
- Berroco's Glace, 100% rayon, worsted weight ribbon (75 yards per hank): 7 (8, 9, 10) hanks of Jewel Teal (2537)
- Size 7 (4.5mm) knitting needles or size needed to obtain gauge
- Size 5 (3.75mm) knitting needles
- Yarn needle

GAUGE:
In Body Pattern with larger needles, 20 sts and 28 rows = 4"/10cm.
TAKE TIME TO CHECK YOUR GAUGE.

SPECIAL ABBREVIATIONS:
Ssk: Sl next 2 sts knitwise, one at a time to right-hand needle, insert tip of left-hand needle into fronts of these 2 sts and k them together.
Sl 1: Slip next stitch purlwise and with yarn on WS of fabric.

P2tog-b: Turn work slightly, insert needle from left to right into second and first sts; p the sts together.

STITCHES USED:
Body Pattern (a multiple of 10 sts; a rep of 12 rows)
Row 1 (WS): Purl.
Row 2: K2; * in next st [(k1, yo) 3 times, k1—7 sts], k9; rep from * across ending last rep k7.
Row 3: Knit.
Row 4: K1; * k2tog, k5, ssk, k7; rep from * across, ending last rep k6.
Row 5: P6; * p2tog-b, p1, sl 1, p1, p2tog, p7; rep from * across, ending last rep p1.
Row 6: K1; * k2tog, sl 1, ssk, k7; rep from * across, ending last rep k6.
Row 7: Purl.
Row 8: K7; * in next st [(k1, yo) 3 times, k1], k9; rep from * across, ending last rep k2.
Row 9: Knit.
Row 10: K6; * k2tog, k5, ssk, k7; rep from * across, ending last rep k1.
Row 11: P1; * p2tog-b, p1, sl 1, p1, p2tog, p7; rep from * across, ending last rep p6.
Row 12: K6; * k2tog, sl 1, ssk, k7; rep from * across, ending last rep k1.
Rep Rows 1–12 for Body Pattern.

INSTRUCTIONS:
BACK
Beg at the lower edge with smaller needles, cast on 79 (89, 99, 109) sts.
Ribbing
Row 1 (WS): P1; (k1, p1) across.
Row 2: K1; (p1, k1) across.
Rep Ribbing Rows 1–2 to approx 1" from beg, ending with a WS row. Change to larger needles, k across, inc 1 st—80 (90, 100, 110) sts. Work Body Pattern Rows 1–12 to approx 11½" from beg, ending with Row 6 or Row 12. P 1 row. Change to smaller needles and k 1 row dec 1 st—79 (89, 99, 109) sts. Work Ribbing Rows 1–2 twice, rep Row 1 again. K 2 rows. Bind off knitwise.

FRONT
Work as for Back.

STRAPS (make two)
With smaller needles, cast on 15 sts. Work Ribbing as for Back until piece measures approx 10 (10, 11, 12)" from beg, ending with a WS row. Bind off loosely and knitwise.

FINISHING
Join side seams. For first strap, place a marker 3" from side seam then 2" from first marker. Sew strap between markers. Rep this process, joining straps to front and back.

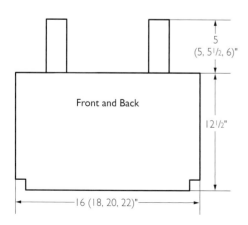

5 (5, 5½, 6)"

Front and Back

12½"

16 (18, 20, 22)"

Lace and Cables Cardigan

photo on page 155

SKILL LEVEL: Intermediate

SIZES: S (MEDIUM, L, XL, 2XL)
Note: *The pattern is written for the smallest size with changes for larger sizes in parentheses. When only one number is given, it applies to all sizes. For ease in working, before you begin circle all numbers pertaining to the size you are knitting.*

FINISHED MEASUREMENTS:
Bust (buttoned): 39 (41, 44, 47, 50)"
Length: 23 (23½, 23½, 24, 24½)"

MATERIALS:
- Patons Grace, 100% cotton, sport weight yarn (136 yards per skein): 10 (11, 11, 12, 13) skeins of Apricot (60603)
- Sizes 3 (3.25 mm) and 5 (3.75mm) knitting needles or size needed to obtain gauge
- Cable needle (cn)
- Seven ½-inch-diameter buttons
- Yarn needle

GAUGE:
In St st on larger needles, 24 sts and 32 rows = 4"/10cm.
TAKE TIME TO CHECK YOUR GAUGE.

ABBREVIATIONS:
KB1: K into back lp of next st.
PB1: P into back lp of next st. Turn work slightly, insert right-hand needle from left to right into st, and p in the usual manner.
C6B: Sl next 3 sts onto cn and leave at back of work. K3, then k3 from cn.
Tw10B: Slip next 8 sts onto cable needle and leave at back of work. (KB1) twice. Slip 6 sts from cn back onto left-hand needle. Bring rem 2 sts on cn to front of work between needles. K6 from left-hand needle, then (KB1) twice from cn.
Ssk (slip, slip, knit): Sl next 2 sts knitwise, one at a time to right-hand needle, insert tip of left-hand needle into fronts of these 2 sts and k tog.

STITCHES USED:
Cable Panel (worked over 10 sts; a rep of 18 rows)
Row 1 (RS): (KB1) twice, k6, (KB1) twice.
Row 2 and following WS rows: (PB1) twice, p6, (PB1) twice.
Row 3: (KB1) twice, C6B, (KB1) twice.
Row 5: Rep Row 1.
Row 7: Tw10B.
Row 9: Rep Row 1.
Row 11: Rep Row 3.
Rows 13, 15, and 17: Rep Row 1.
Row 18: Rep Row 2.
These 18 rows form Cable Panel.

Lace Panel (worked over 14 sts; a rep of 48 rows)
Row 1 (RS): K1, yo, ssk, (k1, p1) 5 times, k1.
Row 2: (K1, p1) 6 times, p2.
Row 3: K2, yo, ssk, (p1, k1) 5 times.
Row 4: (K1, p1) 5 times, p4.
Row 5: K3, yo, ssk, (k1, p1) 4 times, k1.
Row 6: (K1, p1) 5 times, p4.
Row 7: K4, yo, ssk, (p1, k1) 4 times.
Row 8: (K1, p1) 4 times, p6.
Row 9: K5, yo, ssk, (k1, p1) 3 times, k1.
Row 10: (K1, p1) 4 times, p6.
Row 11: K6, yo, ssk, (p1, k1) 3 times.
Row 12: (K1, p1) 3 times, p8.

Row 13: K7, yo, ssk, (k1, p1) twice, k1.
Row 14: (K1, p1) 3 times, p8.
Row 15: K8, yo, ssk, (p1, k1) twice.
Row 16: (K1, p1) twice, p10.
Row 17: K9, yo, ssk, k1, p1, k1.
Row 18: K1, p1, k1, p11.
Row 19: K10, yo, ssk, p1, k1.
Row 20: K1, p13.
Row 21: K11, yo, ssk, k1.
Row 22: K1, p13.
Row 23: K12, yo, ssk.
Row 24: P14.
Row 25: (K1, p1) 5 times, k1, k2tog, yo, k1.
Row 26: P3, (k1, p1) 5 times, k1.
Row 27: (K1, p1) 5 times, k2tog, yo, k2.
Row 28: P5, (k1, p1) 4 times, k1.
Row 29: (K1, p1) 4 times, k1, k2tog, yo, k3.
Row 30: P5, (k1, p1) 4 times, k1.
Row 31: (K1, p1) 4 times, k2tog, yo, k4.
Row 32: P7, (k1, p1) 3 times, k1.
Row 33: (K1, p1) 3 times, k1, k2tog, yo, k5.
Row 34: P7, (k1, p1) 3 times, k1.
Row 35: (K1, p1) 3 times, k2tog, yo, k6.
Row 36: P9, (k1, p1) twice, k1.
Row 37: (K1, p1) twice, k1, k2tog, yo, k7.

Lace and Cables Cardigan

continued from page 169

Row 38: P9, (k1, p1) twice, k1.
Row 39: (K1, p1) twice, k2tog, yo, k8.
Row 40: P11, k1, p1, k1.
Row 41: K1, p1, k1, k2tog, yo, k9.
Row 42: P11, k1, p1, k1.
Row 43: K1, p1, k2tog, yo, k10.
Row 44: P13, k1.
Row 45: K1, k2tog, yo, k11.
Row 46: P13, k1.
Row 47: K2tog, yo, k12.
Row 48: P14.
These 48 rows form Lace Panel.

INSTRUCTIONS:
BACK
Beg at lower edge with smaller needles cast on 117 (123, 131, 141, 149) sts.
Row 1 (RS): P1; (k1, p1) across.
Last row forms seed st pat. Work additional 7 rows in seed st pat. With larger needles work in St st until Back measures approx 15" from beg, ending with a WS row.
Armhole Shaping
At beg of the next 4 rows, bind off 8 (8, 9, 10, 11) sts—85 (91, 95, 101, 105) sts. Dec 1 st each end of row on next and following alt rows until there are 75 (79, 81, 85, 87) sts.
Work even to approx 23 (23½, 23½, 24, 24½)" from beg, ending with a WS row.

Shoulder Shaping
Bind off 7 (8, 9, 9, 10) sts beg next 2 rows, then 8 (9, 9, 10, 10) sts beg following 2 rows. Leave rem 45 (45, 45, 47, 47) sts on a spare needle.

RIGHT FRONT
Beg at lower edge with smaller needles, cast on 57 (61, 65, 69, 73) sts. Work 8 rows in seed st pat as for Back, inc 4 (3, 3, 4, 4) sts evenly spaced across last row—61 (64, 68, 73, 77) sts.
Change to larger needles.
Body Pattern
Row 1 (RS): P2, work first row Lace Panel across next 14 sts, p2, work first row Cable Panel across next 10 sts, p2, k to end of row.
Row 2: P31 (34, 38, 43, 47), k2, work 2nd row Cable Panel across next 10 sts, k2, work 2nd row Lace Panel across next 14 sts, k2.
Cont in est pat to approx 15" from beg, ending with a WS row.
Armhole Shaping
Bind off 8 (8, 9, 10, 11) sts beg next and following alt row—45 (48, 50, 53, 55) sts. Work 1 row even in pat. Dec 1 st at beg of row on next and following alt rows until there are 40 (42, 43, 45, 46) sts. Work even to approx 20½ (21, 21, 21, 21½)" from beg, ending with a RS row.
Neck Shaping
Bind off 15 sts beg next row. Dec 1 st at neck edge on next 7 rows, then on following alt rows until there are 15 (17, 18, 19, 20) sts. Work even to approx 23 (23½, 23½, 24, 24½)" from beg, ending with a WS row.
Shoulder Shaping
Bind off 7 (8, 9, 9, 10) sts beg next row. Work 1 row even. Bind off rem 8 (9, 9, 10, 10) sts.

LEFT FRONT
Beg at lower edge, with smaller needles, cast on 57 (61, 65, 69, 73) sts. Work 8 rows in seed st pat as for Back, inc 4 (3, 3, 4, 4) sts evenly spaced across last row—61 (64, 68, 73, 77) sts.
Change to larger needles.
Body Pattern
Row 1 (RS): K31 (34, 38, 43, 47), p2, work first row Cable Panel across next 10 sts, p2, work 25th row Lace Panel across next 14 sts, p2, k to end of row.
Row 2: K2, work 26th row Lace Panel across next 14 sts, k2, work 2nd row Cable Panel across next 10 sts, k2, p to end of row.
Cont in est pat to approx 15" from beg, ending with a RS row.
Armhole Shaping
Bind off 8 (8, 9, 10, 11) sts beg next and following alt row—45 (48, 50, 53, 55) sts. Dec 1 st at end of row on next and following alt rows until there are 40 (42, 43, 45, 46) sts. Work even to approx 20½ (21, 21, 21, 21½)" from beg, ending with a WS row.

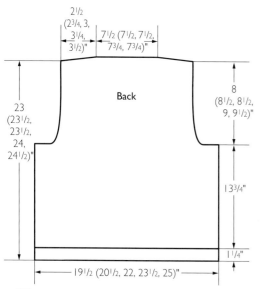

Back

23 (23½, 23½, 24, 24½)"

2½ (2¾, 3, 3¼, 3½)"

7½ (7½, 7½, 7¾, 7¾)"

8 (8½, 8½, 9, 9½)"

13¾"

1¼"

19½ (20½, 22, 23½, 25)"

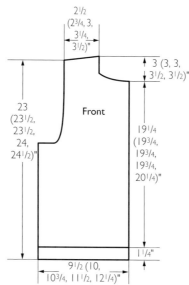

Front

23 (23½, 23½, 24, 24½)"

2½ (2¾, 3, 3¼, 3½)"

3 (3, 3, 3½, 3½)"

19¼ (19¾, 19¾, 19¾, 20¼)"

1¼"

9½ (10, 10¾, 11½, 12¼)"

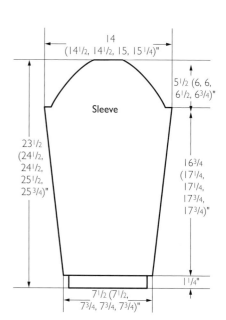

Sleeve

14 (14½, 14½, 15, 15¼)"

5½ (6, 6, 6½, 6¾)"

23½ (24½, 24½, 25½, 25¾)"

16¾ (17¼, 17¼, 17¾, 17¾)"

1¼"

7½ (7½, 7¾, 7¾, 7¾)"

Neck Shaping

Bind off 15 sts beg next row. Work 1 row even in pat. Dec 1 st at neck edge on next 7 rows, then on following alt rows until there are 15 (17, 18, 19, 20) sts. Work even to approx 23 (23½, 23½, 24, 24½)" from beg, ending with a RS row.

Shoulder Shaping

Bind off 7 (8, 9, 9, 10) sts beg next row. Work 1 row even. Bind off rem 8 (9, 9, 10, 10) sts.

SLEEVES (make two)

Beg at lower edge with smaller needles, cast on 45 (45, 47, 47, 47) sts. Work 8 rows in seed st pat as for Back, inc 3 sts evenly spaced across last row—48 (48, 50, 50, 50) sts. Change to larger needles.

Body Pattern

Row 1 (RS): K15 (15, 16, 16, 16), p2, work first row Lace Panel across next 14 sts, p2, k to end of row.

Row 2: P15 (15, 16, 16, 16), k2, work 2nd row Lace Panel across next 14 sts, k2, p to end of row.
Cont in est pat shaping sides by inc 1 st each edge on next and every 6th row 17 (18, 17, 19, 20) times more—84 (86, 86, 90, 92) sts. Work even to approx 18 (18½, 18½, 19, 19)" from beg, ending with a WS row.

Shape Cap

Keeping cont of est pat, bind off 4 (4, 4, 5, 5) sts beg next 2 rows, then dec 1 st each end of next and every alt row until there are 54 (48, 48, 48, 46) sts. Dec 1 st each end of every row until there are 12 (14, 14, 14, 16) sts. Bind off.

FINISHING

Sew shoulder seams.

Neckband

With RS facing using smaller needles, pick up and k27 (27, 27, 30, 30) sts up Right Front neck edge. K45 (45, 45, 47, 47) from Back spare needle, dec 4 sts evenly across. Pick up and k 27 (27, 27, 30, 30) sts down Left Front neck edge—95 (95, 95, 103, 103) sts. Work 7 rows in seed st pat as for Back. Bind off in pat.

Buttonhole Band

With RS facing, using smaller needles, pick up and k115 (117, 117, 117, 121) sts evenly spaced from lower edge to top of neckband along Right Front edge. Work 3 rows in seed st pat as for Back.

Row 4 (Buttonholes–RS): Pat across 2 (4, 4, 4, 2) sts. * Bind off 2 sts, pat across 16 (16, 16, 16, 17) sts (including st on needle after bind off). Rep from * 5 times more. Bind off 2 sts. Pat to end of row.

Row 5: Work in pat, casting on 2 sts over bound off sts. Work additional 2 rows even in pat. Bind off in pat.

Left Front Band

With RS facing, using smaller needles, pick up and k115 (117, 117, 117, 121) sts evenly spaced from top of neckband to lower edge along Left Front edge. Work 7 rows in seed st pat as for Back. Bind off in pat. Sew in sleeves. Sew side and sleeve seams. Sew buttons opposite buttonholes.

Tiny Top

photos on pages 156–157

SKILL LEVEL: Experienced

SIZES: SMALL (M, L)
Note: *The pattern is written for the smallest size with changes for larger sizes in parentheses. When only one number is given, it applies to all sizes. For ease in working, before you begin,* circle all numbers pertaining to the size you are knitting.

FINISHED MEASUREMENTS:

Bust: 31 (34½, 38)"
Length: 18 (18½, 19)"

MATERIALS:

- Elmore-Pisgah, Peaches & Crème, worsted weight cotton (2.5 ounces per ball): 3 (4, 5) balls of Ecru (4)
- Size 7 (4.5mm) knitting needles or size needed to obtain gauge
- Size 6 (4.25 mm) knitting needles
- Cable needle (cn)
- Yarn needle
- 2 ring-type stitch markers
- Size G/6 (4.5mm) crochet hook

GAUGE:

In St st with larger needles, 17 sts and 27 rows = 4"/10cm.
TAKE TIME TO CHECK YOUR GAUGE.

SPECIAL ABBREVIATIONS:

Sl 1: Slip next stitch purlwise and with yarn on WS of fabric.

MB (make bobble): In next st [(k1, yo) twice, k1]; turn; p5; turn; k5; turn; p2tog, p1, p2tog; turn; sl 1, k2tog, psso. Push bobble to RS.

C4B (cable 4 back): Slip 2 sts to cn and hold at back, k2, k2 from cn.

T3B (twist 3 back): Slip 1 st to cn and hold at back, k2, p1 from cn.

T3F (twist 3 front): Slip 2 sts to cn and hold at front, p1, k2 from cn.
RT (right twist): Pass needle in front of first stitch, k second st, k first stitch and slip both sts off needle.
LT (left twist): Pass needle behind first stitch, k second stitch through the back loop, k first stitch and slip both sts off needle.
SFC (single front cross): Slip 1 st to cn and hold in front, p1, k1 from cn.
SBC (single back cross): Slip 1 st to cn and hold in back, k1, p1 from cn.
M1 (make one stitch): On WS, pick up strand of yarn lying between last st worked and next stitch, and p into back of it. On RS, pick up strand of yarn lying between last st worked and next st, and k into back of it.
Ssk (slip, slip, knit): Slip next 2 sts knitwise, one at a time to right-hand needle, insert tip of left-hand needle into fronts of these 2 sts and k them tog.
K1b: K in back loop of next stitch.

STITCHES USED:
Lace (a multiple of 8 sts + 3 sts; over 6 rows)
Row 1 (RS): K2; * yo, sl 1, k1, psso, k3, k2tog, yo, k1; rep from * across, ending k2 instead of k1.
Row 2 and each WS row: Purl.
Row 3: K3; * yo, sl 1, k1, psso, k1, k2tog, yo, k3; rep from * across.

Row 5: K4; * yo, sl 1, k2tog, psso, yo, k5; rep from * across, ending k4 instead of k5.
Row 6: Purl.

Cable Panel (over 18 sts; a rep of 24 rows)
Row 1 (WS): K7, p4, k7.
Row 2: P7, C4B, p7.
Row 3: Rep Row 1.
Row 4: P6, T3B, T3F, p6.
Row 5 and all following WS rows: K the k sts and p the p sts as they appear.
Row 6: P5, T3B, p2, T3F, p5.
Row 8: P5, RT, p4, LT, p5.
Row 10: P4, SBC, SFC, p2, SBC, SFC, p4.
Row 12: P3, (SBC, p2, SFC) twice, p3.
Row 14: P3, k1, p4, k2; then slip the last 2 sts worked onto cn and wrap yarn 6 times counter-clockwise around these 2 sts; then slip the 2 sts back to right-hand needle; p4, k1, p3.
Row 16: P3, (SFC, p2, SBC) twice, p3.
Row 18: P4, SFC, SBC, p2, SFC, SBC, p4.
Row 20: P5, LT, p4, RT, p5.
Row 22: P5, T3F, p2, T3B, p5.
Row 24: P6, T3F, T3B, p6.
Rep Rows 1–24 for Cable Panel.

INSTRUCTIONS:
BACK
Beg at lower edge and above the border, with larger needles, cast on 67 (75, 83) sts. K 1 row. P 1 row.
Eyelets: K2; (yo, k2tog) across, ending k1. Beg with a p row, work 5 St st rows. Rep Lace Rows 1–6. **Next RS Row:** K5; (MB, k7) across, ending MB, k5.
Next Row: P25 (29, 33); place marker (pm); k7, p1, M1, p2, k7; pm; p25 (29, 33).
Next Row: K1, M1, k24 (28, 32); p7, k4, p7, k24 (28, 32), M1, k1—70 (78, 86) sts. Keeping sts outside of markers in St st, beg with Row 1 of Cable Panel. Rep Cable Panel Rows 2–24, then Rows 1–6.
Armhole Shaping
Row 7 (WS): K1, work est pat across, ending k1.
Row 8: Work est pat.

Row 9: K2, work est pat across, ending k2.
Row 10: Work est pat.
Row 11: K3, work est pat across, ending k3.
Row 12: Work est pat.
Row 13: K4, work est pat across, ending k4.
Row 14: K4, ssk, work est pat across to last 6 sts, k2tog, k4.
Row 15: K4, work est pat across, ending k4. Cont working garter st on first and last 4 sts and dec as est on following alt rows, completing Row 24 of Cable Panel then working Rows 1–3. **Next Row:** K4, ssk, k across to last 6 sts, k2tog, k4—54 (62, 70) sts. K 7 rows for neck border.
Neck and Straps
K11 (12, 13), bind off center 32 (38, 44) sts, k to end. Place first 11 (12, 13) sts onto a holder. **Right Strap:** K11 (12, 13). **Next Row:** K2tog, k to end. K 1 row. Dec 1 st at neck edge on each RS row 4 times more. Work even on 6 (7, 8) sts until piece measures approx 8 (8½, 9)" from first armhole dec, ending with a WS row. Bind off knitwise and loosely. **Left Strap:** With the WS facing, return sts from holder to larger needle; join yarn and k across. **Next Row:** K across to last 2 sts, k2tog. Dec 1 st at neck edge on each RS row 4 times more. Complete as for Right Strap.
Lower Border
With the *WS* facing using smaller needles, pick up and k65 (73, 81) sts evenly spaced along lower edge.
Row 1 (RS): K1; (p1, k1b) across, ending p1, k1.
Row 2: P1; (k1, p1) across.
Rep Rows 1–2 for 6 total times. K across. Bind off loosely and knitwise on WS of fabric.

FRONT
Work as for Back.

FINISHING
Join shoulder and side seams. Weave in loose ends on WS of fabric. For border: with crochet hook, sl st around neck and armhole openings.

Front and Back

9½ (11, 12¼)"
1½ (1¾, 2)"
18 (18½, 19)"
5 (5½, 6)"
3"
15½ (17¼, 19)"
7½"
2½"
14½ (16¼, 18)"

Plaid Pullover

photo on page 159

SKILL LEVEL: Intermediate

SIZES: XS (SMALL, MEDIUM, L, XL, XXL)
Note: *The pattern is written for the smallest size with changes for larger sizes in parentheses. When only one number is given, it applies to all sizes. For ease in working, before you begin, circle all numbers pertaining to the size you are knitting.*

FINISHED MEASUREMENTS:
Bust: 35 (39, 42½, 46, 50, 54)"
Length: 19½ (20, 20, 20½, 21, 21½)"

MATERIALS:
- Lion Brand Yarn's Cotton-Ease, 50% cotton/50% acrylic, worsted weight yarn (207 yards per skein): 1 (1, 2, 2, 2, 3) skeins of Bubblegum (102) for Color A; 3 (3, 4, 4, 4, 5) skeins of Vanilla (100) for Color B; 1 (1, 2, 2, 2, 3) skeins each of Banana Cream (157) for Color C and Mint (156) for Color D
- Size 7 (4.5mm) knitting needles or size needed to obtain gauge
- Size 6 (4.25mm) knitting needles
- Size 6 (4.25 mm) circular knitting needle 16" long
- Yarn needle

GAUGE:
In Plaid Pattern with larger needles, 32 sts and 48 rows = 6"/15.25cm. TAKE TIME TO CHECK YOUR GAUGE.

Note: *Always sl sts purlwise unless noted otherwise.*

STITCHES USED:
Plaid Pattern (a multiple of 10 sts + 3 sts; a rep of 12 rows)
Row 1 (RS): With Color C, (k1, sl next st with yarn in back) twice; * k5, (sl next st with yarn in back, k1) twice, sl next st with yarn in back. Rep from * across, ending row with k5, (sl next st with yarn in back, k1) twice.
Row 2: With Color C, (k1, sl next st with yarn in front) twice; * k5, (sl next st with yarn in front, k1) twice, sl next st with

yarn in front. Rep from * across, ending row with k5, (sl next st with yarn in front, k1) twice.
Row 3: With B, sl next st with yarn in back, k1, sl next st with yarn in back; * k7, sl next st with yarn in back, k1, sl next st with yarn in back. Rep from * across.
Row 4: With B, p across.
Rows 5–6: As Rows 1 and 2 using D instead of C.
Rows 7–8: As Rows 3 and 4.
Rows 9–10: As Rows 1 and 2 using A instead of C.
Rows 11–12: As Rows 3 and 4.
Repeat Rows 1–12.

INSTRUCTIONS:
BACK
Beg at lower edge with smaller needles and Color A, cast on 93 (103, 113, 123, 133, 143) sts.
Ribbing
Row 1 (RS): * K1, p1. Rep from * across, ending row with k1. Change to B.
Row 2: * P1, k1. Rep from * across, ending row with p1.
Rep Ribbing Rows 1–2, using B only, to approx 1½" from beg, ending after a WS row. Change to larger needles, and k 1 row, then p 1 row.
Body Pattern
Change to C, beg Plaid Pattern, and work even to approx 11 (11, 11, 11, 11½, 11¾)" from beg, ending after a WS row.
Armhole Shaping
At beg of the next 2 rows, bind off 8 (8, 8, 13, 13, 16) sts—77 (87, 97, 97, 107, 111) sts. Work even to approx 18½ (19, 19, 19½, 20, 20½)" from beg, ending after a WS row.

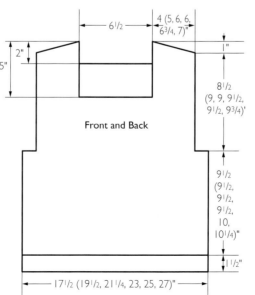

Front and Back

6½
4 (5, 6, 6, 6¾, 7)"
2"
5"
1"
8½ (9, 9, 9½, 9½, 9¾)'
9½ (9½, 9½, 9½, 10, 10¼)"
1½"
17½ (19½, 21¼, 23, 25, 27)"

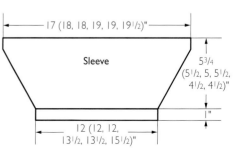

Sleeve

17 (18, 18, 19, 19, 19½)"
5¾ (5½, 5, 5½, 4½, 4½)"
1"
12 (12, 12, 13½, 13½, 15½)"

Plaid Pullover
continued from page 173

Neck Shaping
Work in pat across first 21 (26, 31, 31, 36, 38) sts; join new strands and bind off center 35 sts; work to end of row. Working sides separately and at the same time, work even to approx 19½ (20, 20, 20½, 21, 21½)" from beg, ending after a WS row.

Shoulder Shaping
Attach shoulder edge, bind off 5 (7, 8, 8, 9, 10) sts 3 times and 6 (5, 7, 7, 9, 8) sts once.

FRONT
Same as Back until piece measures approx 15½ (16, 16, 16½, 17, 17½)" from beg, ending after a WS row.

Neck Shaping
Work in pat across first 21 (26, 31, 31, 36, 38) sts; join new strands and bind off center 35 sts; work to end of row. Complete as for Back.

SLEEVES (make two)
Beg at lower edge, with smaller needles and Color A, cast on 63 (63, 63, 73, 73, 83) sts. Rep Ribbing as for Back to approx 1" from beg, ending after a WS row. Change to larger needles and B, and k 1 row, then p 1 row.

Body Pattern
Change to C and beg Plaid Pattern. Beg with next RS row, including new sts into pat as they accumulate, inc at each edge every row 0 (0, 4, 4, 12, 8) times, then every other row 11 (16, 12, 10, 2, 2) times, then every fourth row 3 (0, 0, 0, 0, 0) times—91 (95, 95, 101, 101, 103) sts. Work even to approx 6¾ (6½, 6, 6½, 5½, 5½)" from beg, ending after WS row. Bind off.

FINISHING
Join shoulder seams.

Neckband
With RS facing, circular needle, and B, pick up and k35 sts along back of neckline, 1 st in corner, 29 sts along left side of neckline, 1 st in corner, 35 sts along front of neckline, 1 st in corner, 29 sts along right side of neckline, 1 st in corner—132 sts total. Mark each corner st. Work rnds of K1

P1 rib as follows: Rib to 1 st before marked st; * sl next st and marked st knitwise at the same time, k1, p2sso, work to 1 st before next marked st. Rep from * around. When neckband measures approx 1" from beg, change to A and work 1 more rnd as you bind off in rib, working dec as before. Set in sleeves, sewing bound off sts to sleeve sides for square armholes. Sew underarm and side seams.

Lingerie-Inspired Top

photo on page 158

SKILL LEVEL: Intermediate

SIZES: S (MEDIUM, L, XL)
Note: *The pattern is written for the smallest size with changes for larger sizes in parentheses. When only one number is given, it applies to all sizes. For ease in working, before you begin, circle all numbers pertaining to the size you are knitting.*

FINISHED MEASUREMENTS:
Bust: 30 (32, 34, 36)"
Length: 20¼ (21, 22¼, 23¼)

MATERIALS:
- Classic Elite Provence, 100% mercerized Egyptian cotton (256 yards per hank): 2 (3, 3, 4) hanks of Bright Chartreuse (2681)
- Size 6 (4.25mm) knitting needles or size needed to obtain gauge
- Size F/5 (4mm) crochet hook
- Tapestry needle
- 1½ yards ⅜" satin ribbon
- ⅜" decorative trim
- 39 small scrystal beads
- Sewing needle and matching thread

GAUGE:
In Body Pattern (when slightly stretched), 24 sts and 23 rows = 4"/10cm.
TAKE TIME TO CHECK YOUR GAUGE.

ABBREVIATIONS:
K1b: K in back lp of next st.
P1b: Turn work slightly, insert right-hand needle from left to right into the back lp of next st and p.

Ssk: Slip next two sts knitwise, one at a time to right-hand needle, insert tip of left-hand needle into fronts of these 2 sts and k them together.
Sl 1: Slip next st purlwise and with yarn on WS of fabric.
P2togb: Turn work slightly, insert right-hand needle from left to right into the back loop of 2nd and then first sts, and p them together.

STITCHES USED:
Border (a multiple of 12 sts + 11 sts; a rep of 2 rows)
Row 1 (RS): K1, (p1, k1b) 4 times; * yo, k2tog, k1b, ssk, yo **, (k1b, p1) 3 times, k1b; rep from * across, ending last rep at **, (k1b, p1) 4 times, k1.
Row 2: P1, (k1, p1b) 4 times; * p2, p1b, p2 **, (p1b, k1) 3 times, p1b; rep from * across, ending last rep at **, (p1b, k1) 4 times, p1.
Rep Rows 1–2 for Border.

Body Pattern (a multiple of 2 sts + 1 st; a rep of 2 rows)
Row 1 (RS): K1; (p1, k1b) across, ending p1, k1.
Row 2 (WS): P1, (k1, p1b) across, ending k1, p1.
Rep Rows 1–2 for Body Pattern.

INSTRUCTIONS:
BACK AND FRONT (make alike)
Beg at the lower edge, cast on 167 (179, 191, 203) sts. Work Border Rows 1–2 for 9 total times.
Dec Row 1 (RS): K1, (p1, k1b) 4 times; * k2tog, k1b, ssk **, (k1b, p1) 3 times, k1b; rep from * across, ending last rep at **, (k1b, p1) 4 times, k1—141 (151, 161, 171) sts.
Row 2: P1, (k1, p1b) 4 times; * p1, p1b, p1, (p1b, k1) 3 times, p1b; rep from * across, ending p1, p1b, p1, (p1b, k1) 4 times, p1.
Dec Row 3: K1, (p1, k1b) 4 times; * (sl 1, k2tog, psso), (k1b, p1) 3 times, k1b; rep from * across, ending (sl 1, k2tog, psso), (k1b, p1) 4 times, k1—115 (123, 131, 139) sts.
Row 4: P1, (k1, p1b) 4 times, * p1, (p1b, k1) 3 times, p1b; rep from * across, ending p1, (p1b, k1) 4 times, p1.
Dec Row 5: K1, (p1, k1b) 3 times, p1; * (sl 1, k2tog, psso), (p1, k1b) twice, p1; rep from * across, ending

(sl 1, k2tog, psso), p1, (k1b, p1) 3 times, k1—89 (95, 101, 107) sts.
Row 6: P1, (k1, p1b) 3 times; * k1, p1, k1, p1b, k1, p1b; rep from * across, ending k1, p1, k1, (p1b, k1) 3 times, p1. Beg Body Pattern and work even to approx 11½ (12, 12½, 13)" from beg, ending with a WS row.

Armhole and Neck Shaping
For size S and L ONLY, bind off 1 st at beg of next 2 rows.
For all sizes work as follows:
Row 1 (RS): K1, ssk, work pat across to last 3 sts, k2tog, k1.
Row 2: P1, p2tog, pat across to last 3 sts, p2togb, p1.

Row 3: K1, ssk, pat on next 38 (42, 44, 48) sts, bind off center st, pat to last 3 sts, k2tog, k1.

Right Bodice
Row 1 (WS): P1, p2tog, pat to 3 sts before neck, p1; turn and leave rem sts for later.
Row 2: K1, ssk, pat to last 3 sts, k2tog, k1.
Row 3: P1, p2tog, pat to last 3 sts, p2togb, p1.
Rep Rows 2–3 until 5 sts rem. On next WS row, p1, sl 1, p2tog, psso, p1. **Next Row:** Sl 1, k2tog, psso. Fasten off leaving an 8" tail.

Left Bodice
With the WS facing, join yarn. P1, work est pat across, ending p2togb, p1.
Row 2: K1, ssk, pat to last 3 sts, k2tog, k1.
Row 3: P1, p2tog, pat to last 3 sts, p2togb, p1.
Rep Rows 2–3 until 5 sts rem. Complete as for Right Bodice.

FINISHING
Join side seams. With the RS facing and crochet hook, join yarn at underarm with a slip st. Ch 1, sc evenly around entire bodice; at the 4 bodice outside points, ch 1. For inverted points, draw up a lp in last st before bind off, draw up a lp in st after bind off, yo and draw through all 3 lps on hook—dec made. Slip st in first sc, ch 1; * slip st, ch 1 in each sc around for rickrack edging. At end, fasten off. **Lower Edge Trim:** Join at lower side seam and work (slip st, ch 1) evenly around.

Straps (make two)
Cut two lengths each of ribbon and decorative trim, measuring approx 13½" each. Sew trim to ribbon to form a strap. Attach strap to WS of front bodice point. Try on garment to determine strap length. Sew opposite end of strap to WS of back bodice point. Randomly sew 18 beads to top of strap.

Bow
Make a bow with remaining ribbon. Cut a small piece of trim to wrap around center knot of bow. Sew in place. Sew 3 beads onto front of the trim. Attach bow to front of V-neck.

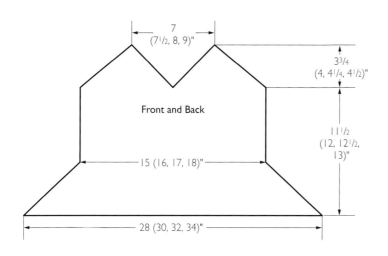

7
(7½, 8, 9)"

3¾
(4, 4¼, 4½)"

Front and Back

15 (16, 17, 18)"

11½
(12, 12½, 13)"

28 (30, 32, 34)"

Faux Cable Twin Set

photos on pages 160–161

SKILL LEVEL: Intermediate

SIZES: XS (SMALL, M, L, XL)
Note: *The pattern is written for the smallest size with changes for larger sizes in parentheses. When only one number is given, it applies to all sizes. For ease in working, before you begin, circle all numbers pertaining to the size you are knitting.*

FINISHED MEASUREMENTS:
Tank
Bust: 34 (36, 38, 39½, 41½)"
Length: 20 (21, 21½, 22, 22½)"

Jacket
Bust: 38 (40, 42, 44, 46)"
Length: 17 (18, 18½, 19, 19½)"

MATERIALS:
- Garnstudio, Paris, distributed by Aurora Yarns, 100% cotton, worsted weight yarn (75 meters per skein): 14 (15, 17, 18, 19) skeins of White (16) for MC; 1 skein each of Red (12) for Color A, Navy (48) for Color B, Yellow (35) for Color C
- Size 7 (4.5mm) knitting needles or size needed to obtain gauge
- Size 5 (3.75mm) circular knitting needle, 16-inch-length; size 5 straight needles
- Yarn needle
- 1 ring-type stitch marker
- 1 JHB International button (Moscow #37359, size1⅛")
- Size F/5 (4mm) aluminum crochet hook

GAUGE:
In Faux Cable Pattern with larger needles, 18 sts and 22 rows = 4"/10cm.
TAKE TIME TO CHECK YOUR GAUGE.

SPECIAL ABBREVIATION:
M1: Lift running thread before next stitch onto left-hand needle, k in back of the running thread to make a new stitch.

STITCHES USED:
Faux Cable (a multiple of 10 sts + 3 sts; a rep of 6 rows)
Row 1 (WS): Purl.
Row 2: Knit.
Rows 3–4: Rep Rows 1–2.
Row 5: Purl.
Row 6: * Skip 2 sts, k the 3rd st on left hand needle, k first st, k 2nd st and sl all 3 sts off needle **, k7; rep from * across, ending last rep at **. Rep Rows 1–6 for Faux Cable.

Note: *Work lower border on Tank and sleeves of Cardigan in St st from a chart, reading from right to left for RS rows and from left to right for WS rows. Loosely carry color not in use along WS of fabric. To change color, bring new color from under present color for a twist to prevent holes.*
IMPORTANT: The first repeat of Chart I begins with a RS row; when working this chart for the second time, it begins with a WS row. So that the motif will look the same, make a mirror image of the first chart.

INSTRUCTIONS:
TANK TOP—BACK
Beg at lower edge, with larger needles and MC, cast on 77 (81, 85, 89, 93) sts. Beg with a k row, work 4 St st rows (k RS rows, p WS rows). Work

Chart 1 from 1–6 across, ending last rep at # 5 (3, 1, 5, 3). After completing Chart 1, work Chart 2 beg at your size and working to B. Rep A–B across, ending last rep by working A–C and then ending at your size. Rep Chart 1 again (REFER TO NOTE on *page 176*). Work Rows 1–5 of Faux Cable. **Row 6:** K2 (4, 6, 3, 5); rep pat across, ending last rep at **, k2 (4, 6, 3, 5). Cont est pat to approx 12½ (13, 13¼, 13½, 13½)" from beg, ending with a WS row.

Armhole Shaping

Bind off 5 sts at beg of next 2 rows, dec 1 st each edge every row 6 (6, 7, 7, 7) times, then dec 1 st each edge every other row 5 times—45 (49, 51, 55, 59) sts. Cont in pat, keeping 1 st each edge in St st for a selvage, to approx 19 (20, 20½, 21, 21½)" from beg, ending with a WS row.

Neck Shaping

Work est pat across first 9 (10, 11, 12, 13) sts; join a new strand and bind off center 27 (29, 29, 31, 33) sts; work to end of row. Working sides separately and at the same time, dec 1 st each neck edge on next RS row. Work even on rem 8 (9, 10, 11, 12) sts to approx 20 (21, 21½, 22, 22½)" from beg, ending with a WS row. Bind off knitwise and loosely.

FRONT

Work as for Back, beg Chart 1 at #6 (4, 2, 6, 4) and work to #6. Rep #1–6 across, ending last rep at #4 (6, 2, 4, 6). Work Chart 2 as for Back, rep Chart 1 as newly est. Work as for Back to approx 18 (19, 19½, 20, 20½)" from beg, ending with a WS row.

Neck Shaping

Work est pat across first 14 (15, 16, 17, 18) sts; join a new strand and bind off center 17 (19, 19, 21, 23) sts; work to end of row. Working sides separately and at the same time, bind

off at each neck edge 3 sts once, 2 sts once, and 1 st once. Work even on rem 8 (9, 10, 11, 12) sts for each shoulder to same length as Back, ending with a WS row. Bind off knitwise and loosely.

FINISHING

Join shoulder seams.

Turtleneck

With RS facing, using smaller circular needle and MC, pick up and k84 (90, 90, 96, 102) sts evenly spaced around neck beg at left shoulder. Place a marker to indicate beg of rnd; join and work k1, p1 ribbing to approx 3" from beg. Bind off in ribbing.

Armbands (make two)

With the RS facing using smaller needles and MC, pick up and k80 (85, 88, 90, 95) sts evenly spaced around armhole opening. K 2 rows. Bind off knitwise. Join side seams, using matching colors.

Lower Edging

With the WS facing and crochet hook, join MC with a slip st near both seams. Slip st evenly around and fasten off.

JACKET—BACK

Beg at lower edge with smaller needles and MC, cast on 91 (95, 99, 103, 107) sts. K 3 rows. Change to larger needles. Work Rows 1–5 of Faux Cable. **Row 6:** K4 (6, 8, 5, 7); rep pat across ending last rep at **, k4 (6, 8, 5, 7). Pat is now set. Beg with the next RS row, dec 1 st each edge every fourth (fourth, fourth, sixth, sixth) row 5 times. Work even on 81 (85, 89, 93, 97) sts to approx 9½ (10, 10, 10, 10)" from beg, ending with a WS row.

Armhole Shaping

Bind off 5 sts at beg of next 2 rows, dec 1 st each edge every row 7 (8, 8,

9, 8) times. Work even on rem 57 (59, 63, 65, 71) sts to approx 17 (18, 18½, 19, 19½)" from beg, ending with a WS row. Bind off loosely and straight across.

RIGHT FRONT

Beg at lower edge, with smaller needles and MC, cast on 46 (48, 50, 52, 54) sts. K 3 rows. Change to larger needles. Work Rows 1–5 of Faux Cable. **Row 6:** K9 (9, 9, 4, 4), rep pat across, ending last rep at **, k4 (6, 8, 5, 7). Pat is now set. Beg with the next RS row, dec 1 st at side edge every 4th (4th, 4th, 6th, 6th) row 5 times—41 (43, 45, 47, 49) sts. AT THE SAME TIME, when piece measures approx 6 (7, 7½, 8, 8½)" from beg, end with a WS row.

Neck Shaping

Dec 1 st at neck edge every other row 0 (3, 5, 7, 9) times then every 4th row 13 (11, 10, 9, 8) times. AT THE SAME TIME when piece measures approx 9½ (10, 10, 10, 10)" from beg, end with a RS row.

Armhole Shaping

Bind off 5 sts, dec 1 st every row 7 (8, 8, 9, 8) times. Work even on rem 16 (16, 17, 17, 19) sts to same length as Back, ending with a WS row. Bind off loosely and knitwise.

LEFT FRONT

Work as for Right Front, reversing armhole and neck shaping. On first Row 6, k4 (6, 8, 5, 7), work Faux Cable across, ending last rep at **, k9 (9, 9, 4, 4).

SLEEVES (make two)

Beg at lower edge with larger needles and MC, cast on 45 sts. Beg with a k row, work 4 rows St st. Work Chart 1 from #1–6 across, ending at #3. Work Chart 2 from X–Z across. Rep Chart 1 as est. With MC, work St st for 5 rows, inc 1 st each edge on

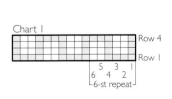

Chart 1

Row 4

Row 1

5 3 1
6 4 2
6-st repeat

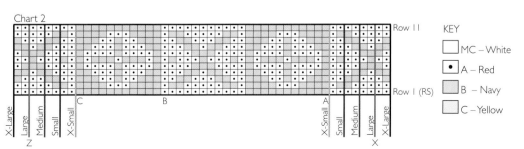

Chart 2

Row 11

Row 1 (RS)

X-Large
Large
Medium
Small
X-Small
Z

C

B

X-Small
Small
Medium
Large
X-Large
A
X

KEY

☐ MC – White
⦿ A – Red
▨ B – Navy
☐ C – Yellow

Faux Cable Twin Set

continued from page 177

2nd row—47 sts. Work Row 6 of Faux Cable as follows: K2, work Faux Cable across, ending last rep at **, k2. Pat is now set. Including new sts into pat as they accumulate, inc 1 st each edge every 2nd row 0 (0, 0, 0, 2) times, every 4th row 0 (2, 6, 12, 17) times, every 6th row 5 (10, 8, 4, 0) times, every 8th row 5 (0, 0, 0, 0) times. Work even on 67 (71, 75, 79, 85) sts to approx 18" from beg.

Cap Shaping
Bind off 5 sts beg of next 2 rows, dec 1 st every row 7 (8, 8, 9, 8) times. On next RS row, bind off rem 43 (45, 49, 51, 59) sts.

FINISHING
Join shoulder seams. Set in sleeves. Join underarm and side seams.

Left Neck and Front Band
With the RS facing, using smaller needle and MC, beg at center of back neck to pick up and k13 (14, 15, 16, 17) sts evenly to shoulder, 47 sts to first V-neck shaping row, and 25 sts to lower edge—85 (86, 87, 88, 89) sts. K 8 rows. Bind off loosely and knitwise on WS.

Right Neck and Front Band
With the RS facing, using smaller needle and MC, beg at lower edge to pick up and k25 sts to V-neck, 47 sts to shoulder, and 12 (13, 14, 15, 16) sts along back neck—84 (85, 86, 87, 88) sts. K 3 rows. K22, bind off 3 sts, k to end. **Next Row:** K across and cast on 3 sts over buttonhole. K 3 more rows. Bind off loosely and knitwise on WS of fabric. Join back neck. Sew button opposite buttonhole.

SLEEVE EDGING (make two)
With the RS facing and crochet hook, join MC with a slip st near seam. Ch 1, sc evenly around. * Slip st, ch 1, in each sc around for rickrack. At end, join and fasten off.

Lower Edging
With the RS facing, join MC with a slip st in corner of lower edge. Ch 1, sc evenly around lower edge. Fasten off.

United We Stand Pullover

photo on page 162

SKILL LEVEL: Easy

SIZES: S (MEDIUM, L, XL)
Note: The pattern is written for the smallest size with changes for larger sizes in parentheses. When only one number is given, it applies to all sizes. For ease in working, before you begin circle all numbers pertaining to the size you are knitting.

FINISHED MEASUREMENTS:
Bust: 39 (41, 42½, 44½)"
Length: 20 (20, 21, 21)"

MATERIALS:
- Marks & Kattens, Bomull, distributed by Swedish Yarn Imports, 50% cotton/50% wool, sport weight yarn (99 yards per ball): 6 (6, 8, 8) balls of Red (1501) for MC and 6 (6, 7, 7) balls of Natural (1474) for CC
- Size 6 (4.25mm) knitting needles or size needed to obtain gauge
- Size 5 (4mm) knitting needles
- Yarn needle
- 5 blue star buttons, 1⅛"
- Sewing needle and off-white thread

GAUGE:
In St st (k RS rows, p WS rows) with larger needles, 22 sts and 28 rows = 4"/10cm. TAKE TIME TO CHECK YOUR GAUGE.

STITCHES USED:
Stripe Pattern (a multiple of 2 sts + 1 st; a rep of 24 rows)
Row 1 (RS): K with MC.
Row 2: P with MC.
Rows 3–10: Rep Rows 1–2.

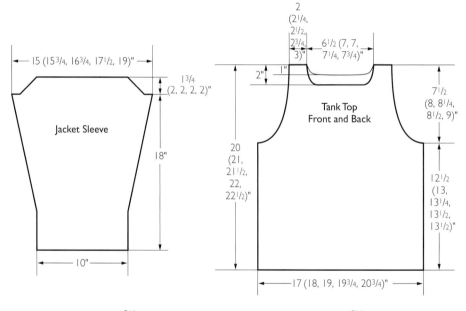

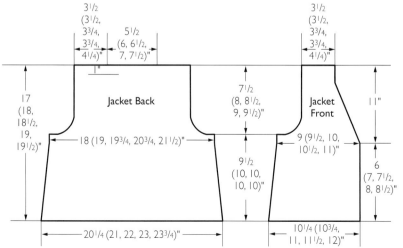

Row 11: With MC, (k2tog) across, ending k1.
Row 12: With CC, (p1, yo) across, ending p1.
Row 13: K with CC.
Row 14: P with CC.
Rows 15–22: Rep Rows 13–14.
Row 23: With CC, (k2tog) across, ending k1.
Row 24: With MC, (p1, yo) across, ending p1.
Rep Rows 1–24 for Stripe Pattern.

Note: One stitch along each edge is counted as a selvage and is not reflected in the final measurements or on the diagram.

INSTRUCTIONS:
BACK
Using MC and smaller needles, cast on 106 (110, 114, 122) sts.
Ribbing
Row 1 (WS): P2; (k2, p2) across.
Row 2: K2; (p2, k2) across.
Rep Ribbing Rows 1–2 to approx 1" from beg, ending with a WS row and inc 1 (3, 3, 1) st(s) on last row—107 (113, 117, 123) sts. With larger needles and MC, beg with a k row and work 0 (0, 6, 6) rows St st. Begin Stripe Pattern, working even until 6 stripes are finished—piece should measure approx 11 (11, 12, 12)" from beg. Place a marker on each edge. Cont in pat until 10 total stripes are complete. Rep Row 24 again. Using MC, work 12 (12, 18, 18) rows of St st.
Neck Trim
Change to smaller needles.

Ribbing
Row 1 (RS): K1; (p1, k1) across.
Row 2: P1; (k1, p1) across.
Rep Ribbing Rows 1–2 to approx 1", ending with a WS row. Work should measure approx 20 (20, 21, 21)" from beg, ending with a WS row. Bind off loosely and knitwise.

FRONT
Work as for Back.

SLEEVES (make two)
Using MC and smaller needles, cast on 46 (46, 50, 50) sts. Work Ribbing as for Back to approx 1" from beg, ending with a WS row. With larger needles and MC, beg with a k row and work 0 (0, 6, 6) rows St st. Begin Stripe Pattern and work 8 (8, 4, 4) rows even. **Next Row (RS):** Including news sts into pat as they accumulate, inc 1 st each edge now, then every 4th row 21 (21, 25, 25) times more—90 (90, 102, 102) sts. Cont in pat until 8 stripes are complete. Rep Row 24 again. Using MC, work 12 rows St st. Bind off loosely and knitwise.

FINISHING
Block all pieces to measurements. Count 30 (30, 31, 33) in from each armhole edge and place a marker at neck edge. Leaving the 47 (53, 55, 57) sts between markers free for neck opening, join shoulder seams.
Note: For an easy shoulder seam, thread yarn needle with an 18" strand of MC. Take needle from front to back and through the back lp of first st on left back, take needle from back to front and through the front lp of first st on left front. Rep this process across to join first shoulder. For the second shoulder, begin at the markers and work as before. Set in sleeves between side markers. Join underarm and side seams. Weave in tails on WS of fabric.

Buttons
Place a marker in the center of the third white stripe on Front. Diagonally above and below center button, place markers 2" apart along the first, second, fourth, and fifth stripes. Sew buttons at the markers.

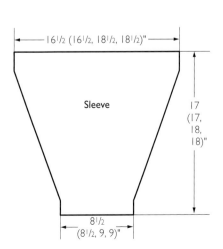

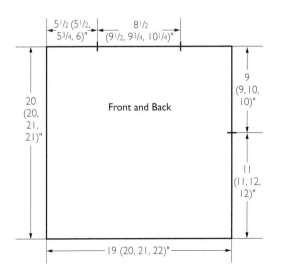

5¹/₂ (5¹/₂, 5³/₄, 6)"
8¹/₂ (9¹/₂, 9³/₄, 10¹/₄)"
9 (9, 10, 10)"
20 (20, 21, 21)"
Front and Back
11 (11, 12, 12)"
19 (20, 21, 22)"

16¹/₂ (16¹/₂, 18¹/₂, 18¹/₂)"
Sleeve
17 (17, 18, 18)"
8¹/₂ (8¹/₂, 9, 9)"

Stars & Stripes Throw

photo on page 163

SKILL LEVEL: Intermediate

SIZE: Approximately 44×56"

MATERIALS:
- TLC Essentials, Article E514, from Coats & Clark,100% acrylic, worsted weight yarn (6 ounces per skein): 6 skeins of Winter White (2316)
- Size 8 (5mm) knitting needles or size needed to obtain gauge
- Size G/6 (4.5mm) crochet hook
- Yarn needle

GAUGE:
In Body Pat, 16 sts and 30 rows = 4"/10cm. Each block measures approx 10½" square.
TAKE TIME TO CHECK YOUR GAUGE.

ABBREVIATIONS:

K2tog-b: K next two stitches together through the back loops.

P1b: Turn work slightly and insert tip of needle through stitch from left to right, p in the usual manner.

Wyib: With yarn in back.

***Note:** Slip stitches purlwise.*

INSTRUCTIONS:

BLOCK (make 20)
Beg at the lower edge, cast on 42 sts. K 5 rows.

Row 6 (WS): K3, p36, k3.

Rows 7–11: Knit.

Rows 12–53: Rep Rows 6–11.

Row 54: Rep Row 6.

Row 55: K23; * k2tog, (yo) twice, k2tog-b; rep from * across to last 3 sts, k3.

Row 56: K3, p1; * p the first yo, p1b in the second yo, (wyib, sl the next 2 sts to right-hand needle, bring yarn to front between needles, slip the same 2 sts back to left-hand needle, pass yarn to back between needles, slip the same 2 sts wyib again—Cluster made); rep from * to last 26 sts. P1, p1b, p1, k23.

Row 57: K25; * k2tog, (yo) twice, k2tog-b; rep from * to last 5 sts, k5.

Row 58: K3, p1; * Cluster, p1, p1b; rep from * to last 26 sts, Cluster, p1, k23.

Row 59: Rep Row 55.

Row 60: K3, p1; * p1, p1b, Cluster; rep from * across to last 26 sts, p1, p1b, p21, k3.

Rows 61–62: Rep Rows 57–58.

Rows 63–64: Rep Rows 55–56.

Row 65: Rep Row 57.

Row 66: K3, p1; * Cluster, p1, p1b; rep from * to last 26 sts, Cluster, p21, k3.

Rows 67–70: Rep Rows 55–58.

Rows 71–72: Rep Rows 59–60.

Rows 73–74: Rep Rows 57–58.

Rows 75–77: Knit.

Rows 78 (WS): Bind off loosely and knitwise.

FINISHING
Whip st blocks together through the garter st bumps along edges with 5 panels of 4 blocks each. Then whip st the panels together.

Crochet Border
With RS facing, join yarn with a sl st in any corner. Ch 1, 3 sc in same corner. Sc evenly around working 3 sc in each corner. At end, slip st in first sc. **Rnd 2:** Ch 1, sc in same sc as joining, 3 sc in next sc, sc in each sc around working 3 sc in each corner. At end, join with a slip st in first sc and fasten off.

Garden Party Sweater and Purse

photos on pages 164–165

SKILL LEVEL: Intermediate

SIZES: Girls' 4 (6, 8, 10)
***Note:** The pattern is written for the smallest size with changes for larger sizes in parentheses. When only one number is given, it applies to all sizes. For ease in working, before you begin circle all numbers pertaining to the size you are knitting.*

FINISHED MEASUREMENTS:

Chest: 24 (26, 28, 30)"
Length: 12½ (13½, 14½, 14½)"
Purse: Approximately 6×7

MATERIALS:

- Sandnes Uldvarefabrik (Swedish Yarn Imports), Mandarin Classic, 100% cotton, sport weight yarn (121 yards per ball): 4 (5, 5, 6) balls of White (1012) for MC
- Size 4 (3.5mm) knitting needles or size needed to obtain gauge
- Size 3 (3.25mm) knitting needles
- 2 packages of "Dress It Up" daisy multicolor buttons/2 Part 67
- 1 skein each of DMC floss: Red (666), Pink (894), Yellow (743), Orange (740), and Purple (327)
- 1 small organza potpourri bag for purse lining
- Size E/4 (3.5mm) crochet hook
- Tapestry needle
- 1 stitch holder
- Sewing needle and white thread

GAUGE:

In St st with larger needles, 24 sts and 28 rows = 4"/10cm.
TAKE TIME TO CHECK YOUR GAUGE.

STITCHES USED:

Eyelet Pattern [a multiple of 8 sts + 8 (6, 12, 10) sts; a rep of 16 rows]
Row 1 (RS): K3 (2, 5, 4); * k2tog, yo, k6; rep from * across, ending last rep k2tog, yo, k3 (2, 5, 4).
Row 2: P all sts.
Row 3: Knit.
Rows 4–7: Rep Rows 2–3.

Row 8: Rep Row 2.
Row 9 (RS): K7 (6, 9, 8); * k2tog, yo, k6; rep across, ending last rep k2tog, yo, k7 (6, 9, 8).
Rows 10–15: Rep Rows 2–3.
Row 16: Rep Row 2.
Rep Rows 1–16 for Eyelet Pattern.

INSTRUCTIONS:
TOP
BACK—BORDER

Beg at lower edge, with smaller needles and MC, cast on 109 (114, 119, 124) sts. P 1 row. K 1 row.

Ruffle Rib

Row 1 (RS): P4; (k1, p4) across.
Row 2: K4; (p1, k4) across.
Rep last 2 rows to approx 2½" from beg ending with a RS row and dec 22 (21, 20, 19) sts evenly spaced across last row—87 (93, 99, 105) sts.

Gathering Rib

Row 1 (RS): K1; (p1, k1) across.
Row 2: P1; (k1, p1) across.
Rep last 2 rows to approx 3" from beg, ending with a RS row and dec 15 sts evenly spaced across last row—72 (78, 84, 90) sts.

Last Border

P 2 rows. K 2 rows. P 2 rows.

UPPER BODY

Change to larger needles. Beg with a p row, work St st to approx 7 (8, 8½, 8½)" from beg, ending with a RS row.

Armhole Shaping

Bind off 6 sts at beg of next 2 rows—60 (66, 72, 78) sts. Dec 1 st, every other row 5 times—50 (56, 62, 68) sts. Work even to approx 9½ (10½, 11, 11)" from beg ending with WS row.

Keyhole Opening

K 25 (28, 31, 34) sts; join new strand and work to end of row. Work sides separately and at the same time to approx 11½ (12½, 13½, 13½)" from beg, ending with RS. Bind off 13 (14, 15, 16) sts at each neck edge; dec 1 st each neck edge once. Bind off rem 11 (13, 15, 17) sts for each shoulder.

FRONT

Work as for Back—Border.

Upper Body

Change to larger needles. Beg with a p row, work 7 St st rows. Begin Eyelet Pattern, working Rows 1–16. Cont est pat, shaping armholes as for Back. Work even to approx 11 (12, 13, 13)" from beg, ending with a WS row.

Neck Shaping

Work in pat across first 14 (16, 18, 20) sts; join new strand and bind off center 22 (24, 26, 28) sts; work to end of row. Working sides separately and at the same time, dec 1 st each neck edge, every other row 3 times. Work even on 11 (13, 15, 17) sts for each shoulder to approx 12½ (13½, 14½, 14½)" from beg, ending with a WS row. Bind off rem sts for each shoulder.

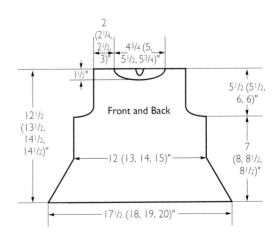

Garden Party Sweater and Purse
continued from page 181

FINISHING
Join shoulder seams. Using the photo as a guide, embroider Lazy Daisies with floss around desired eyelets. Sew on 5 daisy buttons (you may mix and match flower center with petals to complete color combos) with the first at center of Last Border and the rem 4 spaced at 1½" intervals (2 on each side of center). Join side seams.

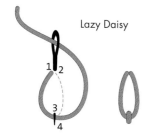

Lazy Daisy

Crochet Edging
With the RS facing, join MC with a sl st at underarm. Ch 1, sc evenly around. At end, join with a sl st in first sc. Do not turn. Working from left to right rather than right to left, sc in each sc around for reverse single crochet. At end, join and fasten off.
For Neck: With the RS facing, join MC with a slip st in corner of left back neck edge. Ch 1, sc evenly around to opposite neck edge; do not turn. Ch 1, working from left to right, sc in each sc around for reverse single crochet. Fasten off. With RS facing, join MC with a sl st ¾" from top of left back neck edge. Ch 7, slip st in corner. Fasten off. Sew on a daisy button to opposite edge. Weave in loose ends on WS of fabric. Without touching iron to fabric, lightly steam.

PURSE
Beg at the top, with smaller needles and MC, cast on 44 sts. P 1 row. K 1 row. Rep Ruffle Rib as for Back Border to approx 1¼" from beg, ending with RS row and dec 14 sts evenly spaced across last row—30 sts. P 2 rows. K 2 rows. P 2 rows. Beg with a p row, work 9 rows St st.
Eyelet Pattern
Row 1 (RS): K2; * k2tog, yo, k6; rep from * across, ending last rep k2tog, yo, k2.

Row 2: P all sts.
Row 3: Knit.
Rows 4–7: Rep Rows 2–3.
Row 8: Rep Row 2.
Row 9: K6; * k2tog, yo, k6; rep from * across.
Rows 10–15: Rep Rows 2–3.
Row 16: Rep Row 2.
Rep Rows 1–16 once more. Rep Rows 1–8. P 1 row on RS for turning ridge at base of Purse. Beg with a p row, work 7 St st rows. Rep Eyelet Pattern, Rows 1–16 once. Work 10 St st rows. P 2 rows. K 2 rows. P 2 rows, inc 14 sts across last row—44 sts. Rep Ruffle Rib for approx 1". P 2 rows and bind off.

FINISHING
Decorate eyelets with Lazy Daisies. Fold Purse in half along turning ridge. With RS facing and crochet hook, join MC with a slip st through both layers of fabric in lower edge. Ch 1, sc in same place as joining. Sc evenly along entire edge to join, leaving ruffle free. At end, ch 50 for handle. Being careful to keep the ch untwisted, sc evenly along second side to join. At end, turn. Ch 1, sc in each sc to the ch. * Ch 9, skip 9 ch, sl st in next ch; rep from * for 4 more times. Sc in each sc along first side and fasten off. Sew 3 daisy buttons to each top edge of purse opening, in the center and others spaced ¾" on either side. Sew in potpourri bag for lining. Without touching iron to fabric, lightly steam.

Fish Place Mat
photo on pages 166

SKILL LEVEL: Intermediate

SIZE: 12×16"

MATERIALS:
- Classic Elite's Provence, 100% mercerized cotton, DK (double knitting) weight (256 yards per hank): 1 hank each of Portland Teal (2690) for MC, Bleach (2601), Black (2613), and Zinnia Flower (2619)
- Size 5 (3.75mm) knitting needles or size needed to obtain gauge
- Yarn needle

GAUGE:
In St st, 22 sts and 28 rows = 4"/10cm. TAKE TIME TO CHECK YOUR GAUGE.

STITCHES USED:
Seed Stitch (a multiple of 2 sts; a rep of 2 rows)
Row 1 (RS): (K1, p1) across.
Row 2: (K the p sts, p the k sts) across.

Notes: The place mat is worked in St st (k RS rows, p WS rows) with seed st borders. Work the fish motif from a chart, reading RS rows from right to left and WS rows from left to right. Before working the motif, roll a small ball of yarn for each color. When starting a new color, tie new color around color in use with a slip knot. When changing yarn color within the design, twist new color around color in use. Seed st borders are not reflected on chart.

INSTRUCTIONS:
With MC, cast on 66 sts. Work 8 seed st rows.
Row 9 (RS): With MC, work 5 seed sts, k across to last 5 sts, work seed st to end.
Row 10: With MC, work 5 seed sts, p across to last 5 sts, work seed st to end.
Repeat Rows 9–10 for 5 more times.
Row 21 (RS): With MC, work 5 seed sts, k27, with white k2, with MC k to last 5 sts, work seed st to end. This completes Row 1 of chart. Continue as set until chart is complete. Repeat Rows 9–10 for 6 times. Work 8 seed st rows. Bind off knitwise.

FINISHING
Weave loose ends into WS of work, closing holes as necessary.

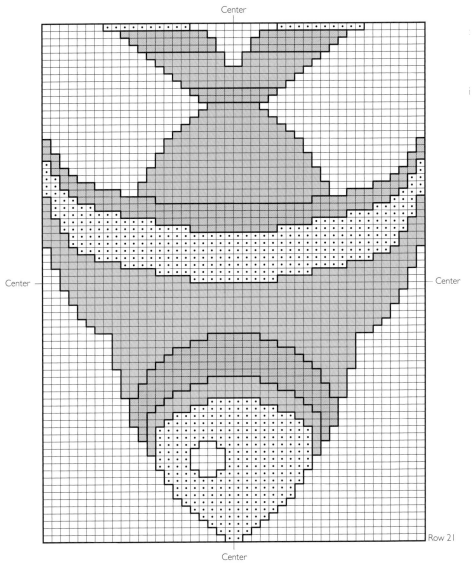

Center

Center — — Center

Row 21

Center

- Portland Teal (2690)
- Bleach (2601)
- Black (2613)
- Zinnia Flower (2619)

Summer Sun Top
photo on page 167

SKILL LEVEL: Easy

SIZES: S (MEDIUM, L, XL, XXL)
***Note:** The pattern is written for the smallest size with changes for larger sizes in parentheses. When only one number is given, it applies to all sizes. For ease in working, before you begin, circle all numbers pertaining to the size you are knitting.*

FINISHED MEASUREMENTS:
Bust: 36 (38, 40, 42, 44)"
Length: 20½ (21, 21½, 22, 22½)"

MATERIALS:
- Coats & Clark's Aunt Lydia's "Baby Denim," 75% cotton/25% acrylic, worsted weight yarn (400 yards per ball): 2 (2, 3, 3, 3) balls of Baby Yellow (1023)
- Size 6 (4.25mm) knitting needles or size needed to obtain gauge
- Size 6 (4.25mm) circular needle, 22-inch length
- Tapestry needle
- 2 ring-type stitch markers

GAUGE:
In St st, 19 sts and 28 rows = 4"/10cm.
TAKE TIME TO CHECK YOUR GAUGE.

STITCHES USED:
Dotted Chevron (over 54 sts and 10 rows)
Row 1 (RS): K17, p2, k16, p2, k17.
Row 2: K2; (p14, k4) twice, p14, k2.
Row 3: K1; (p2, k5, p2, k5, p2, k2) twice, (p2, k5) twice, p2, k1.
Row 4: P2; (k2, p3, k4, p3, k2, p4) twice, k2, p3, k4, p3, k2, p2.
Row 5: K3; (p2, k3, p2, k3, p2, k6) twice, (p2, k3) 3 times.
Row 6: P4; (k2, p6, k2, p3, k2, p3) twice, k2, p6, k2, p4.
Row 7: K5; (p2, k4, p2, k3, p4, k3) twice, p2, k4, p2, k5.
Row 8: P6; (k2, p2, k2, p5, k2, p5) twice, k2, p2, k2, p6.
Row 9: K7; (p4, k14) twice, p4, k7.
Row 10: P8; (k2, p16) twice, k2, p8.

INSTRUCTIONS:
BACK
Beg at the lower edge, cast on 86 (90, 94, 100, 104) sts. Beg with a p row, work St st (p WS rows, k RS rows) until piece measures approx 13" from beg, ending with a WS row.
Armhole Shaping
Bind off 8 (8, 8, 9, 9) sts at beg of next 2 rows, dec 1 st each edge every other row 3 (4, 5, 6, 7) times. Cont in St st on rem 64 (66, 68, 70, 72) sts to approx 20½ (21, 21½, 22, 22½)" from beg, ending with a WS row.
Bind off knitwise and loosely.

FRONT
Work as for Back to approx 13" from beg, ending with a WS row and placing markers each side of center 54 sts. Shape armholes as for Back. AT THE SAME TIME, when piece measures 13 (13½, 14, 14½, 15)" from beg, end with a WS row. Keeping sts outside of markers in St st, work Row 1 of Dotted Chevron over center 54 sts. Work Dotted Chevron through completion of Row 10. K 1 row, p 1 row. Rep Rows 1–10 of Dotted Chevron again. Work rem of front in St st to approx 16½ (17, 17½, 18, 18½)" from beg, ending with a WS row.
Keyhole Opening and Neck Shaping
K across first 31 (32, 33, 34, 35) sts; join a new strand and bind off center 2 sts; k to end. Work sides separately

Summer Sun Top
continued from page 183

and at the same time, to approx 19½ (20, 20½, 21, 21½)" from beg. Bind off 18 sts at each neck edge. Work even on rem 13 (14, 15, 16, 17) sts for each shoulder to same length as Back, ending with a WS row. Bind off rem sts for each shoulder knitwise and loosely.

SLEEVES (make two)
Beg at the lower edge, cast on 58 (62, 64, 66, 68) sts. Beg with a p row, work St st to approx 2" from beg, ending with a WS row. Inc 1 st each edge now and every fourth row 1 (1, 1, 2, 2) times—62 (66, 68, 72, 74) sts. Work even to approx 5½" from beg, ending with a WS row.

Cap Shaping
Bind off 8 (8, 8, 9, 9) sts at beg of next 2 rows, dec 1 st each edge every other row 12 (13, 14, 15, 15) times—22 (24, 24, 24, 26) sts. Work even to approx 9½ (10, 10, 10¼, 10½)" from beg. Bind off 2 sts at beg of next 6 rows. Bind off rem 10 (12, 12, 12, 14) sts.

Lower Border
With WS facing, pick up and k1 st in each cast on st along edge. Bind off loosely and knitwise.

FINISHING
Join shoulder seams. Set in sleeves. Join underarm and side seams.

Lower Border
With WS facing and circular needle, pick up and k1 st in each cast on st along edge. Bind off knitwise and loosely.

Neck Border
With RS facing and circular needle, beginning on back and near shoulder seam, pick up and k38 sts along back neck, 7 sts along side of neck, 18 sts along front neck, 21 sts around keyhole, 18 sts along front neck, 7 sts along side of neck. 109 sts. Place a marker to indicate beg of rnd. P 2 rnds. Bind off loosely and knitwise. Weave in loose ends on WS of fabric.

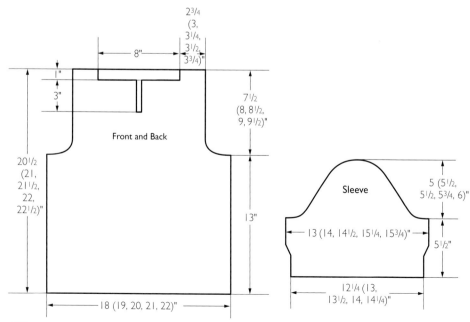

Front and Back

2¾ (3, 3¼, 3½, 3¾)"

8"

1"

3"

7½ (8, 8½, 9, 9½)"

20½ (21, 21½, 22, 22½)"

13"

18 (19, 20, 21, 22)"

Sleeve

5 (5½, 5½, 5¾, 6)"

5½"

13 (14, 14½, 15¼, 15¾)"

12¼ (13, 13½, 14, 14¼)"

basic knitting tools

Use the tools shown *at right* for knitting projects. Pack a basic tool kit (including the needles for the project) that you can easily move from one project bag to the next.

A Flexible straight needles

B Tape measure

C Knitting needle point protectors

D Circular needles

E Tapestry needles

F Double-pointed needles (dpns)

G Thread cutter pendant

H Row counters (two different styles)

I Stitch marker rings

J Split ring markers

K Cable needle

L Crochet hook (for picking up dropped stitches)

M Stitch holder

N Knitting gauge

O Spool knitter and needle (for trims)

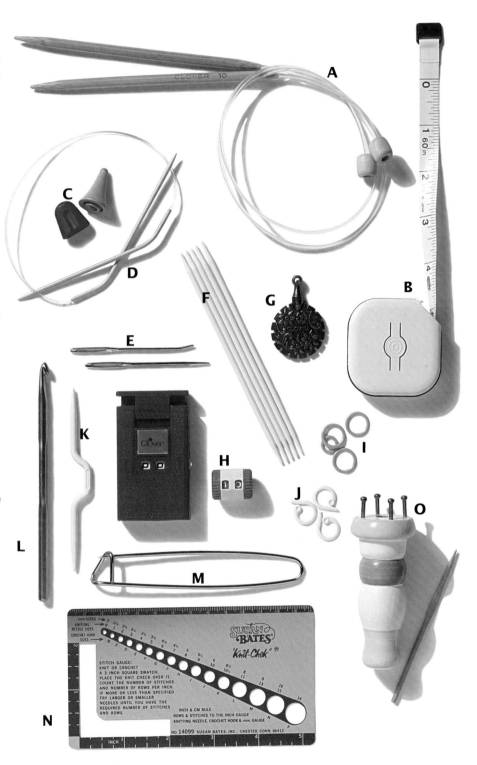

Common Abbreviations

NOTE: Less common abbreviations are defined at the beginning of patterns referring to such terms.

KNIT ABBREVIATIONS

approx	approximately
beg	begin(ning)
CC	contrasting color
cn	cable needle
cont	continue
dec	decrease
dpn	double-pointed needle
est	established
inc	increase
k	knit
k2tog	knit 2 together
lp	loop
M1	make one stitch
MC	main color
p	purl
pat	pattern
psso	pass the slipped stitch over
p2sso	pass 2 slipped stitches over
p2tog	purl 2 together
rem	remain(s)(ing)
rep	repeat
rnd(s)	round(s)
RS	right side
tog	together
skp	slip, knit, pass over
sl	slip
ssk	slip, slip, knit
ssp	slip, slip, purl
st(s)	stitch(es)
St st	stockinette stitch
yb	yarn back
yf	yarn forward
yo	yarn over
WS	wrong side

CROCHET ABBREVIATIONS

beg	begin(ning)(s)
ch	chain
dc	double crochet
dec	decrease
est	established
hdc	half double crochet
inc	increase
lp(s)	loop(s)
rep	repeat
rev sc	reverse single crochet
rnd	round
RS	right side
sc	single crochet
sl st	slip stitch
sp(s)	space(s)
st(s)	stitch(es)
tog	together
tr	treble crochet
WS	wrong side

Pattern Sizes

Sizes for each of the projects in this book are noted at the beginning of the instructions. When one size is written out in capitalized letters, it is to note the size of the modeled garment. The instructions are written for the smallest size with changes for larger sizes in parentheses. When only one number is given, it applies to all sizes. For ease in working, before you begin, circle all numbers pertaining to the size you are knitting.

Metric Conversions

To convert inch measurements to centimeters, simply multiply the inches by 2.5.

Needles and Gauge Notations

The needle you choose affects the gauge, or stitches and rows per inch, of your finished knitting.

Knitting Needles

Unlike crochet, which uses only one hook, knitting requires at least two knitting needles to make the knitted fabric. Knitting needles usually are pointed at one end and have a knob at the other. They're available in plastic, bamboo, wood, steel, and aluminum.

Gauge Notations

Most patterns include a gauge notation. The gauge, or the number of stitches or rows per inch, is determined by the size of the needles and the weight of the yarn. Always work a gauge swatch to see if your tension equals the gauge specified in your instructions. If you have too many stitches per inch, you are working too tightly. You need to change to larger needles. If you have too few stitches per inch, you are working too loosely. You need to change to a smaller needle. For your practice sessions, choose medium-size needles (size 8 or 9 is good to start)

SKILL LEVEL RATING KEY

Beginner: Basic stitches including increasing, decreasing, and finishing skills.
Easy: Simple stitch patterns and/or shaping.
Intermediate: More complicated stitch patterns and charts.
Experienced (Advanced): Intricate stitch and color pattern and/or involved shaping and finishing techniques.

and a smooth, light-color yarn so you can see your work easily.

Button Selection Tips

- To create the proper buttonhole size, buy the buttons before you start the buttonholes.
- Take your gauge swatch when buying buttons; it's a better visual than a skein of yarn.
- If you can't find a good color match, choose a contrasting color.
- Glassy, glittery buttons work well with dressy yarns. Bone, wood, or metal is better for heavier, outdoor garments.
- Buttons are made with or without a shank. Shank buttons are suitable for all yarn weights and are the best choice for thick, bulky knits.
- Buy washable buttons if you plan to wash the garment and dry-cleanable ones if the garment requires dry-cleaning. Pay attention to special-care instructions that come with the buttons.

knitting techniques

MAKING A SLIPKNOT

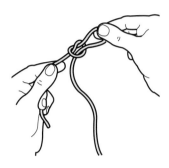

This basic knot comes in handy outside knitting and crochet, too.

Step 1 Let the tail of the yarn hang in front of your palm, and loop the yarn loosely around the first two fingers of your left hand.

Step 2 Pull the yarn attached to the ball underneath the yarn behind your fingers and then through the loop.

Step 3 Hold the tail of the yarn in your left hand and the newly made loop in your right hand. Pull the tail to tighten, and make a slipknot.

CABLE CAST-ON

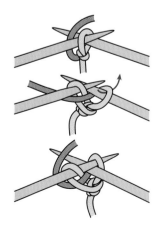

Step 1 Make a slipknot on the left needle.

Step 2 Working into the loop of the knot, knit a stitch; transfer it to the left needle.

Step 3 Insert right needle between the last two stitches. Knit a stitch and transfer it to left needle. Repeat this step for each additional stitch.

KNIT STITCH

Step 1 Insert the right-hand needle from front to back into the first stitch on the left-hand needle. Notice that the right-hand needle is behind the left-hand needle.

Step 2 Form a loop by wrapping the yarn under and around the right-hand needle.

Step 3 Pull the loop through the stitch so the loop is in front of the work.

Step 4 Slip the first or "old" knit stitch over and off the tip of the left-hand needle.

M1 (make one stitch) An increase worked by lifting the horizontal thread lying between the needles and placing it onto the left needle. Work the new stitch through the back loop.

PURL STITCH

Step 1 With yarn in front of the work, put the right-hand needle from back to front into the first stitch on the left-hand needle.

Step 2 Form a loop by wrapping the yarn on top of and around the right-hand needle.

Step 3 Pull the loop through the stitch to make a new purl stitch.

Step 4 Slip the first or "old" purl stitch over and off the tip of the left-hand needle.

P1b
Purl through the back loop.
P2togb
Slip two stitches knitwise, one at a time, from the left needle to the right needle. Return these two slipped stitches to the left needle. Purl the two stitches together through the back loops.

GRAFTING STOCKINETTE STITCHES TOGETHER

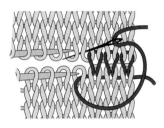

Hold wrong sides together with the needles pointed to the right, thread yarn tail into yarn needle. * Insert needle knitwise through the first stitch on front needle and let the stitch drop from the needle. Insert needle into the second stitch on front needle purlwise and pull yarn through, leaving the stitch on the needle. Insert needle into the first stitch on the back needle purlwise and let it drop from the needle. Insert needle knitwise through second stitch on the back needle and pull the yarn through, leaving the stitch on the needle. Repeat from * across until all stitches have been joined. Adjust tension as necessary. Weave in loose ends.

knitting basics

continued from page 187

3-NEEDLE BIND-OFF

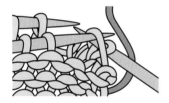

With RS tog, hold in one hand two needles with an equal number of stitches on each and with points going in same direction. Using a third needle of the same size, knit together one stitch from each needle. * Knit together next stitch from each needle, pass first stitch worked over second to bind off; repeat from * across to bind off all stitches.

DUPLICATE STITCH

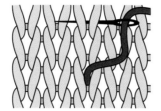

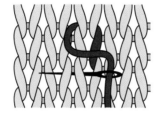

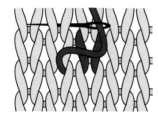

This embroidery stitch imitates the knit stitch, covering the original stitch with a secondary color of yarn to create the pattern. When small areas of color are desired, this is an easy way to add it.

GLOSSARY FOR DECREASING

Knit two together (k2tog): A single decrease, with the facing stitch (the one on top) slanting right. Working from front to back, insert the right-hand needle into the second, then the first stitch on the left-hand needle. Knit both stitches together.

Purl two together (p2tog): A single decrease, slanting to the right when viewed from the knit side. With the purl side of the work facing you, insert the right-hand needle, purlwise, through the first two stitches on the left-hand needle. Purl both stitches together.

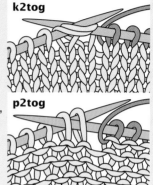

Slip, slip, knit (ssk): A single decrease, with the facing stitch slanting left. Slip the first two stitches knitwise, one at a time, from the left-hand needle to the right-hand needle. Insert the left needle tip into the fronts of both stitches, from left to right, and knit them together.

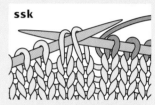

Slip, slip, purl (ssp): A single decrease, slanting to the left when viewed from the knit side. With the purl side of the work facing you, slip two stitches knitwise, one at a time, from the left-hand needle to the right-hand needle. Return the slipped stitches to the left-hand needle, purlwise. Purl both stitches together through the back loops.

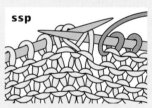

DECREASE TIPS

Although decreases are usually made on right side rows, they sometimes occur on wrong side rows. The following are some general examples.

- **Right-Slanting Decrease:** On right side rows, knit two together (k2tog). Use purl two together (p2tog) on wrong side rows.
- **Left-Slanting Decrease:** The slip, slip, knit (ssk) is used on right side rows. Use slip, slip, purl (ssp) on wrong side rows. Work decreases at least one stitch in from the edges to maintain even edges for seaming or picking up stitches.

crochet techniques

SINGLE CROCHET

Step 1 Insert the hook into the second chain so that two strands are over the top of the hook and one strand is under the hook.

Step 2 Wrap the yarn over the hook; then pull a loop through the chain. (There should be two loops on the hook.)

Step 3 Wrap the yarn over the hook and pull a loop through the two loops.

REVERSE SINGLE CROCHET

(Also known as Crab Stitch) Working from left to right, rather than from right to left, ch 1, single crochet in each single crochet around.

HALF DOUBLE CROCHET

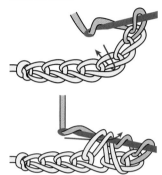

Step 1 Wrap the yarn over the hook; then insert the hook into the third chain from the hook.

Step 2 Wrap the yarn over the hook; then pull a loop through the chain. (There should now be three loops on the hook.)

Step 3 Wrap the yarn over the hook; then draw a new loop through all three loops on the hook.

DOUBLE CROCHET

Step 1 Wrap the yarn over the hook; then insert the hook into the fourth chain from the hook.

Step 2 Wrap the yarn over the hook; then pull a loop through the chain. (There should now be three loops on the hook.)

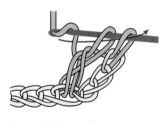

Step 3 Wrap the yarn over the hook; then pull a loop through the first two loops. (There should now be two loops on the hook.)

Step 4 Wrap the yarn over the hook; then pull a loop through the remaining two loops on the hook.

TREBLE CROCHET

Step 1 Wrap the yarn over the hook two times; then insert the hook into the next chain.

Step 2 Wrap the yarn over the hook and pull a loop through the chain. (There should now be four loops on the hook.)

Step 3 Wrap the yarn over the hook and pull a loop through two loops, leaving three loops on the hook.

Step 4 Wrap the yarn over the hook and pull through two loops, leaving two loops on the hook.

Step 5 Wrap the yarn over the hook and pull through the two remaining loops.

index

Rodeo Drive for Lunch p.65

Bright Cardigan and Hat p.23

resources

Aurora Yarns
2385 Carlos St.
PO Box 3068
Moss Beach, CA 94038-3068
(800)637-3207

Berroco, Inc.
PO Box 367
Uxbridge, MA 01569
(800)343-4948

Blue Sky Alpacas, Inc.
2831 199th Ave. NW
Cedar, MN 55011
(888)460-8862

Brown Sheep Co., Inc.
100662 CR 16
Mitchell, NE 69357
(800)826-9136

Chester Farms
3581 Churchville Ave.
Churchville, VA 24421
(877)ONE-WOOL
(877)663-9665

Classic Elite Yarns
300 Jackson St.
Lowell, MA 01852
(800)343-0308

Coats & Clark
8 Shelter Dr.
Greer, SC 29650
(800)648-1479

Elmore-Pisgah, Inc.
204 Oak St.
Spindale, NC 28160
(800)633-7829

JHB International
1955 South Quince St.
Denver, Colorado 80231
(800)525-9007

Lion Brand Yarn Co.
34 W 15th St.
New York, NY 10011
(212)243-8995

Muench Yarns & Buttons
285 Bel Marin Keys Blvd #J
Novato, CA 94949-5724
(800)733-9276

Patons
320 Livingstone Ave. S
Listowel, ON N4W 3H3 Canada
(519)291-3780

Swedish Yarn Imports
126-A Wade St.
PO Box 2069
Jamestown, NC 27282
(800)331-5648

credits

DESIGNERS
Svetlana Avrakh—Pages 66–67, 70–71, and 74.

Gayle Bunn—Pages 51, 55, 72, 112–113, and 155.

Mellissa Leapman—Pages 11, 52–53, 73, and 159.

Lion Brand Yarn Company—Page 56.

Val Love—Pages 122–125 and 166.

Dawn Oertel—Pages 114–115, 162, and 164–165.

Ann Smith—Pages 9–10, 12–18, 19–23, 57–63, 65, 68–69, 76–77, 116–117, 119, 121, 126, 129, 154, 156, 158, 160–161, 163, and 167.

PHOTOGRAPHERS
Andy Lyons Cameraworks
Ed Gohlich
Scott Little

PHOTOSTYLING
Carol Field Dahlstrom
Gayle Schadendorf
Donna Chesnut, Assistant

SPECIAL LOCATIONS
Loews Coronado Bay Resort
4000 Coronado Bay Road
Coronado, CA 92118
(800)81LOEWS
(800)815-6397
(619)424-4000
www.loewshotels.com